Essentials of Physical Activity

Fourth Edition

Fritz Huber, ED.D., C.S.C.S
Chairman and Associate Professor
Department of Health, Physical Education and Recreation
Oral Roberts University

eb
eddie bowers publishing co., inc.

eddie bowers publishing co., inc.
P.O. Box 130
Peosta, Iowa 52068-0130 USA

www.eddiebowerspublishing.com

ISBN 978-1-57879-068-5

Copyright © 2011 by *eddie bowers publishing co., inc.*

All rights reserved. No part of this work may be reproduced, stored
in a retrieval system, or transcribed, in any means— electronic,
mechanical, photocopying, recording, or otherwise—without prior
written permission of *eddie bowers publishing co., inc.*

Printed in the United States of America.

9 8 7 6 5 4 3 2 1

Contents

CHAPTER 1
Lifestyle and Health — 2

    Learning Objectives 2
    Key Terms 2
    Historical Search for Health 3
    The Current Health Search 3
    Major Health Problems Today 4
    The Cost of Poor Health 6
    Changing Lifestyle 6
    Contributors to Health or Disease 7
    Lifestyle and Health 8
    Summary 11
    Questions 12

CHAPTER 2
Concept of Health Fitness — 14

    Learning Objectives 14
    Key Terms 14
    What is Health? 15

Concept of Physical Fitness   15
Principles of Conditioning   17
Adaptation and Progression   18
Types of Exercise   19
Health Benefits from Regular Physical Exercise   20
Exercise and Aging   22
Summary   24
Questions   24

CHAPTER 3

The Cardiorespiratory System   26

Learning Objectives   26
Key Terms   26
Requirements of the Cell   27
The Cardiorespiratory System   27
Summary   35
Questions   35

CHAPTER 4

Cardiovascular Disease Risk Factors and Aerobic Exercise   36

Learning Objectives   36
Key Terms   36
Cardiovascular Disease   37
Risk Factors for Developing Cardiovascular Disease   39
Aerobic Exercise   42
Mode of Aerobic Exercise   46
Progression of Aerobic Exercise Program   47
Benefits of Regular Aerobic Exercise   48
Reversibility Principle   49

Summary 49
Questions 50

CHAPTER 5

The Skeletal Muscular System and Strengthening Exercises — 52

Learning Objectives 52
Key Terms 52
The Skeletal Muscular System 53
Types of Muscle Contractions 54
Mode of Strength Training 55
Anaerobic Metabolism 57
Principles for Training Muscles 57
Summary 61
Questions 62

CHAPTER 6

Starting an Exercise Program for Health Fitness — 64

Learning Objectives 64
Key Terms 64
Medical Clearance 65
Exercising Session 65
Hydration 71
Exercising in the Heat or Cold 72
Exercise Program Design for Health Fitness 75
Summary 77
Questions 77

CHAPTER 7
Body Composition and Health Fitness — 78

Learning Objectives   78
Key Terms   78
Overfatness, Disease, and Related Costs   79
Body Composition   80
Assessment of Body Composition   81
Factors Affection Body Fat   82
Energy Balance Equations   83
Benefits of Exercise for Fat Reduction   85
Eating Disorders   87
Summary   88
Questions   89

CHAPTER 8
The Physically Active Lifestyle and Aging — 90

Learning Objectives   90
Key Terms   90
Making Exercise a Regular Habit   91
Developing a Physically Active Lifestyle   92
Physical Activity and Aging   93
Summary   95
Questions   96

CHAPTER 9
Basic Nutrition for Health Fitness — 98

Learning Objectives   98
Key Terms   98

Contents

Eating for Health   99
Seven Basic Nutrients   99
Vitamins and Minerals Supplementation   111
Purchasing and Preparing Foods   112
Food Groups and Food Pyramids   113
Eat Well-Balanced Meals   116
Snacks and Desserts   117
Guidelines for Controlling Caloric Intake   117
Summary   118
Questions   118

CHAPTER **10**

Managing Stress and Back Injuries 120

Learning Objectives   120
Key Terms   120
Stress   121
Perception of Stress   121
Symptoms of Stress   122
Role of Physical Activity in Stress Management   123
Effective Stress Management   124
Types of Back Problems   125
Decreasing Back Injuries   127
Guidelines for Back Exercises   127
Specific Exercises for Preventing Back Problems   128
Other Lifestyle Factors   129
Summary   131
Questions   131

CHAPTER **11**

Exercise Management for Special Populations 132

Learning Objectives   132

Key Terms   132
Exercising for Special Populations   133
Arthritis and Exercise   133
Asthma and Exercise   134
Cancer and Exercise   136
Diabetes and Exercise   137
Fibromyalgia and Exercise   140
Hypertension and Exercise   141
Obesity and Exercise   143
Pregnancy and Exercise   144
Summary   146
Questions   147

Laboratory Units   146

1. Medical Clearance   149
2. Lifestyle Appraisal   151
3. Measuring One's Heart Rate   155
4. Evaluating Cardiorespiratory Fitness   157
5. Prescribing an Aerobic Exercise Program   161
6. Evaluating Muscular Strength/Endurance   165
7. Prescribing a Muscular Strength/Endurance Exercise Program   169
8. Evaluating Flexibility   171
9. Prescribing a Flexibility and Back Exercise Program   175
10. Body Mass Index   177
11. Estimating Caloric Expenditure   181
12. 24 Hour Caloric Analysis   185
13. Designing a Health Fitness Program   189

Bibliography   197
Glossary of Terms   227
Index   237

Essentials of Physical Activity

CHAPTER 1

Lifestyle and Health

Learning Objectives

This chapter emphasizes the importance of lifestyle to health. Historical accounts of the search for health and statistical evidence of factors that contribute to health and death are discussed. After reading this chapter you should be able to:

1. Discuss various searches for health and understand the multi-billion dollar industry surrounding that search (page 3).

2. Understand the change in leading causes of death from 1900 to 2000 and list the present most common degenerative diseases (page 5).

3. Know the four primary contributors to health and the role each play (pages 7 - 8).

4. List seven lifestyle characteristics that can affect health (pages 9 - 10).

Key Terms

Degenerative diseases
Health
Health-care costs
Life expectancy
Lifestyle

Historical Search for Health

People are increasingly becoming *health* conscious and are seeking knowledge about sound health practices. While it may seem to be a new trend, people have always searched for health. In 1513, Ponce de Leon, at 53 years of age, organized and led an expedition in search of the fountain of youth in the New World. He believed in the legend of a fountain that, when bathed in, would restore youth, vigor, and beauty. Instead of finding it, he discovered Florida and died after he was shot by an Indian's arrow.

Centuries earlier, during the time of Confucius, Chinese emperors hired alchemists to mix doses of gold and mercury into a solution to be drunk because these metals appeared not to tarnish. Unfortunately, mercury is poisonous and caused death, rather than longevity. The ancient Egyptians and Romans ate large quantities of garlic to lengthen their lives. Europeans tried a variety of roots and insects.

The ancient Greeks placed great value on health and fitness. Greek teachers emphasized exercise, good nutrition, sanitation, and discipline. The Old Testament Scriptures tied sound health practices to religious laws, especially in sanitation, cleanliness, and diet.

The late 19th century, in the United States, saw a great migration to the West. Many people went to discover gold or to start a new life, but historians estimate that at least 25% and perhaps as high as 50% went to the West, particularly the Southwest, in search of health.

Many people have searched for health in the form of medicines, tonics, and special foods. In the past, opium preparations have frequently be}n taken as painkillers with the result that large numbers of unsuspecting people became addicted. The same was true for "medicinal liquids" taken to soothe the nerves and calm the stomach. Such liquids usually contained large amounts of alcohol and often led to alcoholism in many that innocently used them. It has been reported that in the late 1800's when a current popular soft drink was first developed, it contained cocaine.

The Current Health Search

Today the search for health seems to have intensified. In "The Morality of Muscle Tone" Barbara Ehrenreich observed that the quest for health has become the new morality of the 1980's and 90's. As politicians, Wall Street, and some religious leaders have abandoned virtue, it has reappeared in "healthism," i.e. health as a transcendent value. Of the books on the weekly Top Ten best-selling list, often two or three are health-related books, usually extolling some new diet.

The estimated $50 million that was spent in the United States on diet, exercise, and health books in 1982, has grown to over $1 billion in 2008. However, that is a small amount compared to the total amount spent for all diet, exercise, and health-related products. The National Sporting Goods Association reported that in 2007 Americans spent $53.5 billion on sport equipment (e.g. stationary bikes, weight training equipment, golf, etc.). Additionally, $20 billion was spent on nutritional supplements and over $17.6 billion on health club memberships. If you combine all expenditures on fitness, sports, and leisure areas, Americans spend more than $330 billion per year.

Entrepreneurs have cashed in on the population's search for an attractive, thin body that is equated to a healthy body and are promoting various products that promise to help reach that goal. Scarcely a day goes by that we don't read several of the following claims in relation to some product: The easy way to health; Lose weight without diet or exercise; or Recommended by a leading medical center. Although exercise has clearly been demonstrated to be beneficial to health, appearance and longevity, many individuals choose to have expensive surgical procedures performed to improve their physical appearance with little regard to their health.

Numerous diet pills, diet aids, body wraps, and electrical stimulation devices are being promoted as beneficial for rapid weight loss, one pound or more per day. If anyone is searching for health, these are definitely not ways to obtain it, since any program that recommends more than two or three pounds weight loss per week is suspect and probably doesn't work or is detrimental to health. If it does work, the weight loss is water that will be rapidly regained. Advertisements that claim quick and easy ways to health should be view with skepticism.

The search for health has led to many "cures" over the centuries with some actually improving the quality of life. Unfortunately, most have had no effect on health other than to waste time and money, with some even causing death. The present consensuses of the allied health professions place the burden of health in the hands of the individual, making it each person's responsibility to adopt a healthy *lifestyle*.

Major Health Problems Today

Health problems today are different from what they were at the turn of the century. Table 1.1 compares the leading causes of death in 1900 to those of 2000. On the one hand, the infectious diseases of 1900 have been significantly reduced or are not present on the 2000 list, and thus accounting for the increased life span. However on the other hand, the incidence of both heart disease and cancer has virtually tripled since 1900, and those diseases are currently the leading causes of death.

Today, modern medicine has eliminated most of the early deaths due to infectious diseases leading to a large increase in *life expectancy* from 1900 to 1950 (see Figure 1.1). With these premature deaths no longer shorting the life span of Americans, *degenerative diseases* have come to the forefront and have taken over as the leading causes of death. Degenerative diseases are primarily diseases of lifestyle. They often begin undetected early in life and progressively cause deterioration in health, as we grow older. Often we feel that we are in a healthy state because we have no outward symptoms, of disease. Sometimes the first symptom of a disease is also the last, since 40 to 50% of all heart attack victims die before they reach the hospital after their first heart attack. Coronary arteries can be occluded (obstructed) as much as 70 to 90% with atherosclerosis (build up of fatty deposits on the inner walls of arteries) before any noticeable symptoms appear. This is why health is far more than just the outward appearance of freedom from disease.

Table 1.1

Leading Causes of Death in 1900 and 2000 in the United States

Causes of Death in 1900	Causes of Death in 2000
• Tuberculosis	• Heart Disease
• Pneumonia	• Cancer
• Diarrhea and Enteritis	• Stroke
• Heart Disease	• Chronic Lung Disease
• Liver Diseases	• Accidents
• Injuries	• Diabetes
• Stroke	• Pneumonia and Influenza
• Cancer	• Alzheimer's Disease
• Bronchitis	• Kidney Disease
• Diphtheria	• Systemic Blood Infection

Figure 1.1

Life Expectancy at Birth from 1900 to 2006 in the United States

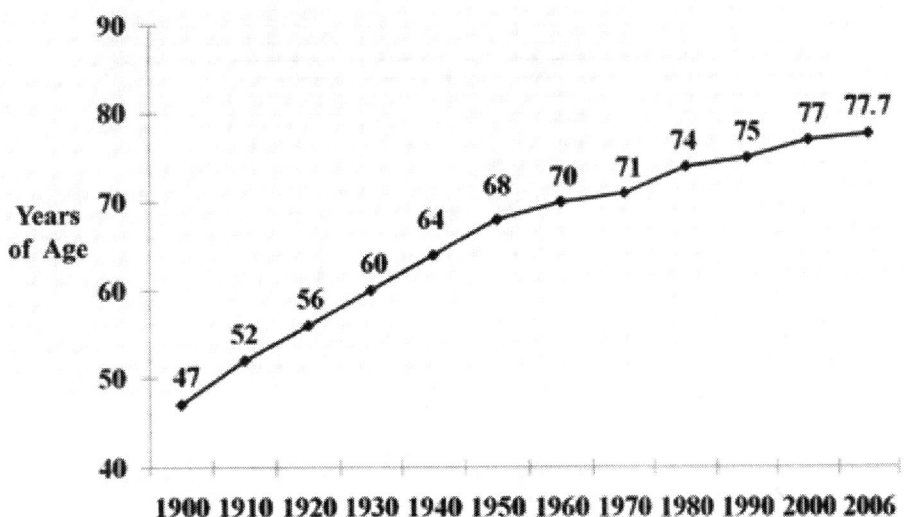

The Cost of Poor Health

In the economic arena, the effects of poor health are becoming vividly clear. In 1996, the total *health-care costs* topped the $1 trillion mark for the first time, up 60% from 1990 (see Fig. 1.2). Presently, health care costs are increasing approximately $100 billion each year. The 2007 expenditure represents 16.2% of the federal budget and is projected to reach 37% by 2030. General Motors spends more on health benefits for its employees than it does on buying steel for making cars. In 2006, the company added between $1500 and $2000 to the price of each new car. Poor health is expensive for everyone. Unhealthy lifestyles are the biggest contributing factor to the staggering health-care costs in the United States.

Figure 1.2
Total Health-Care Costs Increments since 1950 in the United States.

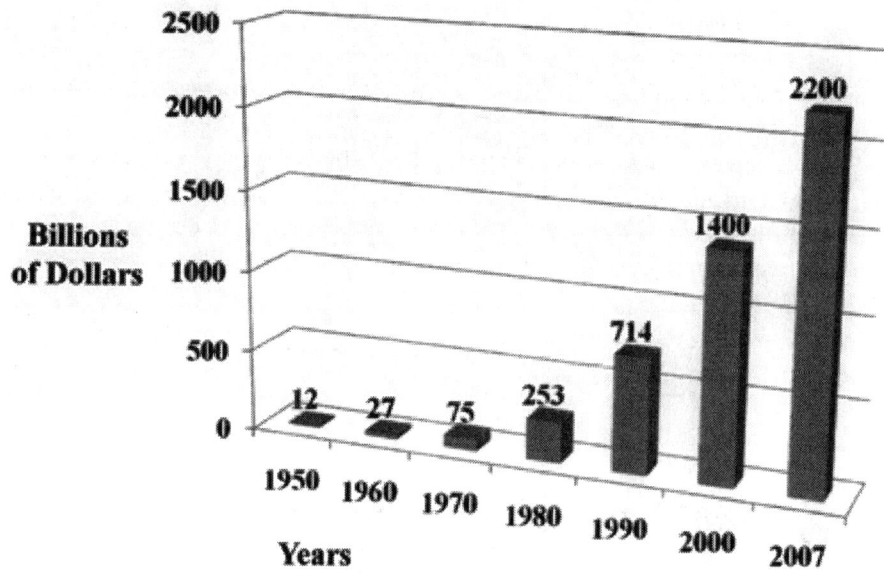

Changing Lifestyle

The way we live today is not the way our forefathers lived. The American lifestyle has changed significantly over the last 100 years. At the turn of the twentieth century, 70% of the American population lived in the country and was physically active in food production. They tilled the soil by walking behind a horse-drawn plow, tended animals, built their own homes, and often fought for survival. The food they ate was not processed or refined.

With advanced technology, occupations became less physically demanding. Walking behind a plow for the farmer gave way to riding on a tractor. Walking to school, church, and the grocery store gave way to riding in the automobile. Wood-burning stoves that required chopped wood for fuel evolved to automatic furnaces. Today, 95% of our population lives in cities and is accustomed to work-saving devices, such as power lawn mowers, elevators, golf carts, and weed eaters. The new discoveries and lifestyle changes have been a mixed blessing for health.

In the years from the birth of Christ to 1900, life expectancy at birth advanced only 20 years (from 25 to 47). In the 100 years since 1900 (see Figure 1.1) however, life expectancy at birth advanced 30 years (from 47 to 77). But before drawing erroneous conclusions attributing the increased life expectancy to lifestyle, we must look more carefully at the reasons for the increased life span.

During the past one hundred years, the medical profession has made many landmark discoveries. Whereas infectious diseases such as typhoid fever, smallpox, diphtheria, tuberculosis, scarlet fever, pneumonia, measles, whooping cough, and others caused by microorganisms killed hundreds of thousands every year in the past, these diseases are almost unheard of today. Medical science has won the battle against most infectious diseases through the use of vaccinations and modern medicines. In 1900 the death rate from tuberculosis was 195 per 100,000 persons, but today it is two per 100,000 persons. We used to fear outbreaks of polio but since the Salk vaccine of the 1950s, this disease no longer presents a threat.

Most of the increase in life expectancy has come from conquering infectious diseases and improvements in living conditions. Public health policies, improved sanitation, vaccinations, antiseptic surgery, and other medical discoveries have all contributed to the increase. In Figure 1.1, the slope of the curve has flattened since 1950. Ironically, the last 50 years is when most of the expensive and technologically advanced medical innovations were introduced. In reality, a person who reaches age 45 today can expect to live only two or three years longer than a person who was 45 years old in 1900.

Contributors to Health or Disease

The United States Department of Health and Human Services Centers for Disease Control and Prevention in Atlanta, Georgia has identified four factors that contribute to the cause of death and disease.

1. **Health Care** - Health care is the organization and administration of health services by professionals in our society. It involves doctors, nurses, hospitals, clinics, ambulances, and related health-care personnel and facilities. Occasionally this area is to blame for the death of a person because of the misdiagnosis of a problem, wrong prescription of medication, or some other neglect or lack of knowledge.

2. **Environment** - The evidence is clear that environment (physical, social, economic, and family) can affect our health. Living and working in high-pollution areas contribute to higher rates of emphysema and lung cancer. Other environmental problems may be stress, toxic materials, transportation, and so forth.

3. **Genetics** - A person's basic cell structure and characteristics are determined by heredity. The tendency toward heart disease, cancer, hemophilia, sickle cell anemia, diabetes and certain other diseases may be present at birth. However, heredity alone rarely causes the disease. Usually the tendency interacting with an individual's lifestyle and environment can delay or hasten the prospects of the disease.

4. **Lifestyle** - The way we live influences our health and can be a major cause of our own diseases and death. In some cases we are literally digging our own graves. Lifestyle involves total behavior, 24 hours a day, seven days a week, 52 weeks of the year. The number of sleeping hours, the food consumed, the fluids drank, the type of work, relationships with others, leisure time activities, plus all other aspects of living, reflects the individual's lifestyle.

Lifestyle and Health

The Centers for Disease Control and Prevention has evaluated 10 common leading causes of death and has allocated the proportion of each of these four contributing factors to the cause of death. Table 1.2 reveals their results.

Table 1.2
The Contribution of Four Factors to the Ten Common Causes of Death in the United States

Ten Common Causes of Death	Health Care (%)	Environment (%)	Genetics (%)	Lifestyle (%)
Heart Disease	12	9	28	54
Cancer	10	24	29	37
Stroke	7	22	21	50
Diabetes	6	0	68	26
Cirrhosis of Liver	3	9	18	70
Influenza and Pneumonia	18	20	39	23
Vehicular Accidents	12	18	1	69
Other Accidents	14	31	4	51
Suicide	3	35	2	60
Homicide	0	35	2	63

These statistics clearly place the majority of the responsibility for maintaining good health with the individual. Over 50% of the causes of all deaths are due to lifestyle (see Figure 1.3). Heart disease and stroke are often combined into a category of cardiovascular disease; these two diseases together account for 40% of all deaths. In cardiovascular disease, lifestyle is the major contributing factor, and when environment is combined with lifestyle, over 65% of cardiovascular diseases have controllable components. When Joseph Califano was secretary of the Department of Health, Education, and Welfare, he concluded that the individual themselves can do more for their own health and well-being than any doctor, hospital, drug, or medical device.

Figure 1.3

Seven Lifestyle Characteristics that Effect life Expectancy.

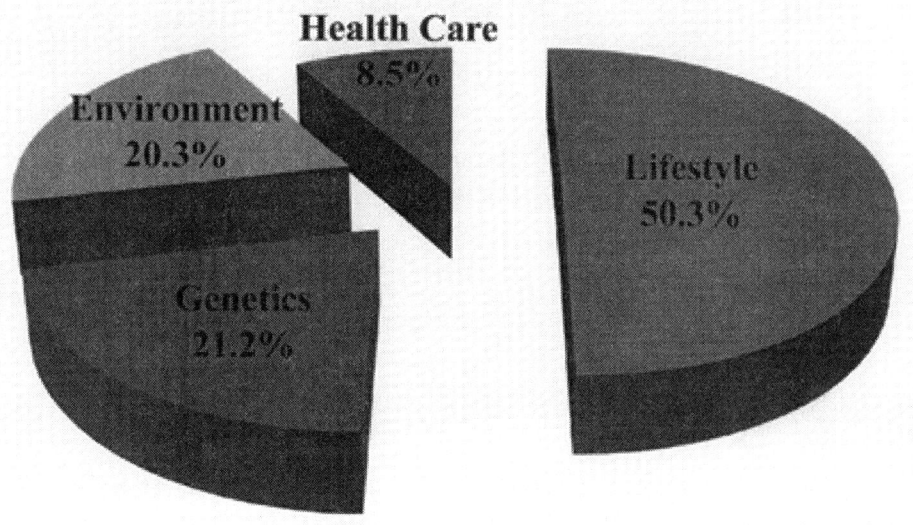

In addition to the statistics from the Centers for Disease Control and Prevention, other research has shown that lifestyle does significantly affect health. The American Institute for Cancer Research reports that 35% of cancer deaths are caused by diet and 30% by smoking. Mormons and Seventh-Day Adventists have been the target of numerous studies because of their healthful lifestyle that emphasizes good diet, exercise, avoidance of alcohol and caffeine, and positive family relationships. Mormons have a cancer rate of only 60% of the national average, and Seventh-Day Adventists have a cancer rate of only 50% of the national average. Additionally, Seventh-Day Adventists have one-third of the bronchitis and emphysema (both related to smoking), half of the expected heart disease, and half of the diabetes of the national average. They also have a greater life expectancy. Studies comparing death rates in Nevada and Utah revealed that the death rate in Nevada was 35% higher for all ages than that of Utah. The primary difference between the two states was the heavy Mormon population in Utah.

Dr. Nedra Belloe and her associates have conducted an ongoing study in California of the relationship between lifestyle characteristics and life expectancy. The seven characteristics they have studied are shown in Table 1.3. The results have demonstrated that if at age 45 you follow three or fewer of the seven lifestyle habits, your life expectancy is an additional 22 years, or age 67. If, on the other hand, you follow six or seven of the habits, your life expectancy increases by 33 years to an age of 78 years.

Table 1.3
Seven Lifestyle Characteristics that Effect Life Exectancy.

1. Exercise moderately.
2. Refrain from smoking.
3. Eat breakfast everyday.
4. Sleep seven to eight hours per night.
5. Maintain a normal healthy body weight.
6. Eat three meals per day and avoid snacks.
7. Drink alcohol in moderation or abstain completely.

Hans Kugler, in his book "Slowing Down the Aging Process", summarizes some of the key lifestyle behaviors and their health benefits for longevity. Smoking two or more packs of cigarettes per day subtracts eight to nine years from your life. You lose one year for each 10 pounds of excess weight you carry plus an additional six to 10 years off for bad nutrition. However if you exercise regularly, can add six to nine years to your life.

Today there are several known cultures that appear to have long life expectancies, many over 100 years and some surpass 120 years. All these cultures follow very similar lifestyles that include a diet low in fat, cholesterol, processed sugar, salt, and calories. In addition, the members lead physically active lives consisting of hard physical work and live in a quiet, peaceful, and relaxing environment filled with few worries, and low stress.

Table 1.4
Three Cultures with Life Expectances Over 100 Years

> **Vilcabambans of Southern Ecuador**
>
> **Hunzkuts from the Himalayas of Northern Pakistan**
>
> **Caucasian group in Russia between the Black and Caspian Seas**

Life insurance companies report that 83% of deaths before age 65 could have been prevented with a healthy lifestyle. Studies at the University of Tennessee and at the Massachusetts General Hospital reveal that lifestyle was a major contributing factor in more than 78% of the hospital admissions.

Summary

The search for health dates far back into history. Currently, the health search is a multi-billion dollar industry. Effective and not so effective items for maintaining health are available to the health and fitness consumer. The cost of health care and prevalence of heart disease virtually command a change to positive lifestyle behavior. The four factors that contribute to the cause of death and disease consist of inadequate health care, the environment, genetics, and lifestyle. Lifestyle is the one factor that each individual can positively control. Life expectancy and quality of life can be improved through proper nutrition, maintaining normal body weight, exercising, adequate rest, refraining from smoking, and drinking alcohol in moderation or abstaining.

Review Questions

1. What personal expenditures have you made in the past year that relates to your "search for Health"?

2. What were the five leading causes of death in 1900 and 2000 and what factors have affected he change between these two periods?

3. Define degenerative diseases; list the most common ones.

4. List and explain the four primary contributors to health and disease.

5. What are seven lifestyle characteristics that can affect life expectancy?

6. What percent of cancer deaths are caused by diet and what percent by smoking?

CHAPTER 2

Concept of Health Fitness

Learning Objectives

This chapter describes an over-all concept of health fitness and the benefits of exercise to one's health. Upon completion you should be able to:

1. Define health and understand the five health fitness components (pages 15 - 16).
2. Explain the components of performance fitness (page 17).
3. Understand the concepts of the four principles of general conditioning (i.e. overload, specificity, individuality, and reversibility) (pages 17 - 18).
4. Explain the four general categories of exercises (page 19).
5. Understand the many health benefits of regular physical exercise to the body (pages 20 - 22).
6. Discuss the relationship exercise has on aging (pages 22 - 23).

Key Terms

Aerobic Exercises
Anaerobic Exercises
Body Composition
Cardiorespiratory Fitness
Flexibility
Flexibility Exercises
Health Fitness
Individuality Principle
Muscular Endurance
Muscle Development Exercises
Muscular Strength
Overload Principle
Performance Fitness
Physical Fitness
Reversibility Principle
Specificity Principle

What is Health

Although it is sometimes difficult to define what is meant by "good health", it is usually easy to identify the effects of "poor health". Some people experience frequent, recurring illnesses that cause them to be hospitalized. Others suffer from less severe problems that prevent them from going about their normal daily activities for a period of time. Most of us experience a feeling of being unwell at some point in our lives.

For many years, health was considered by most people as "absence of disease." If a person was not sick or had no disease, the individual was said to be healthy. The current view of health is that it is more than simply the absence of disease. Suppose you view two persons, neither of whom are sick. Being free from disease, they are considered healthy. One person is overweight, is often tense and anxious, and has difficulty walking up a flight of stairs without breathing heavily. The other is of normal weight, is physically fit, has energy to enjoy numerous activities after a day's work, and is also happy and relaxed. Both have an outward freedom from disease, but they differ significantly in their quality of life and are not really in equally good health.

Just as wealth is more than absence of poverty and happiness is more than absence of sorrow, health is far more than absence of disease. Health is freedom from diseases plus the possession of *physical fitness*, which promotes quality living as well as longevity.

Concept of Physical Fitness

Most authorities agree that there are two general categories of physical fitness. One is fitness related to health that is called *health fitness* and the other category is fitness related to efficiency of movement and sports skill that is called *performance fitness* (see Figure 2.1).

Components of Health Fitness:

1. **Cardiorespiratory Fitness** - Healthy and efficient functioning of the heart, lungs, blood vessels, and the blood is considered *Cardiorespiratory (CR) fitness*. This system functions to deliver oxygen and nutrients to all the cells of the body and remove waste products. Efficient functioning of this system is not only important for sustaining life, but is essential for performing all physical activities. To develop the CR systems, activities must employ large-muscle groups contracting in a rhythmic manner for an extended period of time (e.g. running, walking, swimming, and etc.).

2. **Muscular Strength** -The ability of the skeletal muscles to exert maximal amount of force is called *muscular strength*. Adequate

strength is important for health in order to perform daily tasks more efficiently, to decrease joint and muscle injuries, and to delay the weakening of muscles and bones with aging. To develop muscular strength, weight-training devices are utilized to place a workload above the amount the muscles are accustomed to.

3. **Muscular Endurance** - The ability of the skeletal muscle to perform repetitive contractions and/or maintain a contraction for an extended period of time is called *muscular endurance*. Proper muscular endurance enhances posture, prevents low back pain, improves muscle tone, and self-esteem. To develop muscular endurance, the muscle is repeatedly contracted beyond daily levels (e.g. sit-ups, push-ups and pull-ups).

4. **Flexibility** - The ability to move a joint through the full range of motion without discomfort or pain is called *Flexibility*. Flexibility ensures efficient body movements and is essential for preventing muscle and joint injury. To develop good flexibility, stretching exercises are performed to the point of discomfort and held.

5. **Body Composition** - The ratio of lean tissue (i.e. bones, muscles, and body organs) and fat in the body is referred to as *body composition*. Excess body fat is related to increased health problems (e.g. cardiovascular disease, hypertension, stroke, and cancer) and early death. On the other hand, too little body fat also compromises health by disrupting the reproductive system, decreasing temperature regulation, and limiting protective cushioning of internal organs and joints. To maintain healthy body composition, caloric intake and expenditure must be in balance.

Figure 2.1

Components of Physical Fitness

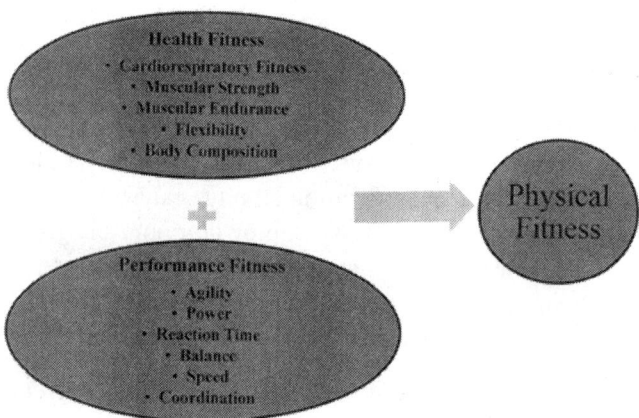

The five components of health fitness are essential to good health and wellbeing. When these components are improved, there is a decreased risk of diseases related to a sedentary lifestyle such as heart disease, type 2 diabetes, and osteoporosis. One advantage of activities that promote health fitness is the fact that they may be done alone or with others. Generally, competition is only with oneself to fulfill individual goals.

Performance fitness includes the five components of health fitness, as well as the following six components:

Components of Performance Fitness:

1. **Agility** - The ability to move the body quickly in different directions, including stopping and starting is called agility.

2. **Power** - The explosive use of strength refers to power and is similar to muscular strength except it is strength per unit of time.

3. **Reaction time** - The ability to react quickly to a stimulus, such as, moving quickly to return a fast tennis serve is termed reaction time.

4. **Balance** - The skill to maintain equilibrium when stationary (static balance) or while moving (dynamic balance) is referred to as balance.

5. **Speed** - The quickness of movement, such as how fast one can run 50 meters is called speed.

6. **Coordination** - The ability to gracefully and smoothly integrate movements of different body parts at the same time is termed coordination. This is necessary when performing an activity such as kicking a ball, catching a ball, and performing dance steps.

These six components of performance fitness are important for an individual to successfully participate in sports activities. These components however, are not essential for a person to have good health, but the health fitness components usually do contribute to success in sports. Many sports such as tennis, gymnastics, basketball, football, badminton, and racquetball rely heavily on both health fitness and performance fitness components. Participation in skill-related sport activities will assist in maintaining a level of health fitness; however these activities by themselves will not develop good health fitness.

Principles of Conditioning

In order to improve physical fitness a conditioning program will be necessary. The components of health fitness improve if increased demands are placed upon the bodily systems that they are dependent upon. Additionally, physical fitness is an individual matter with every person possessing different abilities and needs. Some may need to work more on flexibility while others might need to work to develop muscular strength.

However, to improve physical fitness, there are four basic principles that need to be followed by everyone in order for improvement to occur.

1. **Overload** - The *overload principle* states that exercising at a level of intensity higher than is normally performed will cause the body systems being stressed to adapt to that intensity and enable the body to function more efficiently. The overload principle applies equally to the development of health and performance fitness components. As important as overload is for improvement to occur, the overload must not be excessive so as to cause injury. The principle of overload is accomplished through manipulating combinations of frequency, intensity and time.

2. **Specificity** - The *specificity principle* refers to adaptations in the metabolic and physiological systems are dependent on the type of overload being used. This implies that "you get what you train for." In other words specific exercises must be done to improve specific components of physical fitness for specific organs, muscles, and joints. For example, jogging will improve cardiorespiratory fitness but will not increase flexibility.

3. **Individuality** - The *individuality principle* brings to light the many factors that contribute to individual variation in conditioning response. Genetic factors have an influence on the conditioning response from exercise, but the general adaptation from the overload will be similar from person to person. Clearly, conditioning benefits are optimized when exercise programs are designed to meet the individual needs and capacities.

4. **Reversibility** - The *reversibility principle* states that the beneficial adaptations from the conditioning process are transient and reversible. Simply put, "use it or lose it." The human body is very efficient and will not maintain unused or neglected areas of the body. These areas will be eliminated or converted into another form and stored. In only a few weeks, significant conditioning benefits will be lost.

Adaptation and Progression

As a person overloads the body, it will adjust, and improvements in fitness will occur. As the body adapts to the overload, one must progressively increase the resistance or amount of work performed for continued improvement and increased health benefits. By progressing slowly, the chance of injury is limited and a person will gradually improve. Health fitness should be a lifetime goal that can not be achieved quickly and then forgotten.

Types of Exercise

Following the conditioning principle of specificity, the body will adapt according to the type of overload (i.e. exercise). There are basically four general categories of exercises, and each has specific application for benefiting different systems of the body.

1. **Aerobic** - The primary function of ***aerobic exercises*** is to develop the cardiorespiratory system. By placing an overload on the heart, lungs, and exercising muscles; improvements in oxygen delivery and utilization occur. These types of exercises are beneficial in preventing heart disease and improving functioning of the immune system. Aerobic exercises use large muscle groups in a repetitive, rhythmic motion for an extended period of time. They include walking, jogging, cycling, swimming, and exercise to music. Guidelines for aerobic exercises will be described in chapter 4.

2. **Muscle-development** - The primary purpose of ***muscle-development exercises*** is to develop the muscles of the body that control movement and maintain posture. These exercises include weight training using machine weights and/or free weight as well as calisthenics. They are vital in developing strength, muscle endurance, muscle tone, and good posture. Muscle-development exercises are an essential and important part of a good conditioning program. These will be discussed in Chapter 5.

3. **Flexibility** - The primary reason for ***flexibility exercises*** is to improve or maintain joint range of motion. Through appropriate stretching techniques, risk of injuries is reduced and efficiency of movement is increased. Flexibility exercises consist of stretching either alone or with a partner and require holding the stretched position for 15 to 60 seconds. Flexibility exercises should not be confused with stretching exercises used as part of a warm-up (Chapter 6).

4. **Anaerobic** - The primary function of ***anaerobic exercises*** is to develop performance fitness such as speed, agility, and strength. They include sprinting, strength training, agility drills used in sports activities, and other high-intensity activities of short duration. Anaerobic exercises are especially important for sport skill performance but are not a necessary part of an adult conditioning program for health fitness (chapter 5).

Of the four types of exercise, aerobic, muscle-development, and flexibility form the core of a good health fitness conditioning program. Interestingly, all three must be included for the conditioning program to achieve health fitness.

Health Benefits from Regular Physical Exercise

The benefits of exercise upon the body depend upon the type of exercises performed, the intensity and duration of the exercise, and the number of times the exercises are done each week. Some health benefits occur immediately after performing a single exercise bout, however most require many months of consistent conditioning to reap full benefits. Listed below are some of the beneficial adaptations that can be expected when a comprehensive conditioning program is followed.

1. **Heart** - With aerobic conditioning, resting and submaximal exercise heart rate decreases. The size and weight of the heart will increase along with stroke volume (i.e. the amount of blood ejected from the heart each contraction) during rest and exercise. This allows the oxygen needs of the body to be met with less work by the heart.

2. **Blood and its Vessels** - Regular exercise will increase blood volume augmenting oxygen transport and cooling the body when in a hot environment. It can also improve the blood lipids by lowering cholesterol, low-density lipoprotein (LDL - bad cholesterol), and triglycerides. In addition, high-density lipoprotein (HDL - good cholesterol) will increase. The blood vessels improve by having greater elasticity and distensibility (ability to expand or stretch). Because of this, resting and submaximal blood pressure decreases and lessens the workload of the heart. In addition, the blood vessels increase in cross-sectional area and create more capillaries which function to deliver more oxygen to cells, thus enabling all the body's cells to function better. Also, the blood vessels will increase their ability to dilate and constrict allowing delivery of the blood to areas where the need is greatest at any given time.

3. **Pulmonary System** - Regular exercise improves the functioning of the pulmonary system in several ways. The lungs will have a greater capacity to inhale and exhale and will also allow more oxygen to be diffused into the blood. During submaximal exercise, conditioned individuals breathe less than before they began a conditioning program. This improved ventilatory economy increases the oxygen availability.

4. **Skeletal Muscles** - Aerobically conditioned muscles will utilize more fat for energy than unconditioned. Strength-trained muscles will be stronger and more resistant to fatigue. Also hypertrophy (increase in cross-sectional area) will occur, however the amount is dependent upon type of training, gender, genetics and maturation. Tendons and ligaments also increase in strength, decreasing joint injuries and improving

the function of an injured joint. The development of muscle tissue is a significant factor in slowing down the aging process.

5. **Body Composition** - Both aerobic and strengthening exercises work to decrease excess body fat. Through aerobic conditioning the body improves its ability to mobilize fat from fat stores and use it for energy and increases the amount of fat used in a 24-hour period. Weight training on the other hand, increases muscle mass, which is more metabolically active than fat tissue, causing increased caloric expenditure over the day.

6. **Bones** - Regular exercises consisting of weight baring and strengthening activities increase calcium deposition in the bones being overloaded. Weak bones lead to osteoporosis (porous and brittle bones) which affects 28 million women in the United States and is responsible for 1.5 million fractures each year at a cost of $14 billion. Calcium supplementation alone will not decrease this disorder; exercise is needed.

7. **Psychological** - A regular exercise program favorably modifies the psychological state. These benefits include a reduction in anxiety, a decreased level of depression, and an improved self-esteem. Exercise negates the harmful effects of stress. In addition, regular conditioning can greatly improve ones personal appearance, enhancing self-concept and body image.

8. **Immune System** - Aerobic conditioning improves the natural immune function of the body. Natural Killer cells increase their activity in inactivating viruses and the metastatic potential of tumor cells. In addition, aerobic exercising slows the age-related decrease in T-cell function, which defends against viral and fungal infections, and assists in regulating other immune mechanisms. Also, regular exercise develops the body's antioxidant functions and increases intestinal transit time. However, high intensive exercise or a rapid increase in training has the opposite effect and decreases the body's immune system. Numerous studies have shown that physically fit persons are sick less often, see their doctors less, are hospitalized less, and spend less on medical care than persons who are not physically fit.

The Journal of the American Medical Association published a major study in 1989 where 13,344 people were followed over an average of eight years. Figure 2.2 shows the results indicating that the fit males and fit females had a significantly lower death rate from cancer, cardiovascular disease, and all diseases combined than the unfit males and unfit females

Figure 2.2

Death Rates for Fit and Unfit Males and Females

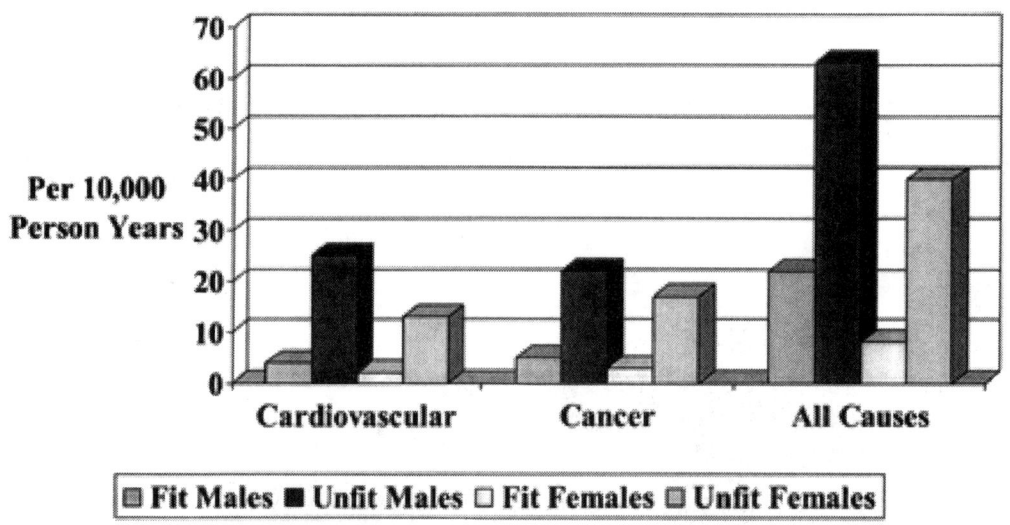

A study from the Massachusetts General Hospital reported that 86% of hospitalizations probably could have been prevented if patients had followed a healthful lifestyle. Separate studies done on employees of Northern Natural Gas, Tenneco, Mesa Petroleum Company, Allen Bradley Co., New York State Department of Education and Civil Services, NASA, and Purdue University reported less sickness, better health, better job performance, and fewer health insurance claims among employees who were physically fit. Businesses are beginning to realize that they can't afford to hire unfit employees. In the last ten years more than three hundred companies have started fitness programs for their employees.

Exercise and Aging

Regular physical conditioning delays or slows the aging process (see Figure 2.3). For years, the decrease in physiological functioning of the aging body was considered to be the normal result of growing old. However, recently researchers have started to separate poor health fitness from the normal physiological decline due to aging. Even if a sedentary lifestyle has been followed for decades, starting a conditioning program will generate benefits and slow the aging process. Studies have shown that even into the ninth decade of life, the body will adapt and improve with a health fitness conditioning program. The sooner an inactive individual begins to exercise (after medical clearance from a physician), the greater the delay in the aging process and the sooner an increase in health benefits. However, it is never too late to begin an exercise program. Even after decades of sedentary living, possibly including a heart attack, a healthier and more productive life can be gained.

Figure 2.3

Percent of Physiological Function of Active and Sedentary Individuals as Compared to a Sedentary 20 Year Old

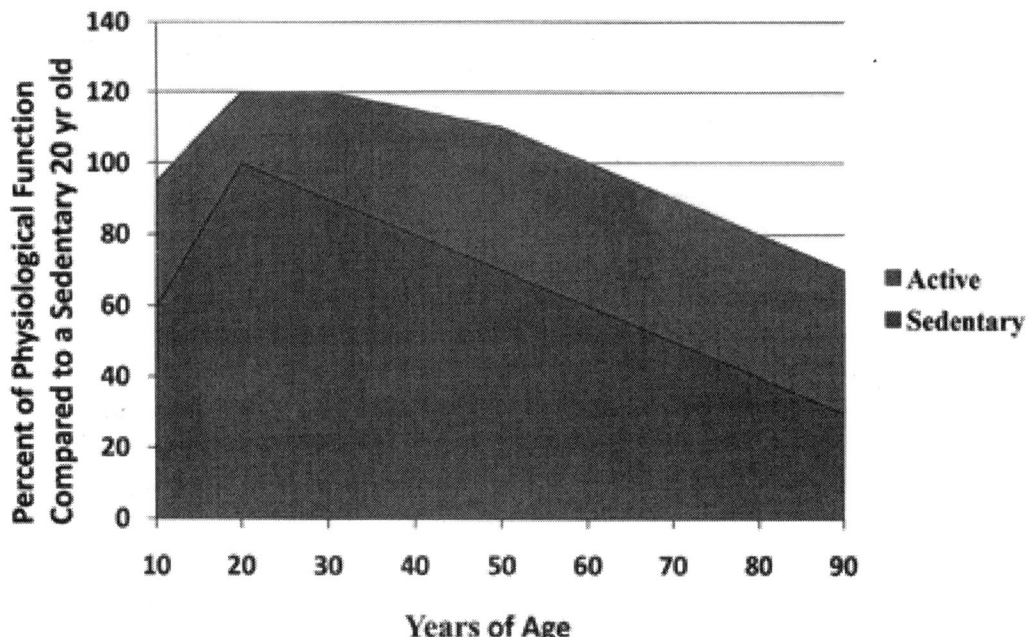

Geneticist Leonard Hayflick has stated that on the basis of his research on cell division and deterioration, mankind could expect a life span of 110 to 120 years. He reports that human cells in a perfect environment continue to divide until they stop according to their genetic code. Evidence is mounting that the way people live their lives is significantly affecting health and life expectancies.

Summary

Health includes absence of disease and the possession of sufficient physical fitness that allows one to live a full life of quality and quantity. Health fitness includes cardiorespiratory fitness, muscular strength, muscular endurance, flexibility, and good body composition. Performance fitness includes agility, power, reaction time, balance, speed, and coordination. To improve health or performance fitness, the principles of overload, specificity, individuality, and reversibility must be followed. Exercises for improving fitness include aerobic, anaerobic, muscle-development, and flexibility activities. A regular conditioning program will benefit all systems of the body and as a result improve the quality of life.

Review Questions

1. Discuss the statement "Health is the absence of disease."

2. List and define the five health fitness components.

3. List and define the six performance fitness components.

4. Explain the four principles of exercise.

5. List and explain the four general categories of exercise, and discuss the benefits of each to different parts of the body.

6. Discuss at least six health benefits from regular physical exercise.

7. Which type of blood lipid is increased with aerobic exercise?

CHAPTER 3

The Cardiorespiratory System

Learning Objectives

This chapter explains the anatomy and physiology of the cardiorespiratory system and its relationship to health fitness. Upon the completion of this chapter you should be able to:

1. Know the four basic needs of cells (page 27).
2. Understand the four components of the cardiorespiratory system (pages 27 - 33).
3. Describe the function of the lungs in exercise (page 30).
4. Describe the four methods that help blood return to the heart (page 31).
5. Understand the significance of systolic and diastolic blood pressure (page 32).
6. Understand the importance of hemoglobin (page 34).

Key Terms

Anemia
Arteries
Arterioles
Atrium
Blood Pressure
Capillaries
Cardiac Output
Coronary Vessels
Diastolic Blood Pressure
Heart Rate
Hemoglobin
Hypertension
Ischemic
Myocardium
Stroke Volume
Systolic Blood Pressure
Valsalva Maneuver
Varicose Veins
Veins
Ventricle

Requirements of the Cell

The basic unit of life in the human organism as well as in all other life forms is the cell. More than one trillion cells are in the human body. It would take about 40,000 blood cells to fill the typewriter letter O. Every minute about three billion cells in our body die, and three billion new cells are formed to replace them.

Every cell has a specific function. Some cells are specialized to cause movement (muscle cells), some are specialized to carry messages (nerve cells), and others are specialized to carry on other functions such as digestion and reproduction. However, for all cells to function, regardless of their structure and purpose, there are four requirements: 1) every cell needs oxygen; 2) every cell needs nutrients (carbohydrates, proteins, fats, vitamins, and minerals); 3) every cell needs water; and 4) every cell needs to get rid of waste products. Of the four requirements, the need for oxygen is the most critical since the body can survive for weeks without food and days without water but only minutes without oxygen.

The Cardiorespiratory System

The cardiorespiratory system functions to deliver a constant supply of oxygen to all the cells of the body and to remove carbon dioxide. The four components of the cardiorespiratory system are 1) heart, 2) lungs, 3) blood, and 4) blood vessels.

1. Heart

The heart is a muscular pumping organ with four chambers (see Figure 3.1): two upper chambers (right and left *atriums*) and two lower chambers (right and left *ventricles*). The heart functions as a double pump that provides the force to transport blood through the body to every cell. Each time the heart muscle (*myocardium*) contracts, it creates a pressure that forces blood into the arteries to deliver oxygen and nutrients to the cells. The heart has a tremendous capacity to vary in the number of times it contracts (i.e. beats) per minute. An adult's *heart rate* may vary from 40 to 80 beats per minute at rest (see Table 3.1) to as high as 160 to 200 beats per minute during maximal exercise.

The resting and submaximal heart rate varies considerably between fit and unfit persons. This is due to the strength of contraction of the myocardium. Table 3.2 shows that at rest a highly fit person's heart will beat almost half as much as an unfit person's heart. The fit (conditioned) heart may beat as much as 43,200 fewer times per day than that of the unfit heart. Obviously the slower the heart beats, the better the heart muscle itself can receive blood to feed its cells. The heart muscle receives its own blood supply only when it is at rest and not contracting.

Figure 3.1

Anatomy of the Human Heart and the Direction of Blood Flow

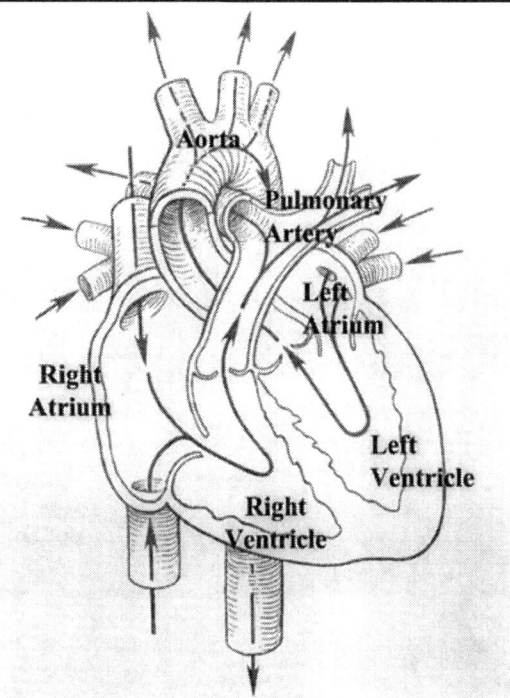

Reprint with permission from Williams & Wilkins Publishing

Table 3.1

Health Fitness Standards for Resting Heart Rate Per Minute in Adults Without Heart Disease

Health Fitness Standard	Resting Heart Rate Per Minute
Excellent	< 60
Good	61 - 65
Average	66 - 70
Poor	71 - 80
Very Poor	> 80

Table 3.2

Cardiac Output at Rest and Maximal Exercise for a Fit and Unfit 20 Year Old

20 Year Old	Activity Level	Heart Rate	Stroke Volume	Cardiac Output
Unfit	Rest	75 bpm	67 ml	5 L
Fit	Rest	50 bpm	100 ml	5 L
Unfit	Maximal	200 bpm	100 ml	20 L
Fit	Maximal	199 bpm	160 ml	32 L

The stronger the heart muscle, the more blood can be pumped and delivered to the cells of the body. The amount of blood pumped from the heart per contraction is called *stroke volume*. When the stroke volume is multiplied by the heart rate per minute, *cardiac output* is obtained. Cardiac output reflects the functional capacity of the circulation to meet the demands placed upon it. At maximum workloads, a highly fit heart can pump 25 to 30 quarts of blood per minute, whereas an unfit heart may pump eight to ten quarts. However, cardiac output at rest and during submaximal exercise is similar in both the fit and unfit. As shown in Table 3.2, the fit heart has a greater stroke volume allowing a slower heart rate and can be used as an indicator of cardiorespiratory fitness.

Coronary Blood Flow. Although tremendous quantities of blood are pumped through the atrias and ventricles every minute, the heart itself does not receive any nutrients or oxygen from this blood flowing through its chambers. Rather, the heart is dependent on its own vascular system called the *coronary vessels*.

The coronary arteries supply the blood to the heart (cardiac) muscle and branch off from the aorta. Cardiac muscle requires a constant supply of oxygen, and when the body is at rest it utilizes up to 80% of the oxygen carried in the blood flowing through the coronary vessels. During increased rate of contraction (e.g. exercise or stress), blood flow through these arteries must also increase to meet the oxygen need of the heart. When fat filled plaque deposits occur in the coronary arteries (i.e. atherosclerosis), the flow of blood to the myocardium is reduced. This presents no problem at rest even with up to 80% blockage, however as greater and greater demands occur, the supply becomes less and less sufficient.

When the demand of the heart muscle for oxygen is not met by the coronary blood flow, the area of the heart deficient in oxygen becomes *ischemic* (i.e. lack of oxygen due to inadequate blood supply). This lack of oxygen can result in angina pectoris, a pain in the chest that usually radiates to the left shoulder and arm, a warning signal of impending heart damage. Ischemia to the myocardium can lead to death of the affected area, called a myocardial infarction, which is more commonly known as a heart attack. The severity of the heart attack depends upon the location and size of the infarction. The heart attack may be unnoticed by the individual, or it may result in their death.

2. Lungs and Breathing

The major function of the lungs is to provide a location for gas exchange between the blood and ambient air. Within the lungs are over 300 million microscopic sacs called alveoli where air is located inside and blood is on the outside. If the alveoli were opened and laid flat they would cover half a tennis court, presenting a great surface area for gas exchange. During respiration, oxygen moves from the inhaled air through the alveoli and into the blood. At the same time, carbon dioxide from the blood diffuses into the alveoli and out of the lungs on exhalation.

As the inspired air moves through the passageways to the lungs it is moistened, filtered of foreign particles, and brought to body temperature. Breathing is an involuntary response regulated by several systems, however the higher brain centers can override allowing for temporary voluntary control. Normal healthy lungs are not a limiting factor in exercise. These organs are very efficient at moving large volumes of air into and out of the body, as well as conducting gas exchange with the blood. Smoking (e.g. tobacco and marijuana) or living in a high pollution environment including one with second-hand smoke will cause damage and ruptures to the alveoli decreasing the efficiency of the lungs and possibly causing early death.

The diaphragm and intercostals are the chief muscles involved in breathing. During exercise, these muscles must work more intensely, and for unfit individuals the constant contraction and relaxation of the diaphragm may lead to a sharp pain in the side of the lower chest. This side ache is due to a lack of oxygen to the diaphragm muscle and will cause an exerciser to decrease the workout intensity. However, this muscle will adapt as the body becomes conditioned, and soon this side pain will no longer occur.

3. Blood Vessels

The blood vessels of the body form the circulatory system through which oxygen and nutrients are transported to all the cells of the body and carbon dioxide and waste products are transported away. This transporting system consists of three different categories of blood vessels: 1) *arteries*, 2) *capillaries,* and 3) *veins*.

Arteries are tubes that carry blood away from the heart and are divided into groups called large arteries, small arteries, and *arterioles*. Large arteries are able to withstand high pressures due to the walls being composed of several layers of connective tissue and smooth muscle. Even though these walls are impervious to gases because of their thickness, they are still elastic but only stretch slightly under high pressure. The large arteries branch into smaller arteries.

The small artery walls have similar construction and characteristics as the large arteries but have fewer layers of connective tissue and smooth muscle. These walls are still too thick for gases to penetrate. The small arteries branch further into smaller vessels called arterioles.

The walls of the arterioles have smooth muscle circling the vessels and function to regulate regional blood flow. This is accomplished by contracting or relaxing the smooth muscles circumferencing the vessel causing the internal diameter to be altered. During exercise the arterioles leading to the liver and digestive system constrict causing a reduction of blood flow to these areas, while at the same time, the arterioles leading to the skin and working skeletal muscles are dilated causing an increase flow. By redistributing blood flow to those areas in greatest need (i.e. exercising muscles), an increase in oxygen is made available. Also with additional blood flow to the skin, the extra heat generated by the contracting skeletal muscles will be better able to dissipate.

The second category of blood vessels is called capillaries. Capillaries are microscopic, thin walled tubes that connect arteries to the veins. This thin wall consists of a single layer of endothelial cells, which allow oxygen in the blood to diffuse into the surrounding tissue and carbon dioxide from the tissue to enter the blood. The capillaries are very narrow vessels, causing the red blood cells to squeeze through in single file. When combined with the low pressure in the capillaries, a red blood cell's transition time through these vessels takes approximately 1.5 seconds. This produces an extremely effective method for gas exchange between the blood and tissue. The density of capillaries in human skeletal muscle is over 2,000 per square millimeter of tissue. Similar capillaries are located in the lungs and lie side by side with the alveoli for gas exchange in the lungs.

The final category of blood vessels is the thinned walled veins, which guide the blood back to the heart. Small veins called venules collect the blood from the capillaries and empty into progressively larger vessels (veins) until reaching the heart. The veins are constructed of less smooth muscle and connective tissue than the arteries making them very expandable but not very elastic. The low pressure of the venous blood requires additional assistance to return the blood back to the heart. This is especially needed when the body is in an upright position and gravity is pulling the blood down into the legs.

Returning Blood Flow - There are four methods the body uses to help return blood in the veins back to the heart. The first is a series of flap-like valves spaced at short intervals in the veins. These thin, membranous valves permit a one-way blood flow toward the heart. Sometimes however, valves in a vein become defective and no longer maintain the one-way blood flow. This condition is called ***varicose veins*** and generally occurs in the surface veins of the legs. Persons who stand motionless or are on their feet for long periods of time, such as dentists, nurses, and checkout counter persons are susceptible to pooling of blood in the veins, leading to varicose veins. This disorder can become painful and lead to other problems requiring surgery.

The second method for assisting venous blood to the heart is the active contraction and relaxing of skeletal muscle. Because the walls of the veins are thin, skeletal muscle contracting in a rhythmic action squeezes the veins to propel the blood similar to milking a cow. After exercising (e.g. running), an active cool down (e.g. walking) should be performed during the recovery to facilitate blood flow to the heart. By standing still after exercising, blood will pool in the legs due to gravity and dilated arterioles, decreasing blood flow to the heart and brain sometimes causing the individual to become faint.

Smooth muscle wrapping the veins also assists blood flow back to the heart and is the third method. This smooth muscle contracts and relaxes causing a "milking" action similar to the skeletal muscle in pushing the blood to the heart against gravity. However, this method is not as effective as compared to the squeezing action of the skeletal muscle due to the small amount of smooth muscle involved.

The forth method the body uses to help return blood to the heart is the change in thoracic pressure. During respiration, intrathoracic pressure decreases with inspiration and increases with expiration. This change in pressure compresses and expands the thin walled veins located in the thoracic cavity. Once again, a "milking" action is created and forces blood to the heart. During weight lifting and other straining type activities, intrathoracic pressure can be increased greatly by holding ones breath, or more accurately called the *Valsalva maneuver*.

Valsalva Maneuver - The Valsalva maneuver is a forced exhalation against a closed glottis and is commonly performed while lifting heavy objects or straining. This procedure stabilizes the trunk and increases the action of muscles attached to the chest. Unfortunately, this increase in intrathoracic pressure collapses the thin walls of the veins located in the thoracic region and greatly reduces blood returning to the heart. Several physiological consequences occur due to performing this maneuver. First *blood pressure* rises abruptly and increases the strain on the heart. For an individual with an underlying heart disease this could be fatal. Following the abrupt rise in blood pressure is a sharp decrease in blood flow to the heart and a drop in blood pressure below resting values. Due to this low pressure, blood flow to the brain is diminished causing dizziness, seeing spots, and fainting. Not holding the breath but exhaling during the straining activity can lessen all of these negative consequences

Blood Pressure - The ejected blood from the left ventricle has a tremendous force behind it that creates pressure against the artery walls and is called *systolic blood pressure*. This surge in pressure causes the arterial wall to distend and snap back to its original size, causing the characteristic pulse felt in the superficial arteries (e.g. carotid and radial). The systolic blood pressure represents the work of the heart.

When the heart relaxes, the pressure against the artery walls decreases as the blood flows away from the heart into the arterioles and indicates peripheral resistance. This pressure is called ***diastolic blood pressure*** and measures how quickly the blood flows from the arterioles into the capillaries.

Average values for blood pressure range widely (see Table 3.3). Blood pressure usually increases with age, and this increase is often accepted as a normal part of aging. However, this increase is not desirable because it may indicate that the vascular system is providing greater resistance to the blood flow due to inelasticity of the arteries.

Table 3.3

Health Fitness Standards for Resting Systolic and Diastolic Blood Pressure

Health Fitness Standard	Systolic	Diastolic
Excellent	105 - 115	60 - 72
Good	116 - 125	73 - 80
Average	126 - 135	81 - 88
Poor	136 - 150	89 - 97
Very Poor	> 150	> 97

Normal resting blood pressure is considered 120/80 mmHg (systolic pressure/diastolic pressure), but 100/70 mmHg and 130/85 mmHg are also normal. Blood pressure varies throughout the day according to activity, stress, and anxiety levels. It is also directly related to cardiac output and arterial resistance to blood flow. High blood pressure (i.e. hypertension) is called the silent killer because there are no outward signs or symptoms and can go undetected until a stroke, heart attack, or kidney failure occurs. It is extremely important that blood pressure is taken regularly. If blood pressure is high, it can be control through diet, sodium restriction, aerobic exercise, relaxation techniques, and if necessary, medication.

If we consider only resting blood pressure, a 35-year-old person with normal resting blood pressure of 120/80 mmHg can expect to live to age 76 years. On the other hand, a person with resting blood pressure of 150/100 mmHg or greater can expect to live only to 60 years of age. This represents 16 years of reduced life expectancy. Individuals should know their blood pressure and, if necessary, take the corrective lifestyle changes to lower it.

4. Blood.

Over 98% of the oxygen transported in the blood is carried by the red blood cells. The blood contains over 25 trillion red blood cells with each housing about 280 million **hemoglobin** molecules. The normal hemoglobin content for an adult male is about 15 grams per 100 milliliters of blood at sea-level conditions and for females it is about 14 grams per 100 milliliters. Oxygen specifically attaches to the iron portion of the hemoglobin in the red blood cell. Therefore, it is critically important to have a good source of iron in your diet. Low iron intake causes a reduced concentration of hemoglobin leading to a disorder called iron-deficiency **anemia**. Symptoms range from sluggishness to a reduced capacity to perform even low levels of exercise. Women are at a higher risk than men for developing iron-deficiency anemia due to iron loss during menstruation. Women on a vegetarian diet are at an even higher risk since the iron contained in vegetables are not as readily absorbed by the body as compared to the iron from meat sources. Inadequate daily iron intake occurs frequently among 30 to 50% of females in the United States.

Water is the single largest constituent of the blood and makes up approximately 50% of its volume (three to four liters). Water in the blood is needed to maintain cardiac output and blood pressure, as well as a medium to transport nutrients and remove waste. In addition, water from the blood is used as the major source of sweat to cool the body. Each day the body loses water through perspiration, respiration, urine, and feces. If this water loss is not replenished, a dehydrated state occurs leading to strain on the circulatory system and poor thermoregulation.

One of the benefits of an exercise program is that it will increase one's plasma volume. This elevated blood volume enhances both the transporting of oxygen and the regulating of body temperature.

Summary

The cell is the basic unit of life in the human organism. Cells have varied functions, but all cells require oxygen, nutrients, and water, and must get rid of waste products. It is the responsibility of cardiorespiratory system to fulfill these needs of every cell. The cardiorespiratory system is made up of the heart, lungs, blood vessels, and blood.

Review Questions

1. What are the four survival requirements of cells?

2. List the four components of the cardiorespiratory system.

3. Define cardiac output and distinguish between a fit person's heart and an unfit person's heart.

4. Describe the differences between systolic and diastolic blood pressure.

5. What blood pressure reading is considered average?

6. Why is hypertension referred to as the "silent killer?"

7. Distinguish between arteries, veins, and capillaries.

8. Diagram and label the structures of the heart.

CHAPTER 4

Cardiovascular Disease Risk Factors and Aerobic Exercise

Learning Objectives

This chapter examines the controllable and uncontrollable risk factors for developing cardiovascular disease. In addition, information will be given on aerobic type exercises that are needed to improve the cardiorespiratory system and decrease the incidence of cardiovascular disease. When you complete this chapter you should be able to:

1. Explain the process of atherosclerosis (page 37).
2. Describe the controllable and uncontrollable risk factors of cardiovascular diseases (pages 39 - 41).
3. Know the consequences of Hypertension and how it can be controlled (page 39 - 40).
4. Understand what makes an exercise aerobic (page 42).
5. Determine your own heart rate training zone for aerobic exercise (pages 44 - 46).
6. Understand the components of the overload principal for developing cardiorespiratory fitness (page 46).
7. Analyze various aerobic activities in terms of their strengths and weaknesses (page 47).
8. Describe the physiological and psychological adaptations from aerobic conditioning (page 48).

Key Terms

Aerobic Exercise
Atherosclerosis
Cardiovascular Disease (CVD)
Cholesterol
Controllable Risk Factors
Diabetes
Frequency, Intensity, and Time
Heart Rate Training Zone
High-density Lipoprotein (HDL)
Hypertension
Low-density Lipoprotein (LDL)
Measuring Heart Rate
Uncontrollable

Cardiovascular Disease

The term *cardiovascular disease* includes more than 20 different diseases that affect the heart (cardio) and arterial blood vessels (vascular). Heart disease and related cardiovascular problems cause 57% of all deaths in the United States. For the year 2008, the American Heart Association estimated the total cost of cardiovascular disease at $448 billion (see Figure 4.1). The underlying cause in 95% of cardiovascular diseases (e.g. heart attack, stroke, and hypertension) is *atherosclerosis*. The atherosclerotic process occurs in the following manner:

1. Chemical changes of various compounds and oxidation of *cholesterol* in *low-density lipoprotein* occur.

2. Lesions (fatty streaks) begin to protrude on the inside of the arterial wall composed of several lipids (cholesterol, triglycerides, and phospholipids).

3. Minerals, especially calcium, also deposit on the inner layer of the arterial wall and are called plaque.

4. The artery narrows, decreasing blood flow through the vessel and to the heart or brain.

Figure 4.1

Costs Related to Cardiovascular Disease in 2008

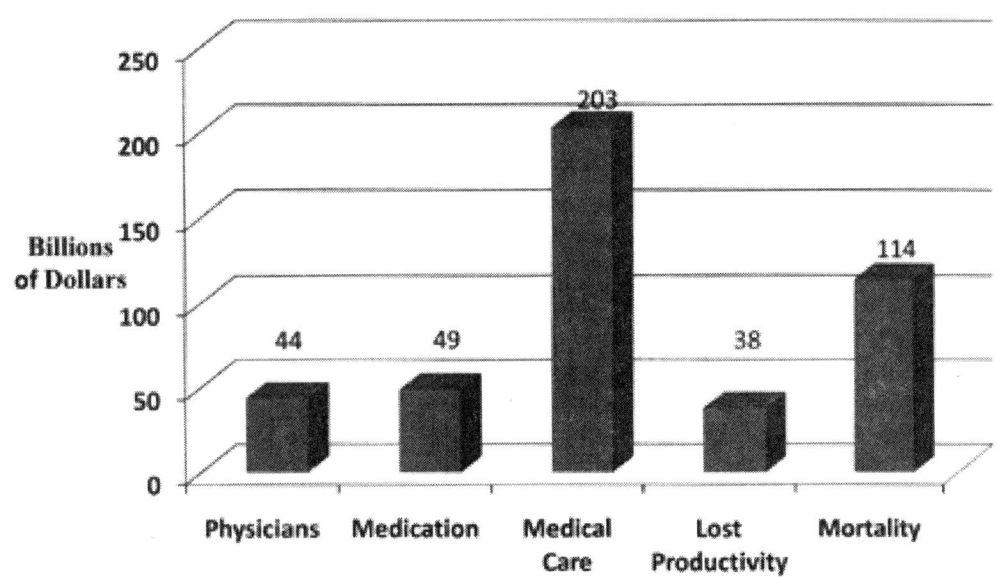

Figure 4.2

Steps Leading to a Heart Attack or Stroke

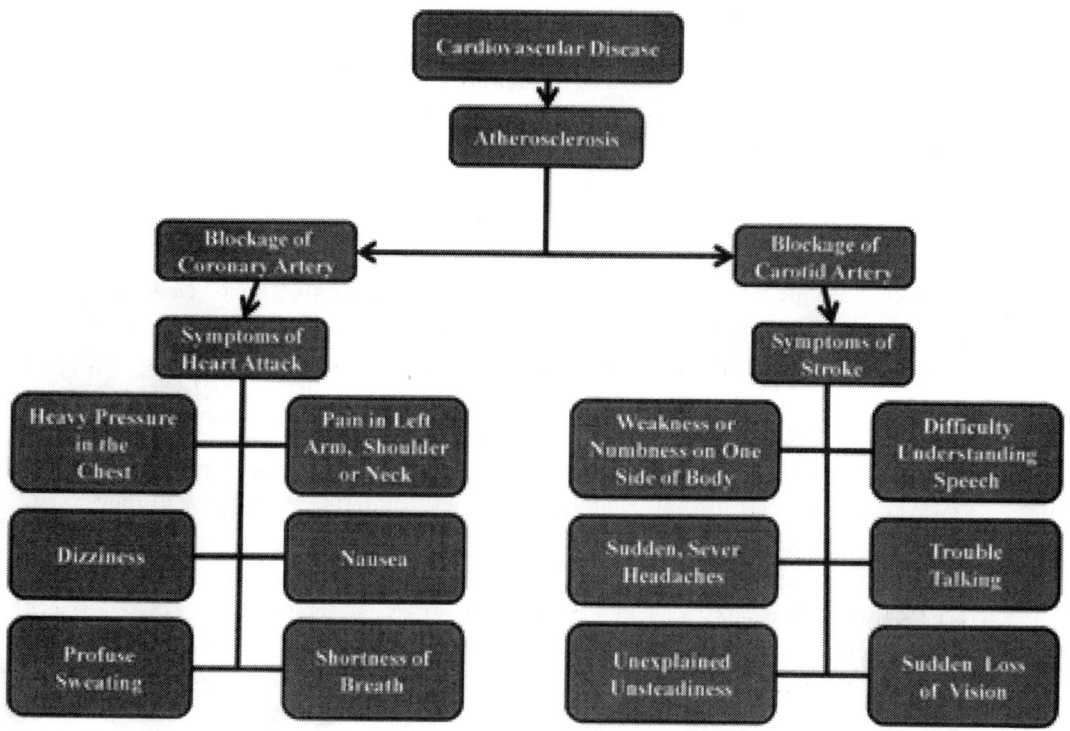

    The atherosclerotic process takes place largely without symptoms during rest and low levels of activity until the arteries are 80% occluded (closed). At this point, if the occluded artery is in the heart, angina pectoris may be experienced during physical activity or periods of stress. If the occluded artery is in the brain, brief blackouts, dizzy spells, or numbness of the face may be experienced (see Figure 4.2).

    At one time authorities considered atherosclerosis to be a part of aging and an old person's disease. Medical evidence discovered over the past 50 years reveals that atherosclerosis is not just an old person's disease but begins in the very young and progresses. Autopsies done on Americans killed in the Korean War revealed that 77% had some degree of coronary atherosclerosis. Unfortunately, recent studies have found that by age five, fatty streaks are common in the coronary arteries of American children.

    As the arteries continue to narrow because of atherosclerosis, a time will come when blood cannot flow through the artery resulting in a heart attack or a cerebral vascular accident. If the blocked artery supplied a very small part of the heart or brain, the heart attack or stroke may go unnoticed. That results in a "silent heart attack" or a "transient ischemic attack" in the brain. If the artery supplied a larger portion of the heart or brain, the person may experience any or all of the symptoms as described in Figure 4.2. If the artery is supplying a major portion of the heart, death may occur immediately as it does in 40 to 50% of the cases.

Risk Factors for Developing Cardiovascular Disease

Many factors have been identified that contribute to the quickening of the atherosclerosis process and cardiovascular disorders. They basically fall into two categories: 1) those that cannot be changed and are called *uncontrollable risk factors*; and 2) those we can change either by ourselves or with the assistance of a physician and are called *controllable risk factors*.

1. Uncontrollable Risk Factors

Heredity - A history of cardiovascular diseases in a family means increased risk for the disease. A history usually means family members (parents, grandparents, brothers, and sisters) have died from some cardiovascular disease before age 60. Influencing factors may be an inherited genetic predisposition of the body to deal effectively with blood fats. Some families have such a strong inherited genetic weakness that few males have lived past age 40.

Gender - Statistics reveal that cardiovascular disease is more prevalent in men than in women, especially before age 45. This is probably due to the protective function of the female sex hormone, estrogen, in delaying the atherosclerosis process. Unfortunately, the beneficial effects of estrogen end after menopause leading to more deaths from cardiovascular disease in women then men after age 55.

Age - Growing older increases the chances of developing cardiovascular diseases. Sixty percent of deaths to persons over the age 65 years are due to heart attacks as compared to only 11% of deaths in persons 15 to 24 years of age.

2. Controllable Risk Factors

Fortunately, research has identified factors related to cardiovascular diseases that can be controlled. These factors are related to lifestyle and make the greatest contribution toward reducing these diseases. Key factors are briefly summarized here and are discussed in greater detail throughout the book.

Hypertension - More than 50 million Americans have *hypertension*, more commonly known as high blood pressure (Chapter 3), with approximately 44% of the blacks and 31% of the whites affected. Hypertension may begin in childhood or during the adult years. It is a silent disease, often with no symptoms and if left untreated, it greatly increases the risk of heart disease, stroke, and kidney failure. The Centers for Disease

Control and Prevention report that while 66% of hypertensives were aware of their high blood pressure, only 24% had it under control. The earlier in life the problem starts, the more severe the consequences. High blood pressure can be controlled through a combination of diet, weight loss to an acceptable body composition, aerobic exercise, and medication.

Smoking - Smoking is estimated to cause 437,500 premature deaths each year (see Figure 4.3) with an estimated 22,700 – 69,000 premature deaths due to second hand smoke. Smoking is responsible for 87% of all deaths due to lung cancer, 30% of all cancer deaths, and 21% of deaths due to heart disease. Additionally, smoking leads to chronic bronchitis, emphysema, and, if done during pregnancy, low birth weights. While the number of persons smoking each year continues to decline, there is still over 29% of all Americans 12 years and older smoking.

Body Fat - As excess body fat increases so does the incidence of cardiovascular disease, type 2 diabetes, hypertension, various cancers, and osteoarthritis. With as little as 20 pounds of excess body fat, the chances of a heart attack triple. In 2005, over 66% of adults in the United States were overweight or obese. On the other hand, very low body fat also leads to a variety of disorders. These consist of abnormal physiological functioning leading to organ malfunctioning, osteoporosis, psychological problems, premature death, and menstrual irregularities for a female. Healthy body composition is 5 to 15% body fat for males and 15 to 25% for females.

Figure 4.3

Disease Distribution of 442,000 Deaths Attributed Annually to Cigarette Smoking

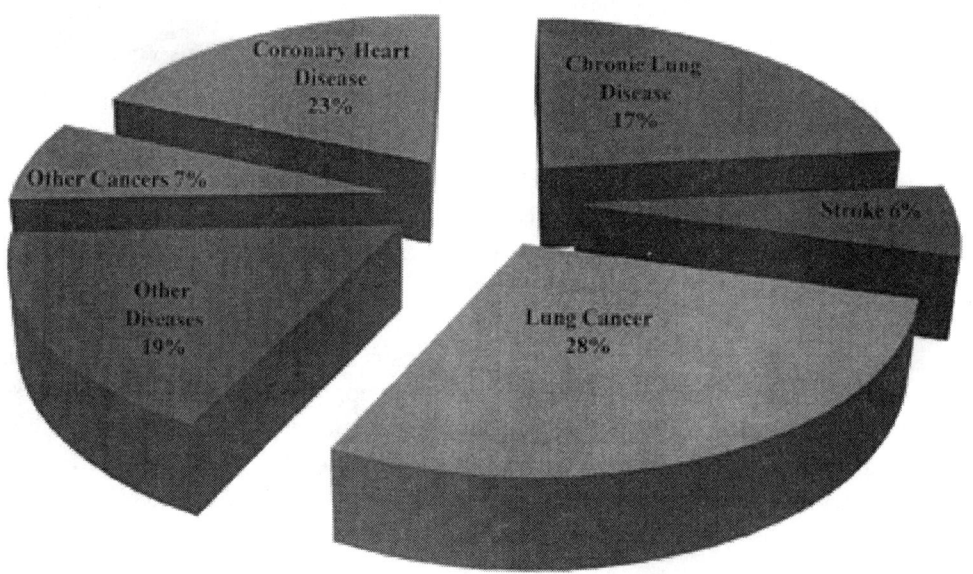

Poor Physical Fitness - The American Heart Association includes lack of physical activity as one of the primary risk factors of cardiovascular disease. In 2006, over 69% of adult Americans were not active enough to meet minimum physical activity recommendations. There is a 2.24 times increased risk of early death for those with any level of body fatness as compared to a fit individual of similar body composition. In addition, regular physical activity reduces the risk of developing hypertension, type 2 diabetes, and colon cancer. A recent study of 17,000 Harvard alumni revealed that those who regularly exercised at least three hours per week suffered 64% fewer heart attacks than those who did not exercise. Also, of those who had a heart attack, 49% who did not exercise regularly died within four weeks, whereas only 17% of those with a good history of physical activity died.

Elevated Blood Fats - A number of fats (i.e. lipids) are found in the blood and are essential for normal physiological functioning. These blood lipids include cholesterol, phospholipids, triglycerides, and fatty acids. Research has shown that high blood levels of cholesterol (see Table 4.1) are related to atherosclerosis. Cholesterol is an essential component for the formation of cell membranes, vitamin D, and sex hormones. The adult body synthesizes enough cholesterol to meet its daily needs; however infants and children require additional cholesterol through the diet. Consumption of animal tissue (e.g. eggs, meat, and cheese) adds cholesterol to the body. In order for cholesterol to be transported through the blood, the liver encases it with a protein and forms a lipoprotein.

There are two main types of cholesterol carrying lipoproteins: 1) low-density lipoproteins (LDL) and 2) *high-density lipoproteins* (HDL). Low-density lipoproteins are the primary transporters of cholesterol and normally carry between 60 and 80% of the total blood cholesterol. These lipoproteins are known as "bad" cholesterol because they have the greatest affinity for the cells of the arterial walls where the cholesterol is deposited. These depositions begin the early stages of atherosclerosis. Aerobic exercise, body fat, and diet affect LDL concentration.

Table 4.1
Blood Cholesterol Level Guidelines

	DESIRABLE	BORDERLINE	UNDESIRABLE
• **Total Cholesterol**	< 200 mg/dl	200 - 239 mg/dl	> 239 mg/dl
• **LDL Cholesterol**	< 130 mg/dl	130 - 159 mg/dl	> 160 mg/dl
• **HDL Cholesterol**	> 44 mg/dl	35-44 mg/dl	< 35 mg/d

Good cholesterol called HDL protects against cardiovascular disease by acting like a scavenger. HDL removes cholesterol from the arterial walls and transports it back to the liver for conversion into bile and excreted through the intestinal tract. Regular aerobic exercise increases HDL levels, whereas smoking, using steroids, and being diabetic decrease the levels.

Emotional Stress - Stress that causes tension within the body can lead to a number of physical ailments including heart disease. Persons under high emotional stress have been found to have elevated blood cholesterol levels, elevated blood pressure, and increased incidence of heart disease.

Diabetes Mellitus - *Diabetes* is a disorder in which the body has chronically elevated blood sugar (glucose) levels. This condition occurs because the body is unable to transfer glucose from the blood into the cells where it can be used for energy. Diabetes is the fifth leading cause of death by disease in the United States. It can cause several diseases including cardiovascular, kidney, and peripheral vascular that lead to blindness and limb amputation.

There are two types of diabetes mellitus. Type 1 is insulin-dependent, requiring daily injections of insulin to maintain normal blood glucose levels and is genetically related. Type 2 diabetes is non-insulin dependent and approximately 90% of the 20.8 million diabetic Americans have this type. The cells in the type II diabetic's body have a resistance to insulin and are related to obesity. Treatment includes diet and exercise to control blood glucose levels and reduce body fat. Diabetics have two to four times higher heart-disease problems than nondiabetics. The life expectancy of a 35 year old untreated diabetic is 63 years, compared to the normal life expectancy of 76 years.

Aerobic Exercise

Aerobic exercise is a term used to describe a type of activity that derives its energy from aerobic metabolism. Exercising muscles requires energy to contract and move the body. For muscles to contract repeatedly for an extended period of time, oxygen is required to maintain the availability of energy for the working muscles. This need for oxygen must be met by the cardiorespiratory system or the contracting muscles will come to a stop. An exercise is considered aerobic if it uses large muscle groups in a repetitive, rhythmic motion for over three minutes. For a list of typical aerobic activities refer to Table 4.2.

Table 4.2

Typical Aerobic Activities for Cardiorespiratory Fitness

- **Aerobic Exercise Machines**
- **Bench-Stepping**
- **Bicycling**
- **Cross Country Skiing**
- **Exercise to Music**
- **In Line Skating**
- **Rope Jumping**
- **Rowing**
- **Running**
- **Stair Climbing**
- **Swimming**
- **Walking**

By improving the cardiorespiratory system, the risk of developing cardiovascular disease decreases. For an aerobic exercise to benefit the cardiorespiratory system, it must follow the overload principle (Chapter 2). This principle has three components: 1) *frequency*, 2) *intensity*, and 3) *time*.

1. Frequency

The minimum frequency of performing an aerobic exercise to produce an improvement in the cardiorespiratory system is three days per week. As the number of days per week of aerobic activity increases, so does the benefit. However for health fitness, no more than five days per week is recommended. Aerobically exercising six or seven days per week only minimally increases health fitness benefits but causes a greater chance of becoming injured.

2. Intensity

Exercise intensity per aerobic session must be in the ***Heart Rate Training Zone*** for positive adaptations to occur in the cardiorespiratory system. The training zone falls between 60 to 90% of your maximum heart rate (see Figure 4.4). Maximum heart rate can be determined by performing a maximum exercise test in a laboratory setting or can be predicted by subtracting one's age from 220. However, when predicting the maximum heart rate there is an error of plus or minus 10 heartbeats per minute. For health fitness, the intensity should be maintained between 70 to 80% of maximal heart rate. Minimal adaptations occur at or below 60% of maximum heart rate, but greater than 80% will also increase the chance of injuries.

Measuring Heart Rate. An easy method to *measure heart rate* is by feeling the pulsing blood as the left ventricle pushes it into the aortic artery. To feel your pulse, use the index and middle fingers pressed gently against the artery. The thumb should not be used as it has a pulse of its own and may cause an incorrect pulse count. The two most common arteries used for taking the pulse during exercise are the 1) carotid and 2) radial.

The *carotid artery* is located on either side of the throat (larynx). It lies in the valley between the Adam's apple and the neck muscle. This artery is usually the easiest to locate quickly, however there are special receptors located in the walls of the carotid that are responsible for detecting changes in blood pressure. By pressing too firmly while taking the pulse, these baroreceptors will send a message to the heart to slow down its contractions. This slowing of the heart rate may cause dizziness or faintness and will cause an incorrect heart rate reading.

The *radial artery* is located on the palm-side of the wrist. This artery can be felt at the wrist, just to the thumb side of the forearm muscle tendons coming from the forearm. With practice the radial artery will be easy to locate, and at this site there are no baroreceptors to slow the heart rate.

Figure 4.4

Heart Rate Training Zone (60- 90%) for Age-Predicted Maximum Heart Rate

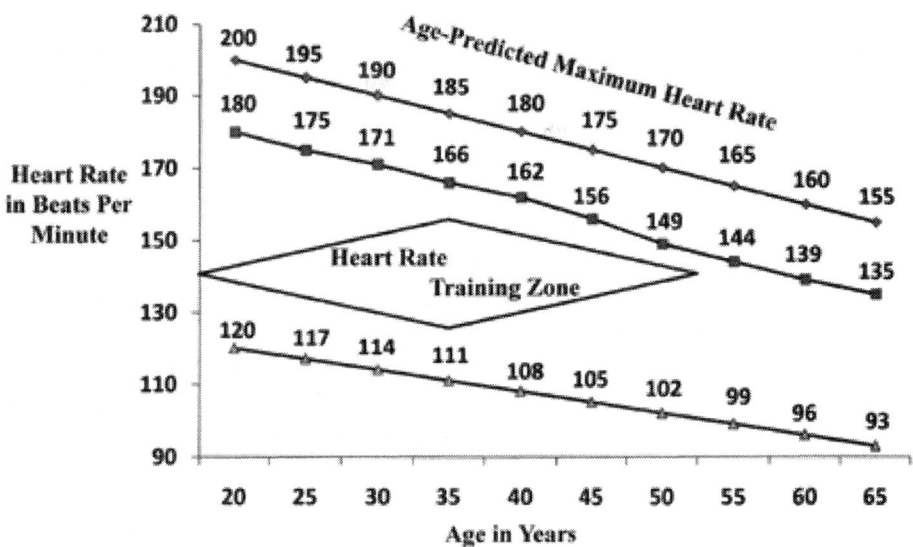

To determine resting heart rate per minute, count your pulse rate for 60 seconds. During exercise take a 10-second pulse count and multiply this number by six for your exercising heart rate per minute. To keep the exercise heart rate at the appropriate training zone, the pulse rate should be checked every five to 10 minutes. If there is difficulty in taking the pulse during the aerobic activity (e.g. swimming), stop and take the 10-second reading immediately. When you stop exercising, the heart rate only stays at that level for approximately 15 seconds before it begins to decrease rapidly. Don't be tempted to take a six-second-pulse count because it is easier to multiply by 10 mentally. This shorter time span magnifies any counting error by a factor of 10 possibly causing the exercise intensity to be out of the training zone.

Another method for determining aerobic exercise intensity is by using the ratings of perceived exertion scale. Swedish physiologist named Gunnar Borg developed this scale. He discovered a relationship between the perception of exercise intensity and heart rate (see Table 4.3). The Borg scale has word descriptions that represent how hard you perceive you are exercising matched up to numbers. A perceived exertion number between 12 and 18 corresponds to the heart rate training zone of 60 to 90% with 14 equaling 70%. This procedure is not as accurate as heart rate but is easier to use.

Table 4.3

Perceived Exertion of Aerobic Exercise Scale

Description	Rating
•	6
• Very, Very Light	7
•	8
• Very Light	9
•	10
• Fairly Light	11
•	12
• Somewhat Hard	13
•	14
• Hard	15
•	16
• Very Hard	17
•	18
• Very, Very Hard	19

Reprint from Borg, 1985

3. Time

The amount of time spent performing the aerobic activity determines the magnitude of benefits to the cardiorespiratory system. The minimum amount of exercise time required for an aerobic exercise to cause physiological adaptations is 20 minutes. However less time is required when the intensity of the workout is high. The reverse is true for lower exercising heart rates, which need a longer duration to gain positive adaptations. Table 4.4 shows the approximate heart rate and time needed to gain similar cardiorespiratory improvement.

Table 4.4

Aerobic Exercise Intensity and Duration for Similar Cardiorespiratory Improvements

INTENSITY % of Maximum Heart Rate	TIME SPENT IN AEROBIC EXERCISE	
	Minimum	Optimal
60 %	40 minutes	60 minutes
70 %	30 minutes	45 minutes
80 %	20 minutes	30 minutes
90 %	10 minutes	20 minutes

Mode of Aerobic Exercise

There are no differences in the cardiorespiratory benefits with different types of aerobic exercise, as long as the frequency, intensity, and time are similar. However, in following the Specificity Principle (Chapter 2), the type of aerobic activity performed will cause specific adaptation to other bodily systems (i.e. muscular, skeletal, and nervous). Because of this, the testing mode must be the same as the aerobic exercise to measure the magnitude of improvements from the conditioning process. If bicycling is used to improve the cardiorespiratory system, the fitness gains will be best demonstrated by being tested riding a bike. Other testing modes (i.e. running, swimming, or walking) will measure cardiorespiratory fitness but will not fully expose the physiological adaptation achieved from the exercise training on a bike.

When deciding which form of aerobic exercise to participate in, a few guidelines should be considered. In following the Principle of Individuality, no single mode of aerobic exercise is the best for everyone. Each method has strengths and weaknesses

Table 4.5

Strengths and Weaknesses of Common Modes of Aerobic Exercise

AEROBIC ACTIVITY	STRENGTH	WEAKNESSES
Aerobic Machines	Develops leg strength. Low Stress to joints. Read or watch TV.	Cost for purchase & upkeep. Ony concentric contraction. Storage of machine.
Cross-Country & Rowing Machines	Develops both upper & lower body. Low stress to joints.	Cost for purchase & upkeep. Only concentric contractions. Storage of machine.
Exercise to Music	Music and variety of movements. Social interaction.	Cost for classes. Mainly develops lower-body.
Lap Swimming	Develops upper-body strength. Low stress to joints. Good for disabilities.	Must be a skilled swimmer. Pool is required. Minimal lower-body use.
Outdoor Cycling	Develops leg strength. Low stress to joints. Use as transportation.	Cost for purchase & upkeep. Little upper-body development. Weather conditions.
Running	Minimal cost. Convenient. Requires minimal skill.	Stressful to joints. Little upper-body development.
Walking	Minimal cost. Convenient. Low stress to joints.	Greater time per session. Little upper-body development.

specific to that activity (see table 4.5). One important factor in choosing is to pick the exercise that will be most enjoyable and will be the easiest to incorporate into ones lifestyle. Regular aerobic exercise requires a commitment and belief that the minimal time spent each week will increase your productivity, longevity, and quality of life. To increase enjoyment and fitness, as well as limiting excessive amounts of stress to individual body parts, it is best to perform several different aerobic activities during the week.

Progression of Aerobic Exercise Program

For the body to continue improving cardiorespiratory fitness, the overload must increase periodically until the desired fitness level is reached. Small progressive increases in the aerobic exercise program will allow the body to adapt to each higher workload without excessive stress causing injuries. The maximal amount of overload increase per week for achieving health fitness is 10%. For example, running 10 miles during a week can be followed by running 11 miles the next week followed by 12.1 miles the week after that. To increase the overload by changing the intensity instead of duration, the heart rate for one workout per week will be increased by 10% (i.e. from 150 beats per minute to 165).

Benefits of Regular Aerobic Exercise

If the aerobic conditioning stimulus follows the Overload Principle, the majority of the physiological adaptations will develop independent of sex and age. These improvements will develop regardless of the mode of aerobic activity. Some of the following changes take place after only one exercise session, however most of these require many months of regular aerobic exercise to be fully acquired.

Metabolic Changes

The skeletal muscles used during the aerobic exercise will become more efficient in deriving greater amounts of energy from aerobic metabolism. These conditioned muscles will develop larger and more numerous mitochondria (i.e. where aerobic metabolism occurs) and increased aerobic system enzymes causing improved oxygen utilization. In addition, the conditioned muscles have a greater capacity to mobilize, deliver, and use fats for energy aiding in maintaining cellular integrity.

Cardiorespiratory

The heart increases in weight and volume with long-term aerobic conditioning. The left ventricular cavity enlarges and the myocardium becomes thicker and stronger. These changes cause an increase in the stroke volume during both rest and exercise. Because of the greater stroke volume, the heart rate decreases at rest and while performing submaximal activity.

Aerobic conditioning reduces both systolic and diastolic blood pressure at rest and during submaximal activity. This decrease is most noticeable in hypertensive individuals, allowing many to avoid medication and its unwanted side effects. Plasma volume increases and blood flow to working muscles become greater. Better distribution of blood also occurs which helps cool the body in a hot environment.

Other Changes

Regular aerobic activity leads to a reduction in body fat percentage. Also there are psychological benefits that include a reduction in anxiety and depression. In addition, aerobic exercise improves mood, self-esteem, self-concept, and general perception of personal worth. Finally, exercise performance increases with the conditioning activity causing faster times and quicker recovery from exercise.

Reversibility Principle

When an individual stops participating in an aerobic exercise program, deconditioning starts to occur. After 10 to 14 days of inactivity there is a significant reduction in both metabolic and exercise capacity with the majority of the acquired conditioning adaptations lost within several months. The rate of decrease is dependent on the conditioned level prior to stopping. However, even highly trained athletes from years of intense aerobic training will loose most of their adaptations within six month of becoming sedentary.

Summary

Risk factors for developing cardiovascular disease that are uncontrollable include heredity, gender, and age. Controllable risk factors include high blood pressure, smoking, obesity, lack of aerobic exercise, elevated blood fats, stress, and diabetes. Regular aerobic exercise can decrease the incidence of cardiovascular disease by improving the cardiorespiratory system. For an aerobic exercise to cause positive adaptations the Overload Principle must be followed. This includes performing the aerobic activity three to four days per week (frequency), at 60 to 90% of age-adjusted maximal heart rate (intensity), and for 20 to 60 minutes per session (time). All types of aerobic exercises produce similar results, however these occur only in the systems and muscles used for the activity. Typical adaptation to an aerobic conditioning program are lower resting and exercising heart rates, a stronger and more efficient heart, increased oxygen utilization, and decreased blood pressure. Once the aerobic conditioning program is stopped the acquired adaptations start to be lost in 10 to 14 days.

Review Questions

1. What condition is the cause of 95% of heart attacks and stroke?

2. Discuss the process of atherosclerosis.

3. List the uncontrollable and controllable risk factors that contribute to cardiovascular diseases.

4. What are the initial symptoms of an individual suffering from a heart attack?

5. Describe the differences between LDL and HDL.

6. Define anaerobic exercise.

7. What are the Overload Principle requirements for aerobic exercise to benefit the cardiorespiratory system?

8. Which two arterial locations are recommended for counting one's heart rate?

9. List the strengths and weaknesses of swimming, cycling, running and aerobics to music as a mode of aerobic exercise.

10. List the cardiorespiratory adaptations from regular aerobic exercise.

CHAPTER 5

The Skeletal Muscular System and Stengthening Exercises

Learning Objectives

This chapter explains the basic anatomy of the muscular-skeletal system and the importance of muscular strength and endurance. It also gives specific guidelines that should be followed in order to develop the muscular system. Upon completion of this chapter you should be able to:

1. Describe the structure of skeletal muscle (page 53).

2. List the characteristics for the three main muscle fiber types (page 53).

3. Demonstrate the three types of muscle contractions (pages 51 - 55).

4. Explain the Overload Principle as it pertains to strength training (pages 57 - 58).

5. Describe specific guidelines for developing muscular endurance and strength (pages 59 - 60).

6. Name five adaptations to strength training (page 60).

Key Terms

Anaerobic Metabolism
Concentric Muscle Contraction
Delayed Onset of Muscle Soreness (DOMS)
Dynamic Strength Training
Eccentric Muscle Contraction
Hypertrophy
Isokinetic
Isometric Muscle Contraction
Isotonic
Motor Neuron
Motor Unit
Muscular Endurance
Muscular Strength
Repetition Maximum (RM)
Resistance
Sets
Static Strength Training
Strength Training
Tendon
Type I Muscle Fibers
Type IIa Muscle Fibers
Type IIb Muscle Fibers

The Skeletal Muscular System

Fitness of the skeletal muscles of the body is of utmost importance. According to the American College of Sports Medicine, strength training that is adequate to develop and maintain muscle should be part of a well-rounded fitness program for adults. Human movement depends on muscles generating forces on the skeletal system causing the bones to move about their joint axes. Skeletal muscles are also responsible for holding fixed body positions such as sitting or standing. In addition, muscle contractions will generate a large amount of heat and may be used to help maintain body temperature in a cold environment (e.g. shivering).

The body has more than 660 skeletal muscles, which account for about 45% of the male's body weight and 35% of the female's weight. Approximately 75% of skeletal muscle is water, 20% is protein, and five percent is composed of various minerals, enzymes, fats, and carbohydrates. The functional unit of the muscle is the muscle cell called the fiber. Each muscle is made up of thousands of individual muscle fibers, with each surrounded by connective tissue. The connective tissue comes together at the end of the muscle to form a ***tendon***, which is attached to a bone.

Human skeletal muscle is not made up of identical fibers with similar contractile and metabolic characteristics. Rather each muscle is composed of several different fiber types. The three main skeletal muscle fiber types are 1) slow twitch (Type I), 2) fast twitch (Type IIb), and 3) intermediate (Type IIa).

Type I muscle fibers possess the potential for great aerobic metabolism. These fibers are well suited for aerobic activities and are resistant to fatigue. However, their contractile rate is slow and their force-generating capacity is low. Type I fibers are recruited first by the body for all types of activity.

Type IIb muscle fibers have a great anaerobic (this concept will be further explained later in this chapter) capability. This fiber can generate 10 times the force during contraction as that of Type I fibers at five times the speed. These Type IIb fibers are used when the body needs to apply maximal force such as when sprinting, jumping, or serving a tennis ball.

Type IIa muscle fibers are called "intermediate" because their characteristics are similar to both Type I and IIb fibers. Type IIa fibers can contract very rapidly and they have the capacity for both aerobic and ***anaerobic metabolism***. These skeletal muscle fibers have the greatest potential for adaptation to the overload placed upon them.

The form of activity determines the specific kind of adaptation (Specificity Principle) that will occur in each muscle fiber type. Through conditioning, all fibers in the exercising muscles will develop their existing characteristic potential based upon the type of overload. Each individual's skeletal muscle fiber type composition is determined by genetics and cannot be changed. The normal fiber type ratio for 95% of the population is 50% Type I (slow twitch) and 50% Type II (fast twitch). This ratio averages out to a range from 60% Type I and 40% Type II to 40% Type I and 60% Type II. Elite athletes of power/strength or endurance events makeup part of the remaining five percent of the population who have less than 40% or greater than 60% Type I fibers, respectively. However, the majority of athletic events require use of both Type I and II fibers to be successful (see Figure 5.1).

Figure 5.1
Skeletal Muscle Type I Fiber Composition of Elite Athletes in Various Sports and Conditioned College Students

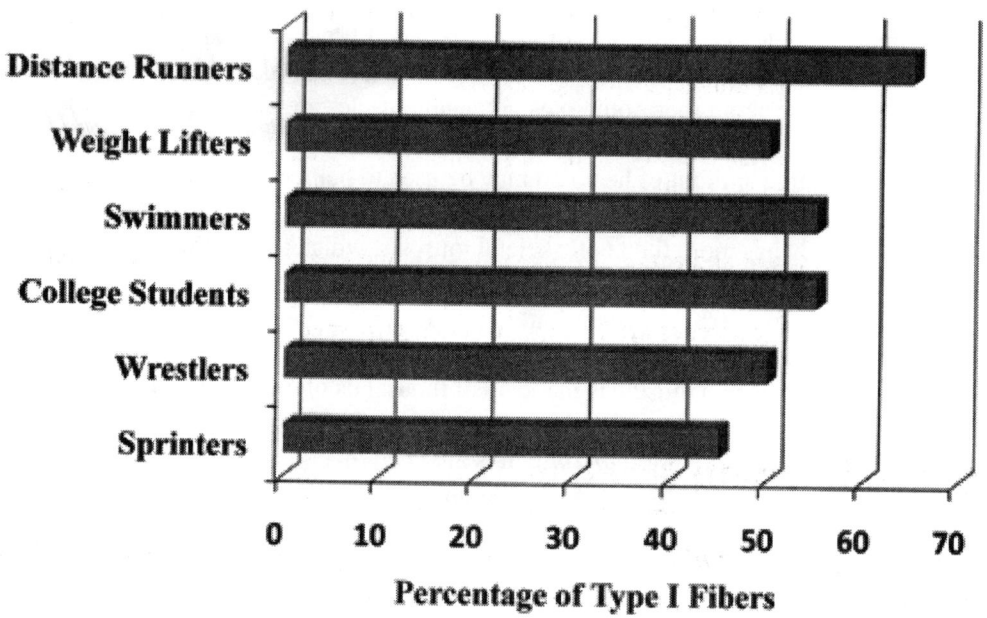

Types of Muscle Contractions

When a person is ready to move, a motor program is engaged and communicated to the appropriate skeletal muscle fibers via the nerve fibers called ***motor neurons***. One motor neuron may attach (innervate) to just a few muscle fibers as in the fingers or several thousand as in the thigh. The motor neuron and all of the fibers it innervates is called a ***motor unit***. All fibers in a motor unit are the same type and when stimulated, all will contract. The body regulates the strength of muscle contraction by recruiting the appropriate number of motor units. The greater the requirement of strength, the greater the number of motor units activated. There are three types of skeletal muscle contractions: 1) isometric, 2) concentric, and 3) eccentric.

1. **Isometric** - The term isometric is derived from two Greek words: 1) "*iso*" meaning the same and 2) "*metric*" meaning measure. An ***isometric muscle contraction*** occurs when the muscle fibers generate a force to shorten the muscle's length, but they are unable to overcome the external resistance. As a result, no movement occurs in the joint or muscle. Nevertheless, the muscle fibers are still creating a tremendous amount of force. An example of an action causing an isometric contraction is pushing against a wall.

2. **Concentric** - The most common type of skeletal muscle contraction is called *concentric muscle contraction*. This action occurs when the muscle fibers contract forcefully enough to overcome any external resistance and actually shortens the muscle's length. When the muscle shortens, it pulls the attached bones toward each other causing movement in the joint. An example of an action causing a concentric contraction is picking up a book.

3. **Eccentric** - When the external resistance is greater than the force generated by the muscle, the muscle fibers lengthen while tension is developed. This type of contraction is called *eccentric muscle contraction* and acts as a brake to control the speed of movement caused by a force. This type of contraction causes the greatest amount of muscle soreness if the muscle is unaccustomed to the amount of force being generated.

Modes of Strength Training

Various *strength training* methods are used to develop *muscular endurance* and *muscular strength*. Each type has specific benefits as well as limitations. However, all resistant type activity comes under one of the two strength training categories: 1) static and 2) dynamic (see Figure 5.2).

Figure 5.2
Strength Training Modes, Methods

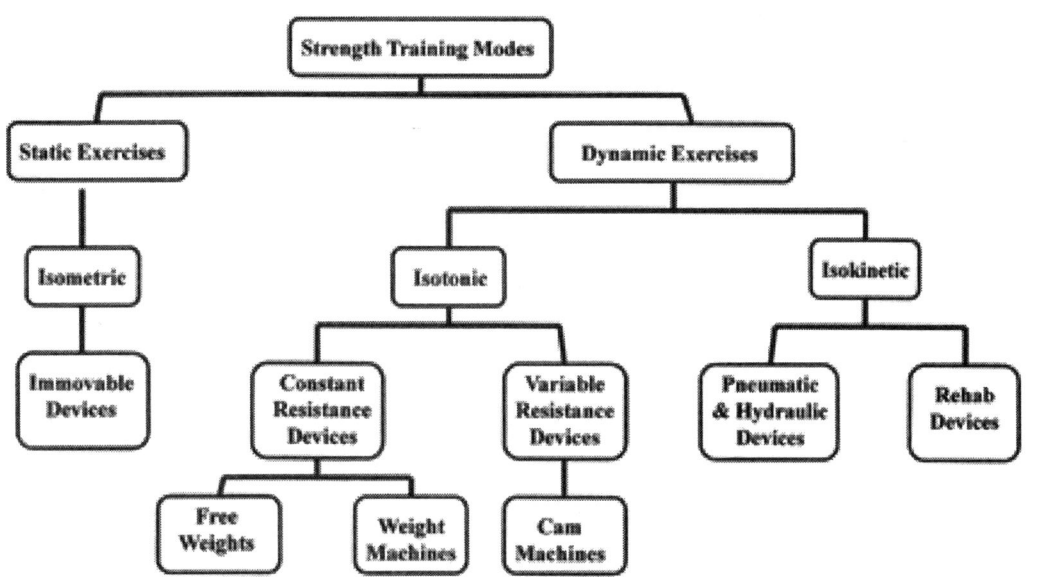

1. **Static Strength Training** - With *static strength training* the muscle generates a force to contract, but there is no change in muscle length. This type of resistance training is generally called isometric and is performed against an immovable object (e.g. wall or doorframe). The big advantage of isometric exercises is the cost because no specialized equipment is needed. The disadvantage is that muscle development from the overload only occurs at the specific angle of training. In addition, the straining nature of isometric exercises may lead to the Valsalva maneuver (chapter 3) which should be avoided by individuals with cardiovascular disease.

2. **Dynamic Strength Training** - Strength training involving muscle and joint movements is called *dynamic strength training* and can be further subdivided into *isotonic* and *isokinetic*. Isotonic is derived from two Greek words: 1) *"iso"* meaning the same and 2) *"tonus"* meaning tension. Isotonic training uses several different methods, but all have resistance that remains constant throughout the range of motion. Typical isotonic devises are free weights (i.e. barbells and dumbbells) and weight machines. All isotonic devices have an inherent limitation (see Table 5.1), that throughout the lifting range of motion there are different positions where the muscles are not overloaded as much as other positions. To overcome this limitation, weight machines have been designed to vary the resistance throughout the lifting motion. This is attempted by having the mechanical levers move during the lifting phase of the exercise. As the levers change, so does the torque, causing a change in resistance through the lifting motion. At best, these devises do alter the amount of torque causing some increase in muscle overload in certain body positions while the weight being lifted does not change.

Table 5.1
Comparison of Various Stregth training Devices

DEVICES	ADVANTAGES	DISAVANTAGES
❏ Free Weights	Good transfer to sport skills. Ease of progression.	Need a spotter. Lifting technique required.
❏ Weight Machines	No spotter required. Little skill needed. Ease of performance.	Cost of equipment. Large weight increments. Not sport specific.
❏ Hydraulic Machines	No spotter required. Variable resistance. Ease of performance.	Cost of equipment. No eccentric contractions. Little transfer to sport skills.
❏ Elastic Bands and Tubing	Minimal cost. Use anywhere. Good for rehabilitation.	Poor strength development.

Isokinetic is derived from two Greek words: 1) *"iso"* and 2) *"kineo"* meaning to move. An isokinetic strength training method involves muscular contraction through a full range of motion performed at a constant velocity. The velocity of movement is the resistance factor instead of weight used in other dynamic training methods. Any force applied against the equipment results in an equal reaction force making it possible for the muscles to exert a maximal contraction throughout the full range of motion. These devises lend themselves for use in the rehabilitation of muscle and joint injuries. Since there is no active external forces being applied against the movement, injured or surgically repaired limbs can be strengthened safely.

Anaerobic Metabolism

Unlike aerobic metabolism (Chapter 4), energy released through the anaerobic system does not require oxygen. The anaerobic system can generate large quantities of energy very rapidly, however this is only possible for a very limited time (less than three minutes). A byproduct of anaerobic metabolism is lactic acid, and accumulation of this product in the muscles interferes with energy production and muscle contraction. The main fuel source for the anaerobic system comes from carbohydrates (glucose), thus fats are not used during intense exercise.

Activities that primarily use anaerobic metabolism are high intensity but short in duration. Examples of these are strength training, sprinting, jumping, and playing intermittent type sports such as football, baseball, and basketball. Some aerobic benefits are gained from intermittent activities if performed with limited rest for an extended time period. However, much greater aerobic benefits will be acquired if aerobic activity is performed for that same amount of time.

Principles for Training Muscles

The four principles of physical conditioning (Chapter 2) hold true for strength training just as they did for aerobic exercise. By incorporating these principles when designing a strength training program, health fitness goals may be more readily achieved. As little as 60 minutes per week of strength training is all that is needed for a successful program.

1. Overload Principle

The Overload Principle consisting of frequency, intensity, and time components must be followed for the skeletal muscles to adapt to strength training. In addition, skeletal muscles require a minimum of 48 hours rest between strength training sessions for cellular repair. If the training workouts consist of just muscular endurance (e.g. sit-ups, pushup, and pull-ups), only 24 hours is needed.

Frequency of strength training refer to the numbers of *sets* (i.e. muscular contractions repeated to failure) performed for a certain exercise. Research has shown that one set per muscle group will cause an increase in strength. As the number of sets increase, so does muscular strength. However, after three sets the law of diminishing return takes over, and the extra amount of time spent does not equal the added increase in strength.

The intensity of strength training depends on the amount of *resistance* the muscles must generate against the force. This is typically the weight lifted, but some strength training devices use elastic bands or hydraulic systems. Intensity is based either on the maximal amount of repetitions (i.e. *repetition maximum* or RM) a weight can be lifted before muscle fatigue set-in or percentage of the maximal amount of weight that can be lifted one time (% of 1 RM). The greater the resistance, the fewer repetitions achieved and the greater the improvement in strength.

Time or the duration of the strength training exercise refers to the number of repetitions per weight lifting set. Muscular endurance and strength are closely related but are separate components of physical fitness. By placing both on opposite ends of a continuum, their relationship to strength training repetitions can be understood (see Figure 5.3). As the maximal amount of repetitions performed increases, the exercise will improve muscular endurance. The opposite is true for muscular strength, however. For developing both muscular endurance and strength, 8 - 12 RM should be utilized.

Figure 5.3
Continuum for Strength Training

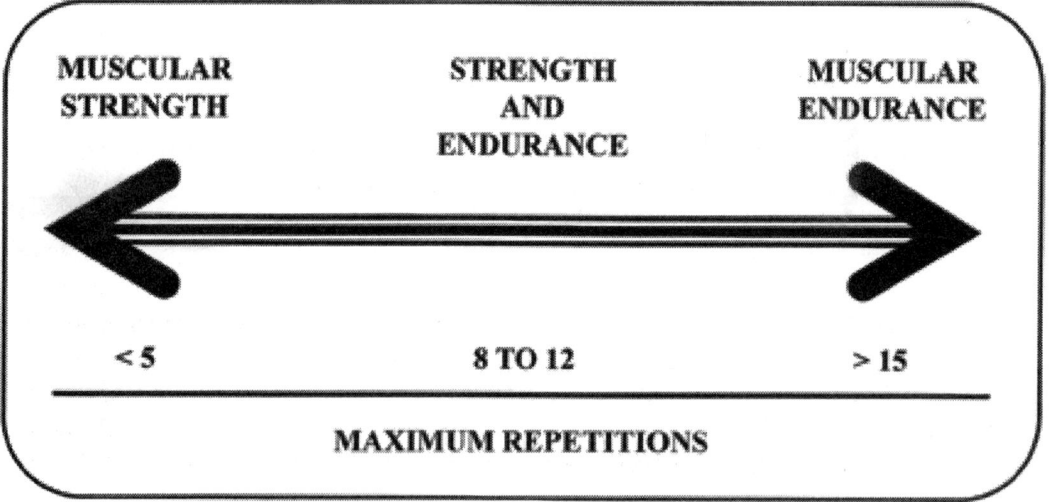

2. Specificity Principle

The adaptations from strength training are specific to the type of overload imposed upon the muscular - skeletal system. The following is a list of guidelines for developing specific muscular function.

1. To develop muscular strength, perform 5 RM or less.

2. For muscular endurance or toning, lift 15 RM or greater.

3. To improve both muscular endurance and strength or for health fitness, perform all strength training exercises 8 to 12 RM.

4. For muscular bulk/body building, lift large volumes of weight per muscle group.

5. One strength training session per week will increase muscular strength, however two sessions are better, and three will show the most gains.

6. Muscular development for sports skills, the strengthening exercises should mimic the skill pattern and speed of contraction.

7. To develop muscular power, the lifting exercises must be performed explosively.

8. A novice starting a strength training program should develop muscular endurance first then progress to muscular strength.

9. During the lifting or straining phase exhaling should occur, and while lowering the weight inhaling should take place. **NEVER HOLD THE BREATH DURING STRENGTH TRAINING** (see Valsalva maneuver Chapter 3).

Muscle Soreness. Along with any increase in physical training, muscle soreness occurs. There are two types of muscle soreness: 1) acute and 2) delayed. Acute muscle soreness begins near the end of the training session or immediately after it stops. This type of soreness is due to ischemic conditions and a build up of lactic acid in the exercised muscles. This is only temporary and within a few hours the soreness will diminish.

The second type of muscle soreness occurs 24 to 48 hours after the unaccustomed workload and is called ***Delayed Onset of Muscle Soreness (DOMS)***. This soreness is much more intense and lasts for several days. The cause for DOMS is actual cellular damage and happens predominately from performing eccentric muscle contractions. After the muscle repairs this damage it becomes stronger and is able to handle this same workload without soreness or damage. This is the natural adaptation process from strength training.

Adaptations to Strength Training. With weekly strength training sessions the body will adapt neurologically and physiologically. To what extent will be based upon the specific type of overload, the months of training, and muscle fiber composition. The following is a list of what can be expected from strength training:

1. The central nervous system increases activation, which improves synchronization of motor units and creates more efficient neural recruitment patterns.

2. Muscle fibers increase in size (***hypertrophy***) but not in number (hyperplasia).

3. Anaerobic metabolism increases.

4. Ligament and tendon strength increases.

5. Bone mineral content increases making the bones stronger and decreasing the risk of osteoporosis.

3. Reversibility Principle

Once the three days per week strength training sessions are discontinued, detraining begins, and the body reverts back to a pretraining state. This reversing of the gained muscular, skeletal, and neural adaptations begins to occur after 10 to 14 days of inactivity. However with two training sessions per week, most adaptations can be maintained. With even one strength training session per week, some gains will remain. Interestingly once the strength training resumes, the previous strength trained state will be regained in less time than the original adaptation.

4. Individuality Principle

The extent of muscular development from a weekly strength-training program is not only dependent on the type of overload but also the individual's gender, age, and genetics.

Regardless of gender, skeletal muscle can generate three to eight kilograms of force per square centimeter of cross sectional area. However, males posses a greater absolute strength due to their greater muscle mass. This occurs because males have much higher levels of testosterone, allowing greater muscular hypertrophy. Even after years of intense strength training, most females will be unable to develop large muscles naturally.

The aging process causes a decrease in skeletal muscle motor units and muscle fiber atrophy leading to a reduction in muscle mass and strength. However, with an active lifestyle including regular strength training this inevitable decline is drastically slowed. Recently, studies have clearly shown that skeletal muscles of elderly individuals who have been sedentary for many decades can adapt to strength training and develop muscular endurance, strength, and hypertrophy even into the ninth decade of life.

Genetic predisposition will determine the extent of skeletal muscle adaptation to high resistant strength training. The greater percentage of Type II fiber in the trained muscle, the greater the amount of muscular hypertrophy, strength, and power. Also the higher the level of testosterone will cause greater and faster adaptation to strength training. This is true for both males and females, young or old.

Summary

Muscular endurance and strength are basic requirements for daily living as well as for sports performance. Skeletal muscles are made-up of three main fiber types with each having specific characteristics. When muscles are stimulated by the nervous system to contract, they generate a mechanical force by pulling on the bones. To develop the skeletal muscles, an overload must be applied. The type and amount of overload will determine the specific adaptations to the muscles regardless of gender, age, or genetics. By manipulating the amount of sets, repetitions, and resistance, muscular endurance and/or strength can be acquired. There are several methods in achieving the desired strength training goal along with a variety of devices to utilize. Strength training requires the skeletal muscles to generate anaerobic energy through metabolism, causing specific adaptations to this system. If weekly training sessions stop, detraining occurs and the acquired benefits are lost. It is never too late to begin a strength training program and reap its many benefits.

Review Questions

1. Muscles account for approximately what percent of total body weight in males and females?

2. What are the recommended sets, repetitions, and resistance for developing both muscular endurance and strength?

3. Define the differences between muscular strength and muscular endurance.

4. List the three major muscle fiber types and two characteristics of each.

5. Discuss gender differences with regard to absolute strength and muscle hypertrophy.

6. Explain the three types of muscle contractions and give an example of each.

7. List five adaptations to strength training.

8. Define DOMS and tell what causes it to occur.

9. Name the three methods of strength training and an advantage of each.

10. How quickly does detraining start to occur?

CHAPTER 6

Starting an Exercise Program for Health Fitness

Learning Objectives

This chapter explains the importance of properly preparing the muscles and joints for physical activity. This includes how to warm-up, cool-down, and increase flexibility for health fitness. After reading this chapter you should be able to:

1. Understand the importance of warming up the body before starting to exercise (pages 65 - 70).

2. Explain the differences between controlled stretching and flexibility training (pages 69 - 70).

3. Describe the importance of proper hydration levels during exercise (pages 71 - 72).

4. List the physiological adaptations from heat acclimatization (page 73).

5. Design a health fitness exercise program for yourself (pages 75 - 76).

Key Terms

Acclimatization
Ballistic Stretching
Controlled Stretching
Cool-down
Dehydration
Flexibility Training
General Warm-up
Hydration
Hyperhydrated
Medical Clearance
Range of Motion
Rehydration
Specific Warm-up
Static Stretching

Medical Clearance

Before beginning any exercise program a physician should be consulted to determine if a complete physical examination is necessary before *medical clearance* is given. This is especially true for individuals with any disease or physical limitation (e.g. overweight or pregnant). According to the guidelines of the American College of Sports Medicine, healthy men under age 40 and healthy women under age 50 with no symptoms of cardiovascular disease and less than two risk factors (Chapter 4) do not require medical evaluation before starting a vigorous exercise program (see Laboratory 1 Medical Clearance).

Exercising Session

Each exercise session should contain four components: 1) warm-up, 2) exercise, 3) *cool-down*, and 4) *flexibility training*. By utilizing all four, the conditioning session will be more productive with a decreased chance of injuries.

1. Warm-up

Prior to any exercise activity a warm-up should be performed. There are several benefits that occur from a properly warmed body (see Table 6.1) including fewer injuries. A good warm-up consists of three parts: 1) *general warm-up*, 2) *controlled stretching*, and 3) *specific warm-up*.

Table 6.1
Physiological Consequences of a Proper Warm-up

1. Increased blood flow through the active muscles.
2. Facilitation of oxygen delivery to the muscles.
3. Greater efficiency of movement.
4. Increased speed of muscle contraction.
5. Facilitation of nerve transmissions.
6. Improved myocardial blood flow.
7. Reduced myocardial workload at the start of exercising.

General Warm-up - The general warm-up includes general body movements utilized to warm the body to a mild sweat or flushing of the skin and to slightly increase respiration. These movements are usually unrelated to the anticipated exercise activity or sporting event and are performed for two to three minutes. Examples of a general warm-up are calisthenics, walking, and jumping rope.

Controlled Stretching - Mild stretching prior to the exercise activity helps to improve joint mobility and function. This type of light stretching is not designed to increase flexibility but to prepare the joints to be utilized during the workout. Each stretching activity requires slow-controlled movements with a three to four second hold at the point of discomfort and may be repeated up to three times. Figures 6.1 to 6.9 are examples of stretching exercises that can be utilized for most physical activities.

Figure 6.1

Shoulder Stretch Across the Chest. Grab your elbow and slowly pull it across to the opposit shoulder. Hold this position while relaxing the stretched muscles. Repeat using the other arm.

Figure 6.2

Shoulder Stretch Behind the Head. Raise an arm overhead and flex it next to the ear. Grab the elbow and slowly pull it behind your head. Hold this position while relaxing the stretched muscles. Repeat using the other arm.

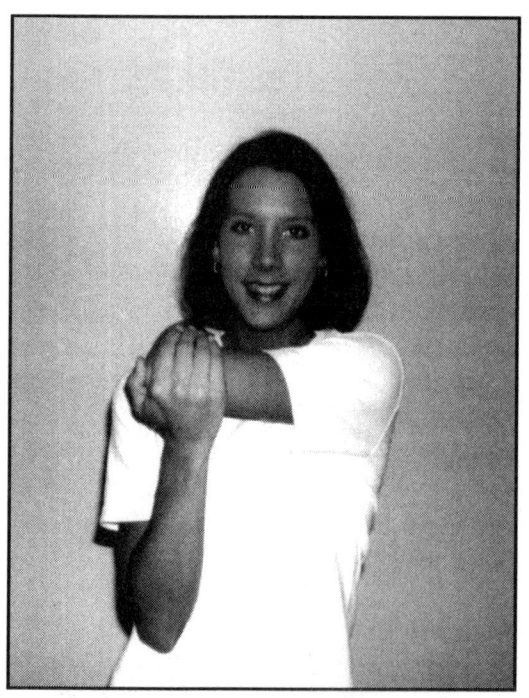
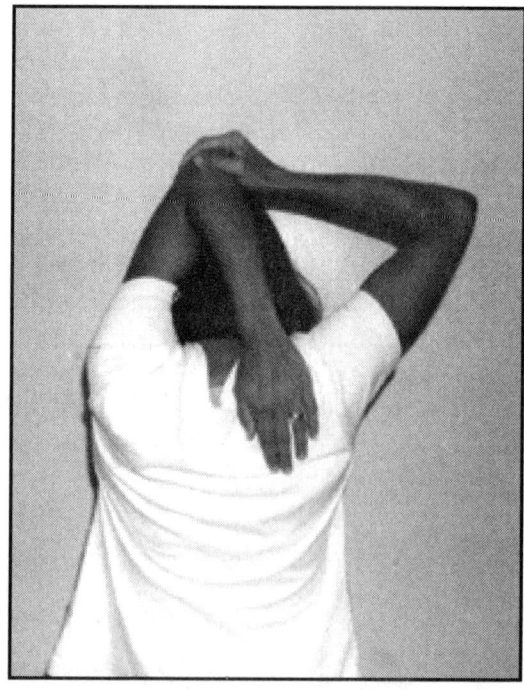

Figure 6.3

Shoulder Stretch to the Side. Grab a tall stationary object with one extended arm at shoulder height. Turn your body away from the arm, stretching the anterior shoulder. Hold this position while relaxing the stretched muscles. Repeat using the other arm.

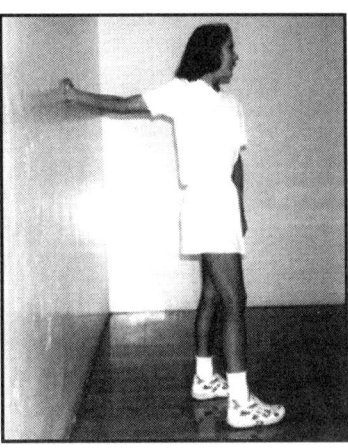

Figure 6.4

Trunk Stretch to the Side. Stand with hands overhead and feet shoulder width apart. Grasp wrist with one hand and pull the arm down the side. Hold this position while relaxing the stretched muscles. Repeat to the other side.

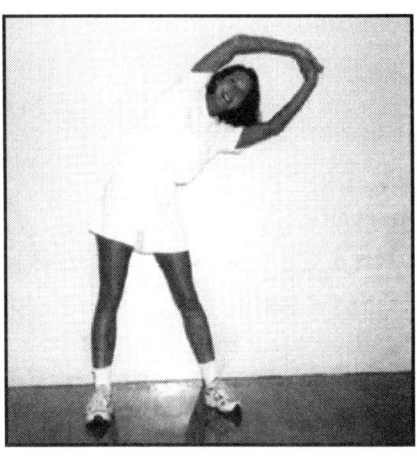

Figure 6.5

Thigh Stretch. Standing near an immovable object, rest one hand against it for balance and support. Flex the opposite side leg and grasp the foot pulling the foot toward the buttocks. Hold this position while relaxing the stretched muscles. Switch legs and repeat.

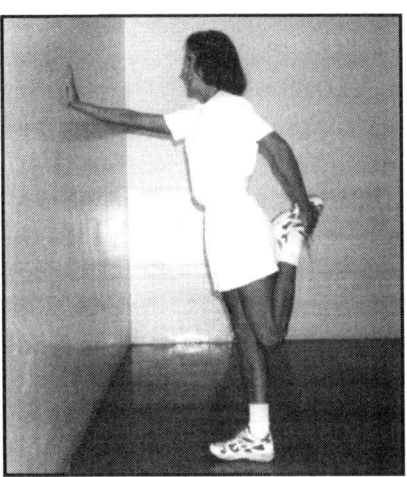

Figure 6.6

Achilles Stretch. Stand facing an immovable object and place hands upon it or balance. Extend one leg back while flexing the other. The extended leg's foot is flexed with the heel in contact with the floor and toes pointing forward. Hold this position while relaxing the stretched muscles. Switch legs and repeat.

Figure 6.7

Groin Stretch. Sit on the floor with knees flexed and soles of feet together. Grasp ankles and pull toward the groin while pressing down with the elbows on the knees. Hold this position while relaxing the stretched muscles.

Figure 6.8

Hip Stretch and Trunk Twist. Sit upright on the floor with one leg flexed across the other. Turn toward the bent leg and using the opposite side arm, press against the knee. Look and twist the trunk as far as possible. Hold and relax the stretched muscles. Repeat by switching the legs and twisting in the opposite direction.

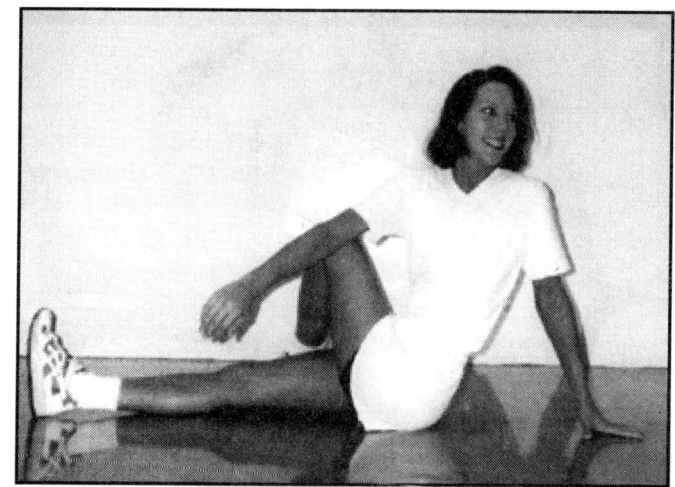

Figure 6.9

Hamstring Stretch. Sit on the floor with one leg flexed and pulled to the groin. With the other leg extended, bend at the waist and lower the chest toward the thigh. Hold this position while relaxing the stretched muscles. Switch leg positions and repeat.

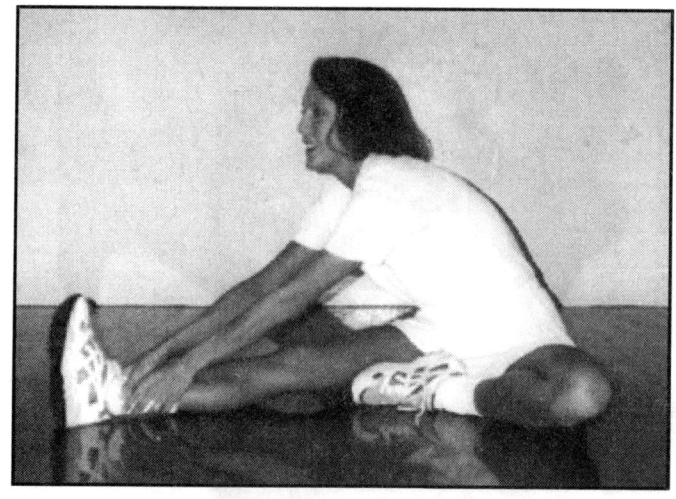

Specific Warm-up - The type of physical activity being performed during the workout will determine the kind of exercises utilized for the specific warm-up. The purpose of this final part of the warm-up is to allow the participant to become familiar with the conditioning, training, or playing environment. The specific warm-up for an aerobic workout would start by performing the aerobic activity at a low intensity. This would be followed by a slow increase in the aerobic exercise intensity until reaching the desired heart rate training zone percentage (Chapter 4). If the exercise activity is going to be strength training, then each lifting exercise will be executed first using little resistance for 10 to 15 repetitions, followed by more intense lifting. For a sporting activity, the specific warm-up would provide a skill rehearsal for the actual activity for which the warm-up is being utilized. Examples include swinging a golf club, throwing a baseball, and warm-up volleying in tennis.

2. Exercise Activity

The largest portion of time spent during the workout session should be devoted to the exercise activity. This is the component for which the majority of physiological, neurological, and psychological adaptations occur if the Overload and Specificity Principles are followed (Chapter 2). For health fitness, the exercise activity should consist of aerobic exercise (Chapter 4) and/or strength training (Chapter 5). If the physical activity is a sport then skill drills and/or game play will take place during this part.

Regardless of the type of exercise being performed, proper athletic attire specific for the physical activity is important to limit the risk of injuries. This includes footwear, undergarments, outerwear, and protective equipment. The price of such apparel may appear costly, however this is minimal compared to the cost of a visit to the emergency room and the associated physical discomfort.

3. Cool-down

The cool-down begins as soon as the exercise session has ended and is designed to bring the body back to near resting levels. A brief period of low-intensity activity such as light jogging, swimming, cycling, or walking will facilitate the body's return to the pre-exercise state. An active cool-down is important immediately after a workout, otherwise the blood will pool in the exercised muscles. This pooling will decrease the volume of blood returning to the heart and will cause a decrease in cardiac output (Chapter 3). If this occurs, blood flow to the brain is diminished causing lightheadedness, dizziness, and possible fainting. By actively contracting and relaxing skeletal muscles, blood flow is "milked" back to the heart maintaining cardiac output. Other benefits of an active cool-down are to facilitate removal of lactic acid, to replenish oxygen stores, and to help dissipate heat.

4. Flexibility Training

Stretching to improve or maintain the *range of motion* of the major joints in the body should be an important component of every exercise session. As a person ages, the connective tissue surrounding each skeletal muscle and its fibers that form the tendon (Chapter 5) loses some of their elastic components. This causes a decrease in muscle-tendon flexibility and joint range of motion, leading to a greater risk of injuries. A sedentary lifestyle also causes a decrease in resilience that magnifies this aging process. Injuries to the muscle-tendon unit will likewise cause a decrease in flexibility due to the scar tissue formed during the healing process. However, if controlled stretching is performed as the body is repairing this injury, the joint range of motion will be maintained and the healed site will be less susceptible to future injury.

A planned, deliberate, and regular flexibility training program will progressively increase the pliability of the muscle-tendon unit leading to a decreased chance of muscle, tendon, and joint injuries. Beginning a flexibility training program at any age will cause improved functioning in the muscle-tendon unit and will increase its range of motion.

Flexibility training should begin towards the end of the cool-down while the muscles, tendons, and ligaments are warm and pliable. There are two types of stretching methods used for flexibility training. The first method is called *ballistic stretching* and consists of bouncing or rhythmic motions. This technique has the potential for causing injuries to the muscle-tendon unit due to large and uncontrollable amounts of momentum generated from the quick movements. Also the stretch reflex phenomenon causes an increase in muscular tension making it more difficult to stretch the muscle and defeating the purpose of flexibility training.

The second method of flexibility training is called *static stretching* and involves holding a position for a period of time. Static stretching uses slow and controlled movement to reach the held position. This position should be at the point of feeling some discomfort in the stretched muscles-tendon unit but never pain, and is held for 15 to 60 seconds. The longer the stretched position is held and the more times it is repeated the greater the improvements in flexibility. The exercises used for controlled stretching may also be used for flexibility training (see Figures 6.1 to 6.9).

Static stretching can be performed alone or with the help of a partner. Partner static stretching has the potential to more efficiently improve muscle-tendon flexibility and joint range of motion. There are two basic stretching techniques used with a partner, and these are designed to utilize the neuromuscular physiology. The first uses reciprocal innervation of the spinal column. When a muscle (agonist) is contracted, the muscle performing the opposite movement (antagonist) will be induced to relax. As this relaxation occurs, the partner stretches the antagonist muscle to the point of discomfort and holds this position for 15 to 60 seconds.

The second method of partner stretching uses the concept of maximal contraction of a skeletal muscle leads to maximal relaxation in that same muscle. This technique requires the partner to resist the maximal contraction of the muscle soon to be stretched. After this maximal isometric contraction (Chapter 5), the partner stretches this muscle to the point of discomfort while it is relaxing and holds this position for 15 to 60 seconds.

For maximum results from partner stretching, each exercise should be repeated up to five times. Disadvantages of this method include the requirement of a partner and the extra amount of time it takes to complete each stretch. If partners are performing this technique on each other, the time doubles.

Hydration

Maintaining proper body *hydration* levels during an exercise session is critical for health, safety, and optimal performance. *Dehydration* leads to heat illnesses (i.e. muscle cramps, heat exhaustion, and heat stroke) and possible death. Normal hydration levels become more difficult to maintain as the exercise session increases and/or the exercising environment has high temperatures with or without high humidity. There are three distinct hydration periods for optimal body fluid levels: 1) pre-exercise, 2) during exercise, and 3) post-exercise.

1. Pre-Exercise Hydration

Proper hydration levels before starting the physical activity is necessary regardless of the length of the exercise session or environmental conditions (i.e. hot or cold). Any fluid deficit prior to exercise can potentially compromise thermoregulation during the session. This dehydrated state increases the cardiovascular strain and limits the body's ability to transfer heat from the contracting muscles to the skin surface where heat can be dissipated. This condition also causes a decrease in performance for both aerobic and anaerobic activities.

During the 24 hour period prior to the exercise session adequate fluids should be consumed to promote proper hydration. Starting about two hours before the exercise activity, approximately 500 milliliters or 17 ounces of water should be ingested. This fluid intake should be consumed gradually to elevate the hydration level above normal values causing a *hyperhydrated* state. If this pre-exercise water is consumed too quickly, the kidneys will slow their reabsorbtion rate leading to excretion of the excess ingested water.

2. Hydration During Exercise

During exercise, humans typically drink insufficient amounts of fluid to negate water loss from sweat. Without adequate fluid replacement during physical activity, internal body temperature rises along with heart rate, and sweat rates decrease. To minimize the chance of developing heat illnesses, fluid intake should equal sweat rate. This approximates 150 milliliters (4 oz) to 350 milliliters (10 oz) every 15 to 20 minutes of exercise. The best fluid replacement is cool water for physical activities lasting under one hour. When exercising longer than one hour, a sport drink with less than 10% carbohydrate concentration and less than seven grams of sodium per liter should be consumed. The carbohydrates (Chapter 8) will help maintain blood glucose levels and delay onset of fatigue.

3. Post-Exercise Hydration

Immediately after the completion of the exercise activity and during the cool-down period, *rehydration* should begin. Any type of fluid is acceptable as long as it does not contain caffeine or alcohol. Both of these drugs are diuretics and defeat the rehydration effort. If a person is a competitive athlete, the rehydration fluid should contain carbohydrates to help replenish the depleted skeletal muscle glycogen stores.

Exercising in the Heat or Cold

The human body must maintain internal (core) temperature within a very narrow range for normal physiological functions. Failure to do so will result in death. The body is very adept at regulating core temperature in varying environmental conditions during exercise. However, certain precautionary procedures should be followed to eliminate the potential for thermal illnesses.

Hot Environment

Exercising in a hot environment places additional stress on the body's cooling mechanisms. Skeletal muscles only use approximately 40% of their generated energy to contract; the other 60% is given off as heat. To dissipate this heat buildup, the body must dilate the arterioles leading to the skin capillaries (Chapter 3) allowing the blood to transport heat from the core to the skin. However, this means that there will be less blood flowing to the exercising muscles for its metabolic needs.

Another mechanism the body uses to remove excess body heat is through the evaporation of sweat. This is the body's major physiological defense against overheating. The water secreted from the sweat glands comes mainly from the blood. This causes a decrease in plasma volume and limits the amount of blood available for skin capillaries to dissipate heat and also limits the amount of oxygen for muscle metabolism. If exercising continues with the diminishing blood volume, core temperature will rise and heat illness will occur. This is precisely the reason for having proper hydration before and during exercise.

Acclimatization to Heat - Physical activities that are non-taxing when conducted in a cool environment become difficult when performed in a hot one. However, repeated exposure to a hot environment while exercising causes the body to adapt, resulting in an improved capacity and less discomfort (see Table 6.2). Major *acclimatization* occurs during the first week of heat exposure and is completed after 10 days. The first few day of exercise in a hot environment should be of low intensity and last less than 30 minutes. Thereafter, the exercise sessions can increase in time and intensity. Elderly individuals without a compromised cardiovascular system can adapt to a hot environment and regulate core temperature as easily as younger individuals.

High humidity and high environmental temperatures decrease the effectiveness of sweating. As relative humidity increases, less sweat evaporates to cool the body and there is a greater risk for developing heat illnesses (see Table 6.3). When an unacclimated individual exercises in a hot and humid environment they are at higher risk regardless of conditioning level. On days with high temperatures and humidity, exercise should be performed outside during the morning or early evening hours or conducted in an air-conditioned building.

Table 6.2

Physiological Adaptations Due to Heat Acclimatization.

> **Improved blood flow to the skin capillaries.**

> **Better distribution of blood flow.**

> **Sweating at a lower core temperature.**

> **Increased sweat output.**

> **Lower concentration of electrolytes in the sweat.**

> **More effective sweat distribution over the skin surface.**

Table 6.3

Heat - Stress Index

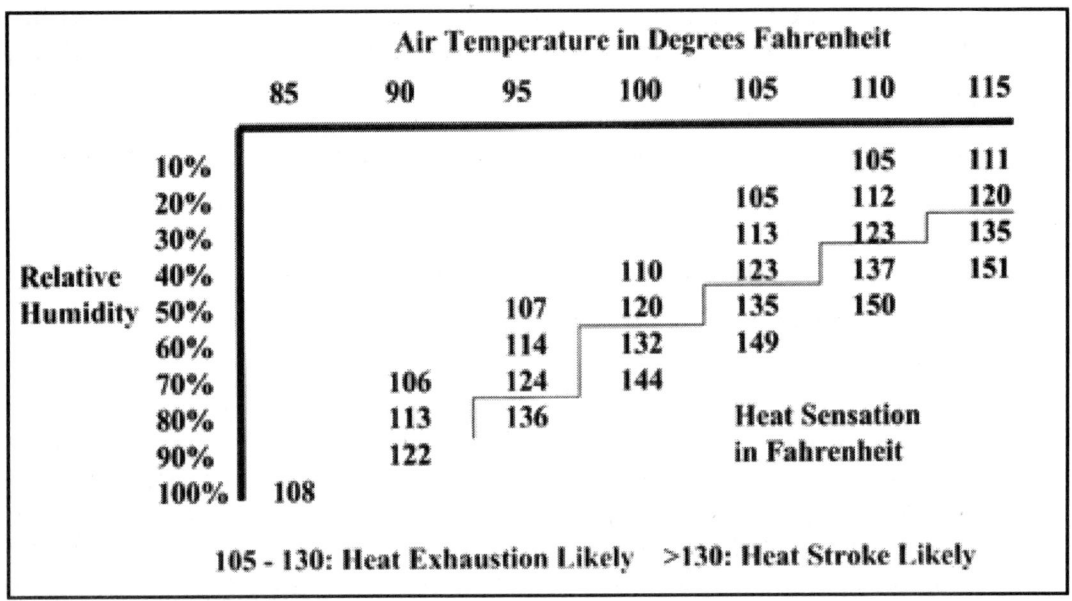

Warm-weather clothing should be of lightweight material and be loose fitting to permit air circulation and sweat evaporation. Light colored clothing is cooler since it reflects heat rays as opposed to dark colored clothing, which absorbs light rays.

Cold Environment

Exercising in a cold environment places less stress on the body to maintain core temperature than a hot environment. The large amount of heat generated by exercising muscles can sustain a constant core temperature in air as cold as - 30 degrees C (-22 degrees F) without the need for heavy clothing. Hydration is still a concern in a cold environment; even though there is less sweating, greater amounts of water vapor are needed to humidify the inspired (Chapter 3) dry, cold air. Asthmatics should not exercise in a cold environment since the dry air may cause an attack.

Clothing for exercising in the cold should consist of several layers so that as the body warms layers can be removed. Also, the material against the skin should be effective in allowing water vapor to escape from the body's surface. Hats and gloves are important, as these coverings will keep the skin surface from freezing in a subfreezing climate.

Exercise Program Design for Health Fitness

When designing an exercise program for achieving health fitness a person must first determine present fitness level after receiving medical clearance from a physician (Laboratory 1). There are several tests that will measure the participant's initial level on each of the five health fitness components (Chapter 2). The evaluating procedures and fitness rating scales are located in the laboratory sections of this book (see Laboratories).

1. Body Mass Index, Laboratory 10.
2. Cardiorespiratory fitness evaluation, Laboratory 4.
3. Muscular endurance/strength evaluation, Laboratory 6.
4. Flexibility evaluation, Laboratory 8.

These fitness tests will assist the individual in discovering areas of health fitness that need more attention and others that only require maintenance. With the results from these laboratories, a health fitness exercise program can be designed that meets the individual's specific needs. To fit all the important components into a busy schedule takes careful planning and requires dedication and sacrifices. However, the benefits to be gained are great (Chapter 2). The exercise program design must follow the four Principles of Conditioning: 1) overload, 2) specificity, 3) individuality, and 4) reversibility. Guidelines on designing a health fitness exercise program can be found on Tables 6.4 and 6.5 and Figure 6.10. Once the exercise program is started, it is important to progressively increase the overload until a fitness level of "Good" (Tables 7.2, 12.3, 12.4 and 12.5) has been reached in all health fitness components.

Table 6.4

Starting Exercise levels for Aerobic, Strength, and Flexibility Training for a Health Fitness Program Based on Classification From Figures 6.10 and Table 6.5

EXERCISE STARTING LEVEL	AEROBIC TRAINING			STRENGTH TRAINING			FLEXIBILITY TRAINING		
	Freq.	Inten.	Time	Day/Wk	Sets	RM	Day/Wk	Reps	Time
I	3	50%	10min	2	1	20	7	3	25sec
II	3-4	60%	20min	2-3	2	15	5	3	20sec
III	3-5	70%	30min	2-3	2-3	8-12	3-4	2-3	15sec
IV	3-6	80%	30min	3	3	8-12	3	2	10sec

Figure 6.10

Determining Starting Level for an Aerobic Exercise Program Based on Body Mass Index and Maximal Oxygen Uptake (VO2 MAX) From a 1.5 Mile Run/Walk

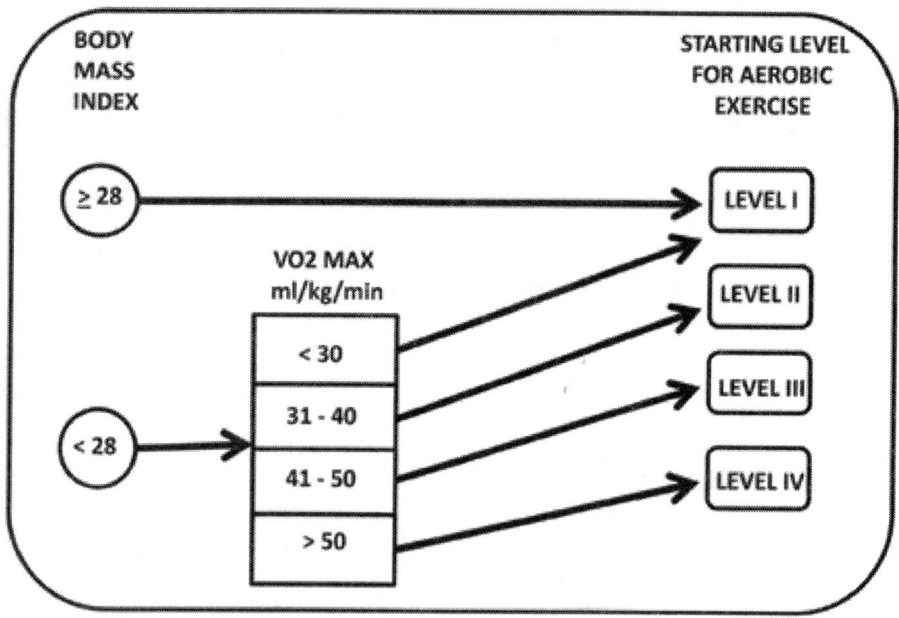

Table 6.5

Determining Starting Levels for a Strength and a Flexibility Training Program Based on Three Muscular and Three Flexibility Tests

CLASIFICATION ON 2 OUT OF 3 MUSCULAR TESTS	Starting Level for Strength Training	CLASIFICATION ON 2 OUT OF 3 FLEXIBILITY TESTS	Starting Level for Flexibility Training
Poor	Level I	Poor or Very Poor	Level I
Fair	Level II	Average or Fair	Level II
Average	Level III	Good	Level III
Excellent or Good	Level IV	Excellent or Very Good	Level IV

Summary

Before beginning an exercise program, medical clearance should be obtained from a physician. When designing an exercise program the first procedure is to determine one's present fitness level on the five health fitness components. With this information an exercise program can be designed to meet the individual's needs. Each exercise session should contain four components: 1) warm-up, 2) exercise activity, 3) cool-down, and 4) flexibility training. The warm-up consists of a general warm-up followed by controlled stretching and ending with a more specific warm-up. After the exercise session a cool-down should be performed to assist the body in returning to pre-exercise level. Flexibility training is designed to increase the range of motion in a joint and can be part of the cool-down. Static stretching is the best method to improve flexibility and can be performed alone or with a partner. When exercising, it is critical to be properly hydrated to decrease the risk of developing heat illnesses.

Review Questions

1. What is the importance of performing a good warm-up before exercising?

2. Explain the difference between controlled stretching and flexibility training.

3. Why is a cool-down period important after exercising?

4. Describe proper hydrating techniques that decrease the chance of heat illnesses.

5. How does the body cool itself in a hot environment?

6. What physiological changes occur when the body acclimatizes to a hot environment?

7. When designing an exercise program for health fitness, what components should be included?

CHAPTER 7

Body Composition and Health Fitness

Learning Objectives

This chapter explains the importance of understanding body composition and energy expenditure in assisting one in achieving a healthy and fit body. Health fitness standards for body fat percentage and body mass index are presented. Caloric intake and caloric expenditure are examined as well as the benefits of having a physically active lifestyle. Upon completion of this chapter you should be able to:

1. Know some of the health problems and diseases associated with being in an overfat condition (page 79).
2. Know the difference between body weight and body composition (pages 80).
3. Explain the difference between essential fat and storage fat (pages 80).
4. Distinguish between acceptable and unhealthy ranges for body fat for males and females (page 80).
5. Understand the technique for measuring body composition using the skinfold method (page 81).
6. Understand the energy balance equations and its relationship to weight control (pages 83 - 85).
7. List the benefits of exercise in fat reduction (pages 85 - 86).
8. Describe three eating disorders and characteristics of each (pages 87 - 88.

Key Terms

Adipocyte
Anorexia Nervosa
Basal Metabolic Rate (BMR)
Binge Eating Disorder
Bioelectrical Impedance
Body Mass Index (BMI)
Bulimia Nervosa
Energy Balance Equations
Essential Fat
Hydrostatic Weighing
Lean Tissue
Overfat
Purging
Skinfold Measurement
Storage Fat

Overfatness, Disease, and Related Costs

In 1990, the American population was 30% overweight (*overfat*), and the resulting increase in diseases due to overfatness (see Table 7.1) threatened to breakdown an already overburdened health care system. This prompted the United States Department of Human Services, in conjunction with over 20 health and fitness organizations, to develop a set of health goals to be achieved by the year 2000. These goals were published under the title "Healthy People 2000: National Health Promotion and Disease Prevention Objectives". One of the goals was to reduce the prevalence of overfatness among American adults to no more than 20% by the year 2000. Unfortunately by the year 2000, 64% of the American adult population were either overweight (33%) or obese (31%) putting over 160 million Americans at a higher risk for a variety of diseases. With most of the Healthy People 2000 physical activity and fitness objectives not met, Healthy People 2010 was created. The Healthy People Consortium headed by federal agencies in concert with state agencies and alliance of national organizations, developed additional objectives 2010. Unfortunately as the decade came to an end, most objectives were not being met and many outcomes were actually below their 2000 level.

Today, the health care cost of overfat-related illnesses in the United States is over $303 billion annually with the American taxpayers financing about half of this cost through Medicare and Medicaid. This staggering number of dollars spent is not due to America's lack of concern about their excess body fat. On the contrary, Americans appear to be extremely concerned with body image as surveys indicate that up to 70% of females and 40% of males are on weight reducing diets. This obsession with weight control has lead to the lucrative industry of diet books and weight-control clinics making over $51 billion annually.

Table 7.1
Various Health Problems Related to Overfatness

√ Coronary Artery Disease	√ Surgical Complications
√ High Blood Pressure	√ Kidney Problems
√ Type 2 Diabetes	√ Cirrhosis of the Liver
√ Cancer	√ High Blood Cholesterol
√ Osteoarthritis	√ Stroke
√ Gout	√ Varicose Veins

Body Composition

Human body mass can be categorized into two main groups. The first is *lean tissue,* which consists of muscles, bones, and organs. The second body mass category is fat, which is subdivided into essential and storage.

Essential Fat

A certain amount of body fat is required for normal physiological functioning and is called *essential fat*. This fat is stored in the marrow of the bones and lipid tissues of the nervous system. In addition, important storage sites of fat are located in or around the heart, muscles, lungs, liver, spleen, intestines, and kidneys. Included in this essential fat is the sex-specific fat for females that is important for hormonal production, menstruation, bone development, and childbearing. Essential fat is 3 - 5% for males and 10 - 15% for females.

Storage Fat

Fat that accumulates in fat tissue (*adipocyte*) is termed *storage fat*. Some storage fat is located in the visceral, but it is mostly located under the skin and is called subcutaneous fat. Storage fat serves as a body insulator against the cold and as protective padding against physical trauma. In addition, it functions as an energy reserve. With just 4.5 kg (10 lbs.) of storage fat, a 68 kg (150 lbs.) male has enough stored energy (35,000 Calories) to run 296 miles nonstop at a nine minute per mile pace.

The acceptable percentage of body fat is different for males and females. For competitive athletes, the body fat percentage is much lower than for those attempting to gain health fitness (see Table 7.2). There are however, minimal and maximal standards of acceptable body fat to maintain a healthy body.

Table 7.2

Body Fat Percentage Standards for Males and Females

STANDARDS	MALES	FEMALES
Unhealthy	<5%	<15%
Athletic	5 - 10%	15 - 20%
Good	11 - 15%	21 - 25%
Acceptable	16 - 20%	26 - 30%
Overfat	>20%	>30%

Assessment of Body Composition

The accurate appraisal of body composition is an important component of health fitness. There are two general techniques used to determine body composition. The first is direct evaluation, through a process of chemical analysis and dissection. For obvious reasons, this method is only performed on animal carcasses or human cadavers.

The second technique utilized for evaluating body composition is through indirect analysis using a variety of methods. A quick review of the most common methods and their limitations are listed below:

1. **Hydrostatic Weighing** - A technique using Archimedes' principle of density to determine body composition and is called *hydrostatic weighing*. Fat has a density of 0.90 grams per cubic centimeter as opposed to average lean tissue, which has a density of 1.10 grams per cubic centimeter. This means that fat has a greater volume per weight allowing it to float in water where as lean mass with a higher density will sink. During hydrostatic weighing the individual is submerged under water where weight is measured. The greater amount of body fat, the lower the underwater weight will be. Several calculations must be made to determine the percentage of body fat. This procedure is highly accurate but does require water submersion, special equipment, and a skilled technician.

2. **Skinfold Measurement** - The second best method for determining body fat percentage is the *skinfold measurement* of specific subcutaneous fatfold sites. This technique is based on the knowledge that in young adults 50% of total body fat is located under the skin. As a person ages, the percentage of subcutaneous fat to total body fat slightly decreases. The most common anatomical locations for taking skinfold measurements are the triceps (back of the upper arm), pectoralis (chest), suprailiac (hip), umbilicus (abdomen), thigh, axilla (side of ribs), and supscapular (upper back). All measurements are taken on the right side of the body in a standing position. A specially designed caliper is used to measure the skinfold thickness in millimeters. With a trained technician, the results are usually within two percentage points of hydrostatic weighing.

3. **Bioelectrical impedance** - A common technique used to measure body composition is called *bioelectrical impedance*. This method is based on the fact that electrical flow is facilitated by high electrolyte water content in the cells of the body. Since fat cells have low water and electrolyte content, impeded electrical flow will be directly related to the quantity of body fat. A painless, low voltage electrical current is introduced to the body and the resistance to the current flow is recorded and converted into a body fat percentage. Though very simple to use, this method is not always reliable. Two factors that can greatly decrease the accuracy are the body hydration levels and room temperature.

4. **Body Mass Index** - The *body mass index (BMI)* is derived by dividing an individual's weight in kilograms by height in meters squared. This method is better than the old height/weight chart used by many insurance companies; however, it still does not consider the proportional composition of the body. The body mass index is easy to calculate (see Laboratory 10) and shows if a person is at a high risk for developing cardiovascular diseases, but does not measure body comosition. The American College of Sports Medicine has stated that a BMI of 21 to 23 for women or 22 to 24 for men is considered desirable. When BMI exceeds 27.3 for women and 27.8 for men, there is a significant increased risk of cardiovascular disease.

Factors Affecting Body Fat

There are two factors affecting a person's amount of body fat (see Figure 7.1). The first factor is genetics, which plays a role in predisposing a person to gaining excess weight and becoming overfat. However this in and of itself will not cause excess accumulation of body fat. This person must also be in a sedentary environment with access to food above the daily physiological requirements. Lifestyle is the second factor in affecting the development of overfatness, determining 75% of the time if a person will acquire excess body fat. This factor includes living environment, social economical status, activity level, and accessibility to high caloric foods.

Figure 7.1

Factors That Contribute to Body Fat

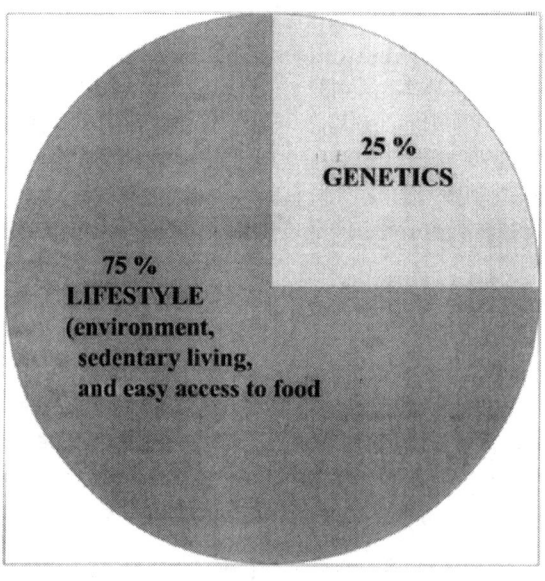

Figure 7.2

Components of Daily Caloric Expenditure

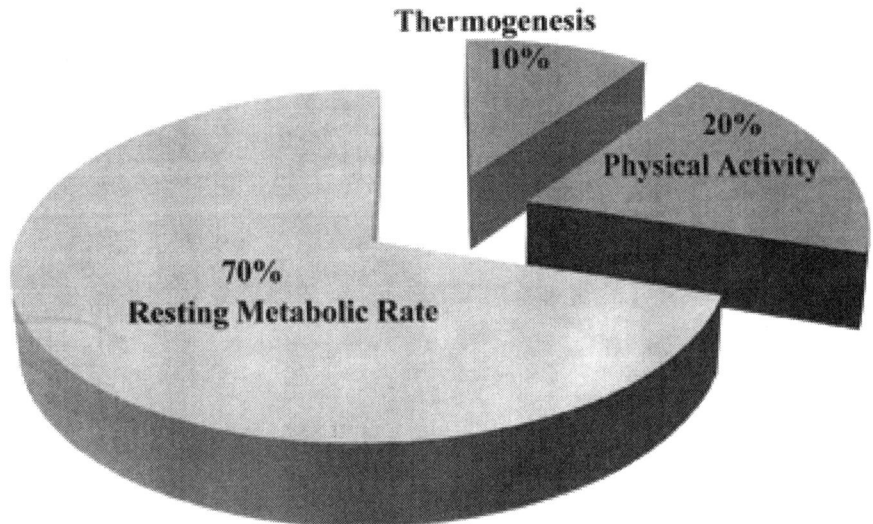

Daily caloric expenditure determines what effect lifestyle has on body fat accumulation. There are three components that determine the amount of calories burned each day (see Figure 7.2). The first component is thermogenesis, which utilizes 10% of daily caloric requirements. This energy is used by the body to break down consumed food into its parts and to transport them throughout the body. The second component in burning calories is physical activity, which includes such things as exercise, gardening, and housework. On the job physical exertion also fits in this category making a combined total caloric expenditure of only 20%.

The third component of daily caloric expenditure is resting metabolic rate and is composed of basal, sleeping, and resting (e.g. sitting, reading, and watching TV) metabolisms. This component burns 70% of the calories expended each day with *basal metabolic rate (BMR)* using the most. BMR is the minimum level of energy required to maintain bodily functions in a resting, awake state and is directly related to the amount of lean body tissue. Women have a 5 - 10% lower BMR than men of the same age and weight, due to their higher percentage of body fat. Also, as a person ages, BMR declines mainly because of a lower physical activity level leading to a decrease in lean body tissue. Clearly the best way to expend more calories each day is to increase lean body mass through regular exercise.

Energy Balance Equations

The three *energy balance equations* state that for body weight to be stable caloric intake must equal expenditures (see Figure 7.3). These equations only look at total

Figure 7.3

The Energy Balance Equations for Body Weight

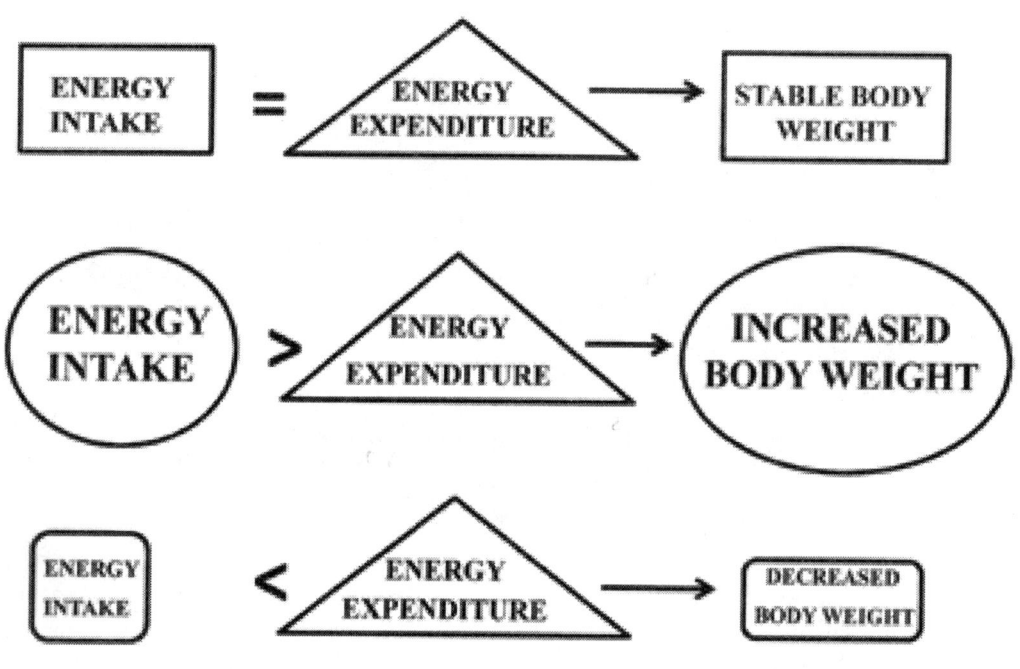

body weight in relationship to caloric consumption and expenditures; they do not specify the type of body mass (fat or muscle) lost or gained. If caloric intake exceeds expenditure, body weight will increase in the form of storage fat as seen in individuals with a sedentary lifestyle. However, if caloric consumption is greater than output due to intense physical activity, then the added weight may be in the form of larger muscles and denser bones as is found with body builders.

There are three ways in which an individual can achieve a decrease in body weight. The first method is to decrease caloric intake while maintaining the present energy expenditure level. This is the least desirable method of losing body weight because the weight loss comes from not only fat stores but also from lean tissue. When following a low calorie diet, the body perceives the environmental condition as one of famine and tries to conserve body fat stores. To accomplish this, BMR is slowed allowing the body to survive with fewer daily calories. Once the goal weight has been reached, the amount of calories needed to maintain this weight would be less than before going on the diet. This causes the individual to either have to maintain this low caloric intake or gain back the weight with a greater amount of body fat than before starting the dieting. Research has found that up to 66% of the weight lost from just dieting is regained within one year, and all is regained by five years. In addition, a low caloric diet will not meet the

Recommended Dietary Allowances for vitamins and minerals, which will lead to deficiencies and possible disorders.

The second method to decrease body weight is by maintaining present caloric consumption and increasing energy expenditure. This technique keeps the body from going into the "starvation mode" and will create additional lean tissue causing an increase in BMR. With the caloric intake staying stable, one should never feel "deprived" of eating and resent the weight loss process. Increased caloric expenditure in the form of exercise also leads to improvements in other health fitness areas. Generally, maintaining caloric intake and increasing caloric expenditures will be the best method for those needing to lose less than 4.5 kg (10 lbs.) of fat. In addition, this method is ideal for athletes where a proper diet of high nutritional value is required for optimal performance.

The final way to lose weight is to slightly decrease caloric intake (< 500 Calories below regular daily amounts) and increase the amount of calories burned each day (~ 500 Calories) through exercise. This method works best for those needing to lose over 4.5 kg (10 lbs.) of fat weight. This combined approach is much less likely to cause hunger pains. Also, exercise protects against the loss of lean tissue and enhances the utilization of fat from the adipocytes.

Benefits of Exercise for Fat Reduction

Regular exercise with or without diet restriction presents many positive benefits for the individual needing to reduce body fat. The best type of exercise for fat loss is a combination of strength training and aerobic activity (see Figure 7.4). Strength training increases lean body mass causing an elevation in BMR. This leads to a higher daily caloric expenditure because lean tissue is more metabolically active than fat tissue. On the other hand, aerobic exercise increases the mobilization and utilization of fat from fat stores (see Figure 7.5). Other benefits from aerobic activity include: an improved cardiovascular system, a decrease in blood pressure, and an increase in HDLs (Chapter 4). With regular exercise, it is possible to increase body weight but actually fit in smaller size clothing. This is possible because fat has a greater volume per weight than muscle. Weight is not a good indicator of fat loss; a better method would be by clothing fit.

Many individuals seek to reduce body fat at specific anatomical locations. This spot reduction is based on the belief that an increase in skeletal muscle activity under the fat storage site will facilitate this fat's utilization. Unfortunately this does not occur; the mobilization of fat to be used for energy comes first from the most metabolically active fat stores. This means that the last place where fat was deposited will be the first fat used, and no type of exercise or special equipment will cause otherwise.

Figure 7.4

The Effects of Eight Weeks of Stength Training, Aerobic Exercise, and/or Low Caloric Diet on Body Composition in Obese Women

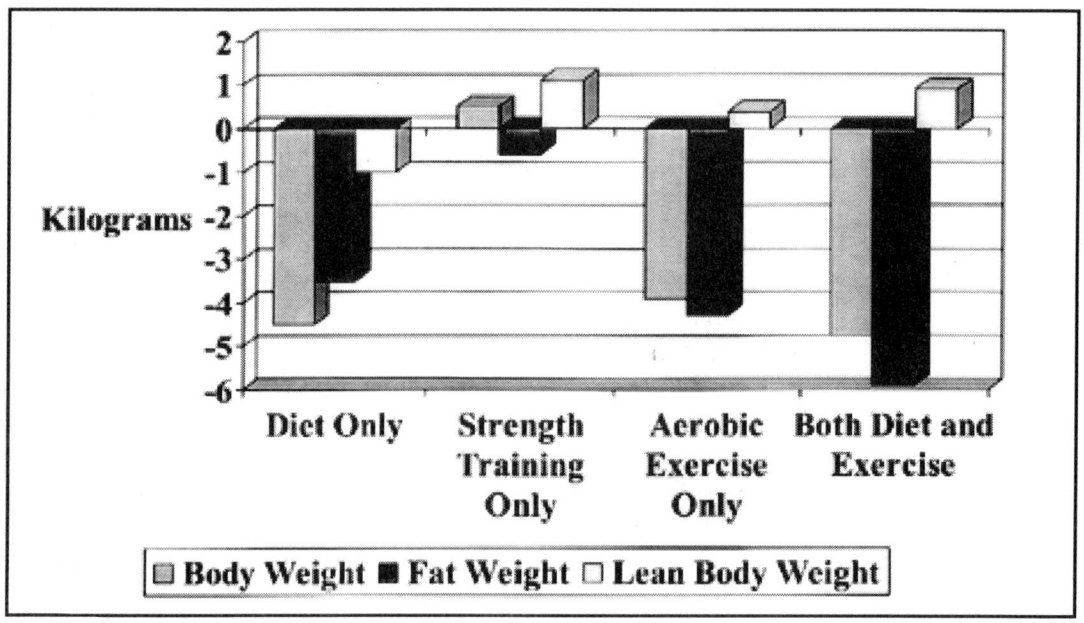

Figure 7.5

The Percentage of Fat and Carbohydrate Metabolized During Aerobic Activity

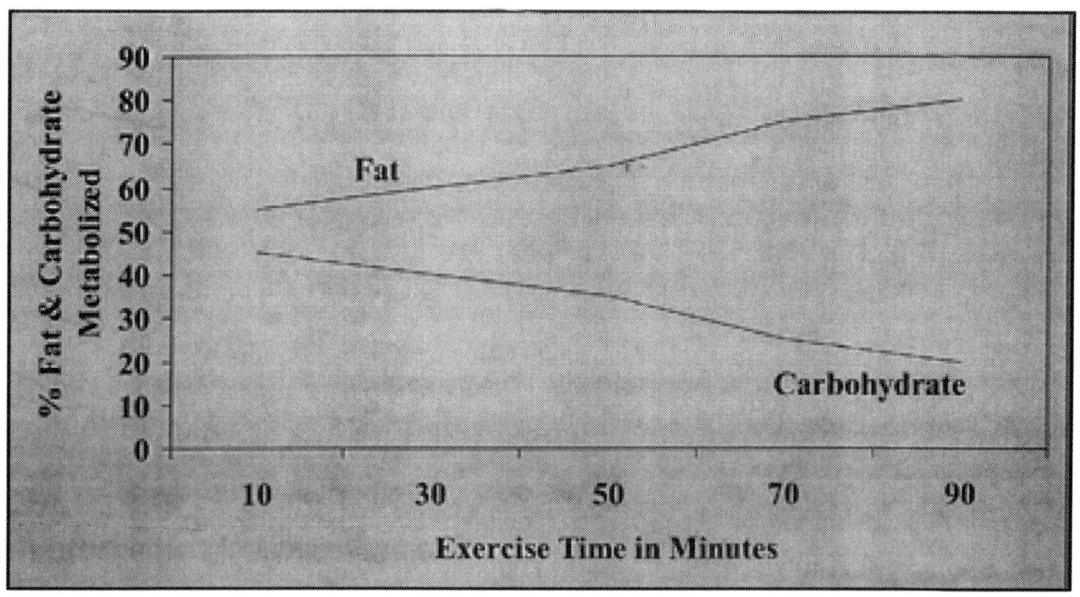

Eating Disorders

Only overfat individuals need to lose weight in the form of fat. Ideal body weight is based on body composition and the attainment of optimal health fitness rather than on body shape or weight. Many healthy-weight or thin women and men are striving to lose additional body weight to achieve some arbitrary weight. An individual's perception of body fatness and strong environmental pressures can cause some to believe they are overfat when in reality they are not. Poor self-concept and an unrealistic body weight goal (see Table 7.3) can lead to eating disorders and possibly death.

In the United States, the prevalence of eating disorders is between 5 - 10% of the population with approximately 90% being female. The greatest number of people with eating disorders is found among young college females who comprise up to 20% of this population. Three common eating disorders recognized by the American Psychiatric Association are 1) *anorexia nervosa*, 2) *bulimia nervosa*, and 3) *binge eating disorder*.

1. **Anorexia Nervosa** - An eating disorder in which a preoccupation with body weight leads to self-starvation is called anorexia nervosa. An anorexic individual possesses a great fear of becoming fat and has a distorted image of their body believing they are fat rather than actually underweight. These individuals typically begin a diet and at first feel in control and please with

Table 7.3

Warning Signs of Eating Disorders

- ✓ A preoccupation with food, calories, and weight
- ✓ Concern about being or feeling fat
- ✓ Self-criticism of one's body
- ✓ Secretly eating or stealing food
- ✓ Unwillingness to eat in front of others
- ✓ Periods of severe caloric restriction
- ✓ Use of laxatives
- ✓ Mood swings
- ✓ An apparent preoccupation with the eating behavior of others
- ✓ Wide fluctuations in weight over short period of time
- ✓ Vomitus or odor of vomitus in the bathroom

their weight loss. To increase the weight loss, they combine exhaustive exercise, laxatives, and diuretics. As they lose excessive weight, their health begins to deteriorate. Typical problems from an anorexia behavior are amenorrhea, digestive problems, anemia, growth of fine body hair, depression, osteoporosis, and abnormalities of the immune system. Anorexics cannot overcome this disease by themselves; a professional trained in eating disorders is required. If help is obtained quickly, many of the physical complications can be reversed.

2. **Bulimia Nervosa** - Another eating disorder is bulimia nervosa and is more prevalent than anorexia nervosa. Bulimia is characterized by eating regular or large meals (binges) followed by intentionally emptying (*purging*) the food out of the stomach by self-induced vomiting, use of laxatives, or intense exercise. Bulimia occurs primarily in young women with a morbid fear of becoming fat. Most bulimics are healthy-looking, good students or athletes, extremely sociable, and pleasant. Medical problems associated with this disease include amenorrhea, tooth erosion, cardiac arrhythmia, ulcers, and kidney damage. Bulimics need assistance in overcoming this disorder and require professional help from a trained eating disorder specialist.

3. **Binge Eating Disorder** - Individuals with binge eating disorder consume large amounts of food in a short period of time; however, unlike bulimia nervosa purging is not included. Binge episodes are often triggered by emotional and/or psychological events (e.g. loneliness and anxiety) instead of physical hunger. These binges usually occur in private and are followed by feelings of guilt, shame, and depression. This disease requires professional help from a trained specialist.

Summary

Overfatness is a serious situation in the United States causing a variety of health problems and early death. Health care costs for overfat-related illnesses are over $117 billion annually. The human body requires a minimal amount of fat for proper physiological functioning. Excess fat is stored in many locations with approximately 50% in the subcutaneous area under the skin in young adults. Lifestyle plays the largest role in affecting body fat accumulation. However, by following the energy balance equations, body mass can be modified. The best method for losing body fat is by a slight reduction in caloric intake and adding exercise consisting of both strength training and aerobic activity. Eating disorders are prevalent on college campuses especially among female students and athletes.

Review Questions

1. Distinguish between body weight and body composition.

2. What are acceptable body fat percentages for males and females?

3. List and explain three techniques for determining body fat percentage.

4. Define anorexia nervosa, bulimia nervosa, and binge eating disorder.

5. List five health problems related to excessive body fat.

6. What are the three methods for losing body weight?

7. Explain why lean tissue has an effect on basal metabolic rate.

8. List the three ways in which energy is expended in the body.

CHAPTER 8

The Physically Active Lifestyle and Aging

Learning Objectives

This chapter recommends establishing a regular exercise routine and sticking to it not for just a few days, weeks, or months but for a lifetime. The message is that regular exercise should be developed as one would develop a lifelong health habit. Guidelines for regular exercise and recommendations for an active lifestyle are discussed. When the chapter is completed you should know:

1. Guidelines for disciplining yourself to have a consistent exercise program (pages 91 - 92).

2. Daily physical activities that can be added to improve health fitness (page 92).

3. The physiological and psychological benefits of being physically active as one ages (pages 93 - 94).

4. The social-cultural benefits of being physically active as an older individual (page 95).

Key Terms

Aging Process
Cognitive Functioning
Exercise Habit
Physically Active Lifestyle
Socio-Cultural
World Health Organization

Making Exercise a Regular Habit

Regular physical exercise, performed on most days of the week, reduces the risk of dying prematurely. In addition, it promotes psychological well being and decreases the risk of cardiovascular diseases that claim the lives of nearly one million Americans every year. Interestingly, even with the knowledge of these benefits, many Americans do not exercise on a regular basis; less than 15% of adults exercise three or more times a week. The greatest benefits from exercising regularly occur later in life; thus causing many young adults not to realize its importance until they are faced with a heart attack or stroke.

Starting an **exercise habit** is not difficult, however maintaining it is. The following are guidelines that can assist in making exercise a regular habit.

1. **Place into the weekly schedule the days and times designated for exercise.** Determine the days of the week that will best accommodate an exercise program, and designate them as "exercise days". Also, find a suitable time during each of these exercise days to reserve for the workout. There are only minimal differences in benefits from exercising during the morning, noon, or night; the key is choosing a time that is most convenient and that causes the least disruption to the daily schedule.

2. **Discipline the mind to exercising during the scheduled time regardless of feelings.** Only an illness or important family event should cause a missed workout. When more than one exercise session must be missed during a week, the workout should be rescheduled. If there are frequent interferences with a particular time, the schedule should be adjusted to avoid the conflict. Missing an exercise session as little as once a month is not a concern, but missing a workout once a week could soon become missing twice a week and eventually lead to the loss of the exercise habit.

3. **Modify exercise rather than discontinue it when an injury occurs.** If an injury prevents the performance of the normal exercise routine then the workout should be modified, not eliminated. There are many types of aerobic and strength training activities that can be utilized without aggravating or making the injury worse. If the disability is permanent, then appropriate modifications should be made to the exercise program. An injury must not be allowed to stop the acquisition of health fitness.

4. **Remember that the more hectic and busier the daily schedule is, the more important the exercise session becomes.** Exercise reduces stress and enhances mental concentration, allowing a greater amount of work to be preformed more efficiently. Solutions to problems come faster, and less mental fatigue occurs.

5. **Continue to exercise regularly into old age.** The need for exercise increases with age because low activity causes muscles to atrophy, bones to weaken, and body fat to increase. A continued sedentary lifestyle often leads to disability, this causes a person to no longer be self-sufficient or have the freedom to move about.

6. **Wear appropriate exercise attire including footwear and undergarments.** Wearing correct clothing for the type of activity will enhance the enjoyment of the exercise and decrease the risk of injury. Also, use the exercise attire just for working out to increase its longevity. Running shoes should be used strictly for running and not for everyday activities. These shoes need to be replaced after every 500 miles of use due to the loss in their protective cushioning. Once the shoes are replaced, they may be used for normal footwear.

Developing A Physically Active Lifestyle

Following an exercise program on a regular basis is only part of having a physically active lifestyle. Exercising one hour per day for six days per week means the other 162 hours in the week may be inactive. While six hours of exercise per week will markedly enhance health fitness, modification of other daily activities will further improve one's health especially if overfatness is a problem. The following are ways to create a more physically active lifestyle:

1. **Use the stairs rather than the elevator or escalator.** When a choice can be made at work, school, or shopping, use the stairs. By just climbing two flights of stairs per day, enough calories will be expended to burn approximately .5 kg (one pound) of fat in a year.

2. **Park farther away from the store or office for the walk to and from the car.** If riding the bus or train for commuting, get off one stop earlier for an extended walk. Walking two additional blocks per day allows an individual to expend enough calories in a year to lose over 2.5 kg (5 lbs.) of fat.

3. **Walk or bicycle; don't ride.** Try to make walking or bicycling the first choice for transportation. Not only will health fitness improve, but also money will be saved from less gasoline used, and the environment will be cleaner.

4. **Avoid laborsaving devices.** Push the lawn mower to cut the grass instead of using a riding or self-propelled mower. When playing golf, walk and pull or carry the golf clubs. By playing 18 holes of golf without riding in a cart, up to five miles could be walked.

5. **Develop hobbies that require physical effort.** Choose leisure activities or hobbies that involve frequent physical movements such as: gardening, dancing, and hiking. Also participate in leisure sports such as: bowling, horseshoes, sailing, and table tennis. While these activities will not produce fitness gains alone, they will increase the amount of physical effort used during the week.

Physical Activity and Aging

At the beginning of the 20th century only four percent of the United States population was over 65 years of age. By the year 2020 this group of senior citizens will increase to 20% of the American population and by 2050 there will be over 89 million senior citizens in the U.S.A. This increase in the number of older adults may have dire consequences for society if they do not embrace physically active and healthy lifestyles. Advancing age is associated with potential sensory, motor, and cognitive changes impacting elderly people's ability to function independently in society.

In recent years, researchers have established that hereditary factors play an important role in how one grows old. However, additional factors influence the aging process and can modify the outcome. The largest aging modifier is a healthy lifestyle consisting of regular physical activity and good nutrition. By participating in regular physical activity throughout one's life a number of physiological, psychological, and socio-cultural benefits occur.

Cardiorespiratory Fitness (Chapter 2) - Maximal aerobic capacity was thought to decline at about 10% per decade with advancing age. However, recent studies have shown that by maintaining one's aerobic activity level, little decline occurs in aerobic capacity. In addition, when sedentary senior citizens increase, even modestly, their levels of physical activity, drastic improvements in cardiovascular function will result.

Blood Pressure (Chapter 4) - Hypertension is a serious medical problem that afflicts more than 73 million Americans. Both systolic and diastolic blood pressure increases with advancing age. However, with a low intensity walking program, significant decreases in both systolic and diastolic blood pressure have been found in hypertensive adults over 60 years of age.

Blood Lipids (Chapter 4) - Aging is associated with an increase in cholesterol levels that can cause development of cardiovascular disease. Studies have found that older individuals on regular aerobic exercise programs have favorable cholesterol levels as compared to sedentary individuals of the same age. An additional area that affects blood lipid levels is body composition. Individuals with healthy body fat percentages have a more positive cholesterol level as compared to overfat persons of the same age.

Muscular Endurance and Strength (Chapter 5) - Muscle endurance and strength decline with advancing age. Adequate levels of muscular strength are critical for the performance of daily living activities. Until recently strength training was considered potentially dangerous for the elderly. However, over the late few years research has shown that strength training can be performed safely in both males and females as old as 90 years of age with strength gains over 100%.

Flexibility (Chapter 6) - Aging is associated with changes in the elasticity of connective tissue resulting in decreases in range of motion of the joints. Most declines in flexibility are directly linked to a decrease in physical activity. Stretching exercises in the older individual will increase flexibility and joint range of motion.

Balance - Age related declines in postural stability and dynamic balance are risk factors for falls and injuries in the older adult population. An exercise program emphasizing walking, flexibility training, and strength training will improve balance and decrease body swaying in senior citizens thus increasing their mobility and self-sufficiency.

Depression and Anxiety - The incidence of depression increases significantly with age and is associated with a decline in physical activity. Participation in regular physical exercise has been shown to reduce mild to moderate levels of depression and to beneficially affect a person's state of mind and anxiety level.

Cognitive Functioning - Decrements in cognitive functioning occur as one ages. However, there is a wide variation in decreases depending upon the cognitive task. Regular exercise has been shown to postpone age-related declines in Central Nervous System processing speed and in both fine and gross motor performance. Elderly people who participate in sporting activities that require adjusting to a constantly changing environment (racquetball and tennis), are able to maintain higher levels of coordination and better reaction times than sedentary individuals of similar age.

Social Functioning - Regular physical activity enhances many sociocultural variables in the elderly. In 1997, the World Health Organization published a summation of their findings (see Table 8.1) indicating that the social benefits of exercise for older individuals are significant.

Table 8.1
A Summary of the Social Beneits of Physical Activity for Older Persons By the World Health Organization

- Empowering Older Individuals in Society
- Enhancing Social and Cultural Integration
- Allowing the Formation of New Friendships
- Widening Social and Cultural Networks
- Permitting Role Maintenance and New Role Acquisition
- Encouraging Intergenerational Activity

Summary

Having a physically active lifestyle requires more than just maintaining a regular exercise program. It also includes making all aspects of one's life more physical. Today, there are many modern devices for saving time and labor. However, avoiding many of these devices will allow a person to reap the benefits of being more physically active. During the aging process, many bodily changes occur; but with regular exercise most of the decline is slowed. Even though an individual has been sedentary into later years, increasing physical activity will reverse many harmful physical and psychological changes and will enhance social functioning.

Review Questions

1. Discuss the recommendations for increasing activity beyond a regular exercise program.

2. List three ways to make exercise a regular habit.

3. What will be the percentage of Americans who are 65 or older in the year 2020?

4. Name three physiological benefits of continuing physical activities into old age.

5. List the social benefits of regular physical activity for the elderly.

CHAPTER 9

Basic Nutrition for Health Fitness

Learning Objectives

This chapter discusses basic nutritional requirements for health fitness. The function of, and the need for carbohydrates, fats, protein, vitamins, minerals, and fluids in the body are explained. Simple and complex carbohydrates, fiber in the diet, and triglycerides are detailed in terms of their affects on the health of the body. Basic food groups, recommended daily menus, calories, and nutritional information are provided in chart and table form. When you complete this chapter you should be able to:

1. Describe the role and function of the seven basic nutrients in the body (page 99).

2. Explain the food sources and recommended daily intake of the seven basic nutrients (pages 100).

3. Describe the seven basic food categories (pages 100 - 111).

4. List the guidelines for controlling caloric intake (page 117).

Key Terms

Antioxidant
Calories
Carbohydrate
Complex Carbohydrate
Fiber
Food and Drug Administration (FDA)
Glycemic Index
Minerals
Protein
Recommended Dietary Allowances (RDA)
Saturated Fats
Trans Fats
Triglycerides
United States Department of Agriculture (USDA)
Unsaturated Fats
Vitamins

Eating For Health

Health is very dependent upon the foods and fluids consumed. Poor eating habits have been associated with hyperactivity in children, physical fatigue, mental fatigue, depression, stunted growth, and numerous other problems. Five of the 10 leading causes of death have been associated with diet: 1) heart disease, 2) cancer, 3) atherosclerosis, 4) stroke, and 5) type 2 diabetes.

The body is composed of the elements outlined in Table 9.1. These elements are constantly being used to provide energy for the body, to build new cells, to repair old cells, and to regulate the various body processes. Since the body is unable to absorb these elements through the skin, they must be gained through daily consumption of foods and fluids.

Seven Basic Nutrients

Nutrients are chemical parts of food and liquids that have specific functions in the body. The two overall functions of nutrients are 1) to provide essential elements the body needs to sustain life and 2) to provide energy for the body. The essential elements needed for health fitness are found in seven basic nutrients (see Table 9.2).

TABLE 9.1

Percentage of the Basic Elements of the Body

NON-METALLIC ELEMENTS		METALLIC ELEMENTS	
Element	Percent	Element	Percent
Oxygen	65	Calcium	1
Carbon	18	Phosphorus	1
Hydrogen	10	Sodium	1
Nitrogen	3	Potassium, chlorine, sulfur, magnesium, and 15+ others	1
TOTAL	96	TOTAL	4

TABLE 9.2

The Seven Basic Nutrients

- CARBOHDRATES
- FIBER
- FATS
- PROTEINS
- VITAMINS
- MINERALS
- WATER

1. Carbohydrates

The primary function of carbohydrates is to provide all the cells of the body with energy. While most cells use a combination of both fats and carbohydrates for energy, the central nervous system (i.e. brain and nerve tissue) uses almost exclusively carbohydrates for energy. In activities of short duration requiring high energy, such as in sprinting and strength training, skeletal muscles use carbohydrates extensively for energy since fat metabolism is a slower energy producing process requiring oxygen.

Carbohydrates must be present in the diet for fats to be completely utilized for energy. If a diet is low in carbohydrates, then proteins from the skeletal muscles will be broken down and used in place of carbohydrates to meet this need. This procedure of catabolizing muscle tissue will cause problems in the body. On the other hand, excess carbohydrate consumption will cause this nutrient to be converted into fat and stored.

When carbohydrates are eaten, enzymes in the mouth, stomach, and small intestine begin to break the carbohydrates down into their simplest form (i.e. sugar). After this process has been accomplished in the small intestine, the sugar can pass through the intestinal wall and is absorbed into the blood stream. Once in the blood it is transported to the liver for conversion into glucose and then released back into the blood stream to be transported to body cells for energy. For glucose to enter most cells in the body insulin is required. Insulin is a hormone secreted by special cells in the pancreas and functions to transport the glucose out of the blood and into the cells. If the cells requirement for energy is low, then the glucose is changed into fat and stored in adipocytes (fat cells)

Types of Carbohydrates - There are two basic types of carbohydrates: 1) simple, which are mainly mono-, and disaccharides and 2) complex or polysaccharides. Simple carbohydrates consist of sugars, (see Table 9.3) and **complex carbohydrates** consist of starch and cellulose (**fiber**). In processed foods, simple carbohydrates go under the names of brown sugar, honey, corn syrup, levulose, and dextrose. Regardless of the name, the body handles them all as sugars and must convert each of them into the usable form called glucose. A complex carbohydrate is composed of many sugars (50 to over 1000) combined together to form a complex molecule. Complex carbohydrates are primarily found in vegetables, grains, seeds, and fruits. Of the carbohydrates in the American diet, approximately half come from starches and half from sugars.

TABLE 9.3

The Six Common Simple Carbohydrate Types

TYPE	SOURCE
Sucrose (table sugar)	Sugar beets and sugar cane
Fructose	Fruits and honey
Galactose	Milk
Lactose	Dairy products
Maltose	Grains and cereals
Glucose	Fruits, corn syrup and honey

Over the last few years, a new system for classifying carbohydrates has been developed; and is known as the glycemic index (see Table 9.4). The glycemic index is a ranking of carbohydrates based on their immediate effect on blood glucose levels. Carbohydrates that digest quickly cause a fast and sharp elevation in blood glucose level are given a high index ranking. Carbohydrates that digest slowly, releasing glucose gradually into the blood over a long period of time are considered a low glycemic food. High glycemic foods can trigger excessive insulin release due to the rapid increase of blood glucose level. High insulin causes the liver to produce triglycerides and very low-density lipoproteins (LDLs) and releases them into the blood. Because of this, high glycemic foods can accelerate atherosclerosis (Chapter 4) making it a contributing factor in cardiovascular disease. In addition, the excess insulin will transport too much glucose out of the blood and into the cells causing low glucose levels (hypoglycemia) leading to weakness and hunger. The person then eats again, when it is really not necessary, demonstrating how high glycemic foods lead to a craving for more sugar.

Over a period of years, the up-and-down effect of high blood glucose and high insulin levels followed by low blood glucose and low insulin can cause the cell to become resistive to insulin. Also, the insulin generating cells of the pancreas can become over-worked and slow their production of insulin. In time the blood glucose level remains elevated and a condition of diabetes develops. Most type 2 diabetes (Chapter 4) is due to this factor and is caused in part by the person's dietary habits, overfatness, and lack of exercise.

When the diet contains excessive amounts of refined simple carbohydrates (sugar) found in soft drinks, bakery goods, and similar products; the body is being robbed of important nutrients. Table sugar is called "empty calories" because it contains no vitamins, minerals, or fiber. Also refined sugar sticks to the teeth and, with the bacteria present in the mouth, causes tooth decay (dental caries).

2. Fiber

Fiber is a type of complex carbohydrate of which cellulose is the most common form and is found primarily in fruits, vegetables, and grains. Since the body does not possess the enzymes necessary to break down fiber, it has no caloric value, and it passes through the small and large intestine relatively unchanged.

TABLE 9.4

Sample of High Glycemic and Low Glycemic Foods

HIGH GLYCEMIC FOODS	LOW GLYCEMIC FOODS
Sugar	Legumes
Potatoes	Whole Fruits
Bananas	Whole Wheat
White Bread	Brown Rice
White Rice	Beans
Sodas	Nuts
Fruit Juice	Leafy Vegetables

Function of Fiber - Although several specific purposes of fiber have been established, much is yet to be learned about its importance in the diet. Fiber promotes regular bowel movements by absorbing water in the large intestine making the stools soft and large. Thus, elimination from the body is easily preformed with no straining or pushing. With a high fiber diet, constipation is rare and so are hemorrhoids.

High-fiber diets also quicken the transit time of food from intake to elimination. Waste products of metabolism stay in the large intestine three times longer with a low-fiber diet. This allows the waste products some of which may consist of toxic chemicals and carcinogenic agents (i.e. cancer causing), a longer time to irritate the large intestine. This may be a strong factor in diverticulosis, colitis, and possibly colon cancer. Authorities recommend one to two bowel movements a day.

Lack of fiber in the diet has also been associated with high blood cholesterol, appendicitis, gallbladder diseases, diabetes, and obesity. Fiber is absolutely an essential part of a healthful diet, not so much for what it does but for what it prevents.

Sources of Fiber - The amount of fiber required each day in the diet is one gram per 100 calories (20 – 35 grams). A typical American eats 14 to 15 grams daily, but vegetarians eat as much as 30 to 40 grams. Most current authorities recommend a safe amount of fiber of at least 25 grams per day. If a person does not normally have one to two bowel movements per day with soft stools, chances are there is not enough fiber in the diet. Like any nutrient, too much of a good thing can lead to problems. Excess fiber in the diet can lead to diarrhea, gas, and cause dehydration and mineral loss.

The sources of fiber should vary (see Table 9.5). Bran found in grain serves as one of the best sources of fiber. However, if the grain has been refined, the bran is lost and

TABLE 9.5
Fiber Content in Selected Fruits, Vegetables, and Grains

FOOD	SERVING	FIBER GRAMS
Broccoli	1 medium stalk	6
Apple	1 medium	5
Almonds	¼ cup	5
Cabbage	½ cup	4
Peas	½ cup	3
Potato	1 medium	3
100% whole wheat bread	2 slices	2
Banana	1 medium	2
Orange	1 medium	2
Strawberries	½ cup	1
Carrots	¼ cup	1

the fiber is gone. During the refining process most of the vitamins, minerals, and fiber is lost. After a food is refined, some of the vitamins and minerals are restored (enriched); and occasionally additional vitamins are added (fortified), but the fiber is still absent. Therefore, unrefined grains are best in order to receive the fiber they possess. While bran from grains is a good fiber source, at least half the fiber should come from vegetables and fruits. Cooking vegetables and fruits causes them to lose some of their fiber. Therefore, people should eat raw vegetables and fruits as much as possible.

Breakfast cereals are an excellent source of fiber if properly selected. Table 9.6 lists the breakdown of carbohydrates in selected high-fiber cereals. A breakfast of Corn Bran, Multi Bran Chex, or 40% Bran Flakes topped with strawberries or a banana can start the day off with a low glycemic index and high fiber meal.

3. Fats

Fats provide most cells of the body with energy. At rest about 66% of the cells' energy comes from fat and 34% from carbohydrates. Fats are also important as carriers of vitamins (A, D, E, and K), as protectors of vital body organs, and as insulators of the body. They are also an important part of cell walls and hormones, and serve to depress appetite. Excess fat in the diet is stored in adipocytes (Chapter 7).

Some fat in the diet is essential for normal body functioning; however, most American consumes too much fat everyday. At the turn of the century, fat accounted for 25 to 30% of Americans' daily caloric intake compared to 40 to 45% today. Teenagers tend to have poor dietary habits, and often 50% of their diets are fat. Problems from excess fat intake include overfatness and elevated blood fats leading to cardiovascular disease (Chapter 4).

TABLE 9.6

Fiber Amounts in Selected Breakfast Cereals

CEREAL (1 Serving)	TOTAL CHO (grams)	STARCH (grams)	SUGAR (grams)	FIBER (grams)
All Bran	21	7	5	9
Raisin Bran	31	11	14	6
40% Bran Flakes	23	13	5	5
Multi Bran Chex	25	15	6	4
Cracklin Bran	21	10	7	4
Shreded Wheat	19	16	0	3
Grape Nuts	23	17	3	3
Cheerios	20	19	1	2
Total	23	18	5	2
Special K	20	16	3	1
Fruit Loops	25	12	13	0
Apple Jacks	26	12	14	0

Types of Fats - Triglycerides are the most common fats in the diet and are either saturated or unsaturated. Saturated triglycerides (saturated fats) are found primarily in animal products such as beef, pork, lamb, lobster, shrimp, milk, cheese, butter, cream, and eggs. Two plant sources that also contain high saturated fat are coconut and palm oil. Although fats are essential for health, saturated fats are not and should be reduced in the diet.

Unsaturated fats, which are polyunsaturated and monounsaturated, do not appear to cause health problems to the same degree as saturated fats. They are found primarily in vegetables but also are in oils (e.g. safflower, canola, corn, peanut, olive, soybean, and cottonseed) and margarine used in baking and cooking.

Another type of fat is cholesterol that is required by the body and is manufactured by the liver. Cholesterol is found in most cells and is a basic structure for several hormones. It is normally present in the blood attached to lipoproteins such as HDL and LDL (Chapter 4).

Trans fatty acids (**trans fats**) are not a natural occurring fat but are formed during a manufacturing process. Trans fats are created when hydrogen atoms are forced into unsaturated fats to make them solid at room temperature. This food processing technique is called hydrogenation and can be found on nutrition labels with terms as "hydrogenated" or "partially hydrogenated" oils. In 2006, the **Food and Drug Administration (FDA)** began to require all nutritional labels to list the amount of trans fat in the food.

Dietary Fat Sources - The daily requirement for fat appears to be between 10 and 30% of caloric intake. To evaluate fat intake, count the grams of fat eaten each day. Table 9.7 presents a recommendation for daily fat intake on the basis of a person's situation. Reduction of daily intake of fat is possible by increasing low-fat foods and decreasing or avoiding fatty foods. By substituting low-fat meat and milk products, a person can significantly reduce fat intake. One baked potato is 100 calories, but one cup of French fries is 480 calories. One cup of whole milk is 150 calories compared to 85 calories in one cup of skim milk. The difference in calories is exclusively due to the fat in the fried potatoes and in the whole milk.

TABLE 9.7

Daily Amount of Fat Grams Intake According to Different Situations

THE PERSON IS/HAS:	Grams of fat/day
° Overfat, sedentary, or has high blood lipids.	<40
° A history of heart disease in the family.	<40
° Acceptable body fat, average blood lipids, and regular exerciser.	40 - 60
° Lean body fat, low blood lipids, and exercises vigorously daily.	60 - 80

TABLE 9.8

Fat Types and Their Effect on Blood Cholesterol Levels

TYPE OF FAT	MAIN SOURCE	STATE AT ROOM TEMPERATURE	EFFECT ON BLOOD CHOLESTEROL
Mono-Unsaturated	Olive, canola & peanut oil	Liquid	Lowers LDL Raises HDL
Poly-Unsaturated	Corn, fish & soybean oil	Liquid	Lowers LDL Raises HDL
Saturated	Whole milk, butter, cheese, coconut & red meat	Solid	Raises LDL Raises HDL
Trans Fatty Acid	Margarine, vegetable shortening & hydrogenated vegetable oil	Solid or Semi-solid	Raises LDL Lowers HDL

The type of fat is more important than the amount when looking at blood cholesterol levels. High blood cholesterol levels greatly increase the risk for cardiovascular diseases (Chapter 4) but the amount of cholesterol in the food consumed has minimal effect on this level. The biggest influence on blood cholesterol levels is the type of fats in the diet (see Table 9.8). Substituting mono and polyunsaturated fats for saturated and trans fats can achieve a healthier diet.

4. Protein

The major functions of **proteins** are to build, repair, and maintain cells. They form the major part of muscle tissue and are essential for muscle contraction. They are an important part of hemoglobin as well as numerous hormones. Excess proteins in the diet are converted to fat and stored. Normally the body does not use proteins for energy, but in emergencies, proteins can be converted to carbohydrates and used for energy.

The basic units, or building blocks, of proteins are amino acids. There are over 100 naturally occurring amino acids, but only 20 are required for the human body. These 20 amino acids can be combined in numerous ways to make the approximately 50,000 different protein containing compounds in the human body. Ten amino acids cannot be synthesized by the body and are called "essential" amino acids. A complete protein is one that contains all the essential amino acids, whereas an incomplete protein does not contain all the essential amino acids. Sources of complete protein include eggs, milk, meat, fish, and poultry.

The average American consumes too much meat. Most people plan their meals around the meat they are serving; and at restaurants the main entree is usually meat. The daily need of protein is about 0.8 to 1.2 gram per kilogram of body weight for the normal adult and 1.5 to 2 grams per kilogram of body weight for the adolescent, the body builder, and the pregnant woman or nursing mother. This means that adults need only three to four ounces of protein per day to meet all their protein needs.

High-Protein Diet - Several potential health problems are associated with a high-protein diet. Persons on a high-protein diet eat an excess amount of meat. The high-meat diet will result not only in excess protein consumption but also in high fat intake, with the fat being in the form of cholesterol and saturated fat. Beef and pork are 20 to 40% fat, chicken and turkey without the skins and fish contain only 10 to 15% fat. The digestion of protein releases acids that the body neutralizes with calcium which may be taken from the bones. Long-term usage of high-protein diets could weaken bones and lead to osteoporosis (Chapter 2).

The excess protein in the diet does not build excess cells; instead it is converted in the liver to fat and stored in adipocytes. When the body converts protein to fat, ammonia is produced. Since ammonia is toxic to the body, it is changed into urea and eliminated by the kidneys in the urine. Since urea is also toxic, water is drawn from the body cells to dilute it, and excess water is lost from the body in the urine. Therefore, a high-protein diet can cause the body to lose excess amounts of body water and leads to dehydration. Many persons on high protein diets enjoy quick and large weight losses. However, the weight loss is only water, not fat, and will return as soon as the diet is ended.

Vegetarian - Many people, including current nutritional scientists, believe the human body functions best by only consuming vegetables, fruits, and grains. It is possible to receive all the essential amino acids without eating meat. A very important point, however, is that the vegetarian must emphasize a variety of foods in the diet, especially soybeans, peas, lentils, and beans, and must supplement these with cheese, milk, and eggs. By consuming a variety of nonmeat foods from these areas, all the essential amino acids can be attained. The only nutrient missing in a vegetarian diet is Vitamin Bl2, which occurs naurally in meat sources only, can be obtained through a vitamin supplement.

5. Vitamins

Vitamins are organic substances required for optimal health. They help regulate nearly all metabolic reactions, help convert carbohydrates and fat into energy, and assist with bone and tissue repairs. The body cannot manufacture vitamins so they must be ingested daily into the body. The *Recommended Daily Allowances (RDA)* for vitamins has been established by the National Research Council of the Food and Drug Administration and is revised periodically as new research becomes available (see Table 9.9)

TABLE 9.9

Adult RDA Amounts for Vitamins, Their Function and Major Source

VITAMIN	MALE/FEMALE	PRIMARY BODY FUNCTION	MAJOR SOURCE
A	.9 mg/.7 mg	Tissue growth and repair, especially skin and membranes; night vision	Vegetables (carrots, sweet potatoes, spinach), cantaloupe, watermelon
D	.005 mg/.005 mg	Bone calcification	Milk, fish, sunshine (naturally formed in the body due to the sun's rays
E	15 mg/15 mg	Prevent cell membrane damage and scar tissue, may help to delay aging	Wheat germ, walnuts, sunflower seeds, almonds
K	.12 mg/.09 mg	Assists in the clotting of blood	Vegetables, especially spinach cauliflower, cabbage
B-1 Thiamin	1.2 mg/1.1 mg	Aids in carbohydrate metabolism	Wheat germ, rice, peanuts, sunflower seeds, soybeans
B-2 Riboflavin	1.3 mg/1.1 mg	Health skin, aids in metabolism to give us energy	Wheat germ, soybeans, cheese
B-3 Niacin	16 mg/14 mg	Converts fats and proteins to energy, may help lower cholesterol	Soybeans, fish, chicken, sunflower seeds, wheat germ, sesame seeds
B-5 Pantothenic Acid	5 mg/5 mg	Aids in nerve impulse transmission, aids in obtaining energy from foods	Soybeans, wheat germ, rice, broccoli, sweet potatoes, milk, fish
B-6 Pyridoxine	1.3 mg/1.3 mg	Metabolism and synthesis of proteins	Wheat germ, sunflower seeds, soybeans, beans, rice, fish
B-12	.0024 mg/.0024 mg	Needed for the formation of red blood cells	Fish, dairy products, eggs, meat, (not found in plants)
C Ascorbic Acid	90 mg/75 mg	Holds cells together, strengthens blood vessels, helps wounds to heal, may fight infections and viruses	Fruits, especially citrus, melons and strawberries; vegetables, especially broccoli, spinach, greens, cauliflower
Biotin	.03 mg/.03 mg	Aids in fatty-acid production and metabolism of proteins	Soybeans, wheat germ, peanuts, mushrooms, fish, eggs
Folacin	.4 mg/.4 mg	Production of body protein (hemoglobin, RNA, and DNA)	Beans, spinach, soybeans, peanuts wheat germ, oranges

Although taking less than the RDA for an extended period of time may lead to health problems, an excess of the RDA will not improve a person's health. In fact, consistently consuming excessive amounts of certain vitamins can lead to medical problems. Americans spend over $15 billion each year on vitamin and mineral supplements of which most exceed the body's needs. In the United States, health problems due to a vitamin deficiency are rare.

Types of Vitamins - Two major categories of vitamins are fat-soluble and water-soluble. Fat-soluble vitamins are A, D, E, and K and must be ingested with fat. If fat is not present, they will pass out of the digestive tract and will not be absorbed into the body. Therefore, when taking a vitamin supplement, it should be taken with a meal. Once absorbed into the body, fat-soluble vitamins can be stored in fat, muscles, and the liver to be used when needed.

Water-soluble vitamins are readily absorbed into the body but are just as readily passed out of the body in urine and perspiration. They are not stored in the body and, therefore, need to be ingested daily. Water-soluble vitamins include B, B2, B6, B12, C, niacin, pantothenic acid, biotin, and folacin.

Antioxidants - During the process of aerobic metabolism or by exposures to tobacco smoke and radiation, free radicals are created. A free radical is a chemically unstable molecule or ion containing an unpaired electron (radical) and can exist independently (free). Free radicals will react with other molecules (fats, protein, and DNA) to replace its missing electron. This process causes damage to cell membranes and mutation of genes. Free radicals have been linked to aging, cancer, cardiovascular disease and arthritis.

Antioxidants protect the body from free radical damage by limiting their formation. In addition, antioxidants can donate electrons to free radicals as well as repair damage caused by free radicals. The most noted antioxidants are vitamin E, vitamin C, and beta-carotene, which are found in vegetables and fruits. Regular exercise improves the body's normal physiological antioxidant defense system but repeated strenuous exercise may cause an increase in free radical formation and cellular damage.

6. Minerals

Minerals comprise four percent of body weight and are essential for many vital body processes. Not only are minerals needed for health, but also the proper balance among minerals is critical. Minerals work closely together, and each affects the other. Mineral imbalances can cause dehydration, heart attacks, and many other health problems.

Minerals are divided into two categories: 1) major minerals and 2) trace minerals. Major minerals are those for which the body has a large daily requirement of over 100 milligrams and include calcium, phosphorus, sodium, chlorine, potassium, magnesium, and sulfur. The specific role of the major minerals in the body is fairly well understood.

Trace minerals are needed daily in smaller amounts. These include copper, iodine, zinc, iron, manganese, and more than fifteen others. Table 9.10 outlines the minerals, their RDA's, primary functions in the body, and major dietary sources.

TABLE 9.10

Adult RDA Amounts for Minerals, Their Functions and Major Source

MINERAL	MALE/FEMALE	PRIMARY BODY FUNCTION	MAJOR SOURCE
Calcium	1000 mg/1000 mg	Needed for formation of teeth and bones, nerve impulse transmission	Dairy products, broccoli, sesame seeds, salmon
Phosphorus	700 mg/700 mg	Formation of teeth and bones, acid-base balance of blood	Dairy products, fish, eggs, whole wheat, beans, nuts
Sodium	1500 mg/1500 mg	Nerve impulse transmission, water balance, acid-base balance of blood	Common salt, processed foods
Chlorine	700 mg/700 mg	Forms stomach acid, maintains acid-base balance of the blood	Common salt, processed foods
Potassium	2000 mg/2000 mg	Functions with sodium for nerve impulse transmission, water balance	Abundant in most plant and animal foods
Magnesium	420 mg/320 mg	Part of enzymes that metabolizes nutrients into energy	Peanuts, wheat germ, spinach, meat, milk
Sulfur	NK	Important part of all proteins	Meats, dairy products, beans
Iron	8 mg/18 mg	Important part of hemoglobin	Vegetables, grains, meat, poultry
Copper	.9 mg/.9 mg	Helps to combine iron with hemoglobin	Beans, nuts, seafood
Fluorine	4 mg/3 mg	Helps prevent tooth decay	Most drinking water, fish
Zinc	11 mg/8 mg	Component of enzymes and proteins	Red meat, seafood
Iodine	.15 mg/.15 mg	Important part of thyroid hormones	Vegetables, fish, dairy products
Nickel	NK	Facilitate iron absorption	Nuts, legumes, chocolate
Selenium	.055 mg/.055 mg	Antioxidant	Organ meat, seafood
Manganese	2.3 mg/1.8 mg	Bone formation	Nuts, legumes, whole grains
Molybdenum	.045 mg/.045 mg	Coenzyme	Legumes, whole grains, nuts
Chromium	.035 mg/.025 mg	Maintain blood glucose level	Meat, fish, poultry

NK – Not known but needed in small amounts

7. Water

The human body is made up of 50 to 70% water making it extremely important to consume enough fluids daily. The body requires approximately eight glasses of water a day. Some of this liquid may be in the form of milk, soup, and juices, but it is best to get most of the fluids from water.One should drink enough fluids daily so that the urine becomes so diluted it is almost clear and colorless at least once during a 24 hour period.

Most fruits and vegetables are also good sources of water such as tomatoes, eggplant, cauliflower, lettuce, strawberries, and watermelon which consist of over 90% water. The amount of water ingested daily will vary from eight glasses in a normal day to an equivalent of 10 to 12 on hot or exercising days when extra fluid is lost through perspiration.

Caffeine-containing drinks such as coffee, tea, and colas should be avoided or the amount decreased significantly. Caffeine is a diuretic as well as a central nervous system stimulant and can cause irregular heartbeats, formation of acid-pepsin digestive juices in the stomach, and fibrocystic breast disease in women. A cup of coffee contains 100 to 150 milligrams of caffeine; a cup of tea contains 50 to 75 milligrams; a 12-ounce cola contains 60 milligrams; and a cup of hot chocolate contains about 50 milligrams.

Vitamins and Minerals Supplementation

With a good balanced diet, all the vitamins and minerals required by the body can be obtained. However, with busy schedules, diets often contain many processed and refined foods causing most individuals to not meet their RDA. Therefore, it seems prudent to take one multivitamin plus mineral supplement per day with not more than 100% of the RDA as a good insurance policy against any possible deficiency. Megadoses of vitamins and minerals should be avoided as they will not improve health or athletic performance but can lead to many health problems (see Table 9.11).

Natural vs. Synthetic - The human body identifies vitamins and minerals by their chemical structures. Vitamin C has the same chemical structure whether it is derived from citrus fruit or if it is synthetically made. People who promote "natural" or "health" food are doing so to capitalize on the public's interest in good health and willingness to pay more for it. Today, the supplement and health food industry is a billion-dollar business.

TABLE 9.11

Health Problems Associated With Megadoses of Vitamins

Vitamin C	Gout, Hemolytic Anemia, and Diarrhea
Vitamin B6	Liver Disease and Nerve Damage
Vitamin B2	Vision Impaired
Vitamin E	Headaches, Fatigue, Blurred Vision, Muscular Weakness, and Gastrointestinal Disturbance
Vitamin A	Nervous System Damage
Vitamin D	Kidney Damage

Purchasing and Preparing Food

Purchasing and preparing food are two important aspects of good nutrition. When grocery shopping, a person should purchase most of their food from the fresh produce and fresh frozen section. Most of the daily caloric intake should come from fresh, whole foods, not processed ones. Buy fruits and vegetables that are in season, and plan meals around them. Recipes for delicious meatless dishes using vegetables and rice are plentiful. By shopping at roadside markets with locally grown produce, the nutritional value of foods is usually superior.

When choosing meats, poultry and fish should be first choices. Many grocery stores have fresh fish, both freshwater and ocean varieties. Chicken is always an economical buy, and there are numerous appetizing ways to prepare it. Both chicken and fish, properly prepared, provide a dish high in protein and low in fat.

Each individual needs to become a label reader and not get confused by the words fortified and enriched. These products have lost most of their vitamins and minerals with only a handful of nutrients added back. Emphasize brown rice over white rice, since brown rice has not been refined. Buy cereals with as much of the whole grain in them as possible. Read the nutritional breakdown on the box and notice the fiber content. Look at the complex carbohydrate and sugar content keeping it high in complex carbohydrates and low in sugar. Notice bread ingredients because some breads claim to contain whole-wheat flour and look brown due to the caramel coloring. Look for ingredients such as wheat bran, wheat germ, wheat berries, or perhaps a combination of grains such as rye, barley, or oats. The coarser and grainier the bread, the healthier the product will be.

When preparing fruits and vegetables, peel and trim as little as possible. Raw fruits and vegetables keep vitamins and minerals. If cooking the fruit or vegetable, scrub it immediately prior to cooking but do not soak it. Cook as briefly as possible and serve immediately. Microwave cooking of vegetables is also good because little water is used.

Skin the poultry and bake, broil, stir fry, or boil it, then use it in salads and casseroles. Fish is also healthier if it is broiled or baked. Experiment with various recipes and seasonings to find something just as tasty as fried chicken or fish.

Several other practices will help to maintain a healthful eating style. Use vegetable oils instead of solid shortening not only in frying but also in baking. For instance, if a cookie recipe calls for one cup of butter, use half oil and half margarine. The amount of sugar called for in most recipes can be cut by one-third to one-half and not affect the taste or texture. To increase fiber in the diet, bran and wheat germ can be mixed in or sprinkled on most foods without affecting taste or texture. Bran is great in muffins and breads.

Food Groups and Food Pyramids

The United States Department of Agriculture (USDA) in 2005 revised the Food Guide Pyramid (see Figure 9.1). Unfortunately, the USDA pyramid does not take into account the types of fats, the Glycemic index, or daily exercise. In 2002, the Harvard School of Public Health created the Healthy Eating Pyramid and updated it in 2008 (see Figure 9.2) to fill in the gaps of the USDA Food Guide Pyramid using the latest research and in a more user friendly format. The following describes the components of the Healthy Eating Pyramid.

1. **Exercise** - The Healthy Eating Pyramid has its foundation based on daily exercise and maintaining a healthy body weight. These two important elements have a direct role on health and how the consumed food will affect the body.

2. **Whole Grain Foods** - The body uses carbohydrates for energy and the best sources are whole grains such as oatmeal, whole-wheat bread, and brown rice. Digestion of whole grains is slower (low glycemic index) than processed carbohydrates such as white flour. Whole grains keep blood glucose and insulin levels from rising quickly followed by a sharp decline, delaying hunger and possibly preventing the development of type 2 diabetes (Chapter 4).

3. **Healthy Fats and Oils** - Plant oils as well as omega-3 fatty acids improve cholesterol and protect the heart when used in place of saturated fats and highly processed carbohydrates. Good sources of healthy unsaturated fats include olive, canola, corn, peanut, and other vegetable oils. Omega-3 fatty acids can be found in cold-water fish such as salmon and tuna.

4. **Vegetables and Fruits** – Consuming vegetables and/or fruits with each meal will deliver many benefits including a decrease chance of having a stroke or heart attack. The fiber helps against certain types of cancers and lessens the risk of developing diverticulitis. Also they contain important vitamins that support good eye health and loaded with antioxidants.

5. **Nuts, Seeds, Beans, and Tofu** – These plant products are good sources of not only protein, but also vitamins, minerals, and fiber. Most can be purchased in an unrefined state that can be stored for extended periods of time with minimal loss of nutritional value.

6. **Fish, Poultry, and Eggs** – These foods are excellent sources of protein. Fish is rich in heart- healthy fats and poultry can be low in saturated fat. Recently, eggs have been found not to be as bad as once thought. Even though they contain high levels of cholesterol, research is showing that dietary cholesterol has a limited effect on blood cholesterol levels. Eggs are also good sources of vitamins and minerals.

7. **Dairy or Vitamin D/Calcium Supplements** – Low fat or no fat dairy products are good sources of calcium, however to build strong bones

Figure 9.1
The United States Department of Agriculture Food Guide Pyamid

Chapter 9 / Basic Nutrition for Health Fitness 115

vitamin D and exercise are also needed. Individuals that are lactose intolerant can meet their calcium need through supplements.

8. **Use Sparingly: Red Meat and Butter** – Red meat and butter contain high levels of saturated fat that can lead to atherosclerosis (Chapter 4). Fish and poultry are better meat choices and using butter substitutes are recommended. However, stay away from trans fats found in many spreads.

9. **Use Sparingly: Refined Grains; Potatoes; Sugary drinks and Sweets; Salt** - These highly refined carbohydrates cause a fast increase in blood glucose level that can lead to weight gain, heart disease, diabetes and other chronic disorder. This group should be used sparingly and should be replaced by whole-grain carbohydrates. High salt (sodium) intake has been found to increase risk of heart attack and stroke as well as hypertension in those individuals that are sodium sensitive.

10. **Multivitamin** – Taking a multivitamin/mineral supplement will offer some protection against a nutrient deficiency. However, supplements cannot replace healthy eating or correct an unhealthy eating pattern.

FIGURE 9.2

The Harvard School of Public Health Healthy Eating Pyramid

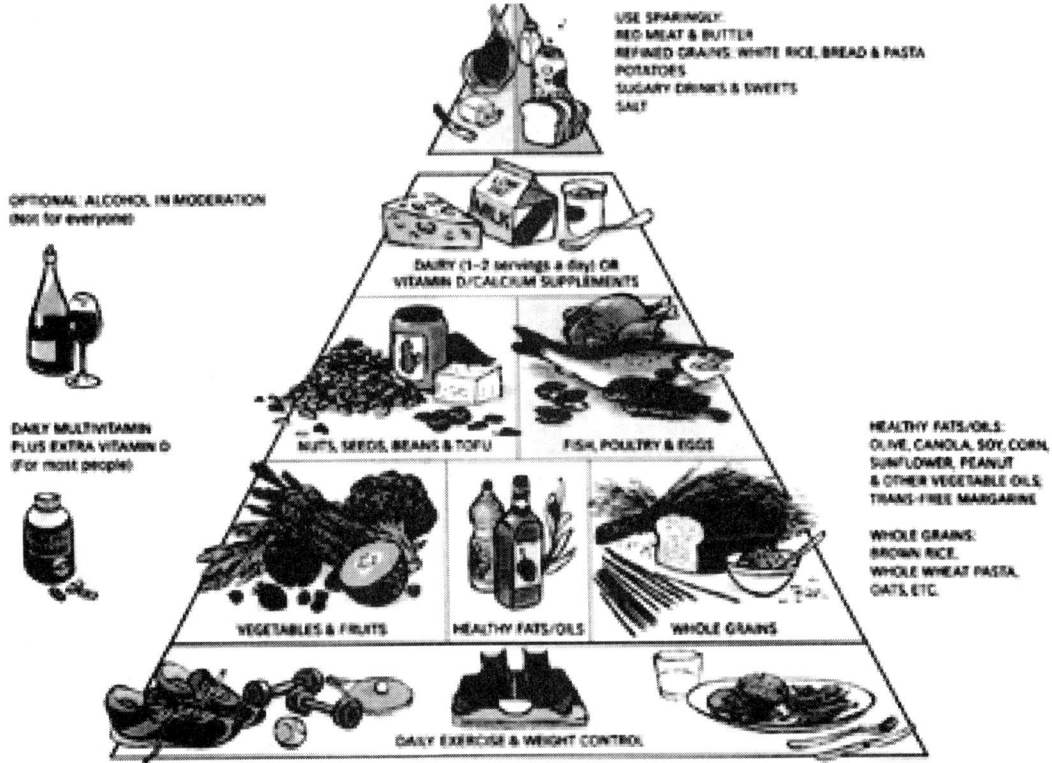

Eat Well-Balanced Meals

People today tend to skip meals, especially breakfast. Lack of time is the usual excuse, but it is important to eat balanced meals each day. Each person needs to determine how many calories to consume each day in order to lose, maintain, or gain weight. For each meal (i.e. breakfast, lunch, and dinner), approximately 30 % of the total daily calories should be consumed. The remaining 10 percent may be divided up into midmorning, midafternoon, or evening snacks. Do not wait until evening to consume all the calories since it appears that food eaten after 2:00 P.M. tends to be stored as fat. Eating most of the calories before 2:00 P.M. gives the body more hours to digest and burn them.

The following examples are suggestions for what one-day of meals, including snacks, might look like:

Breakfast
1. 6 ounces orange juice or 1 whole orange
2. Bowl of high-fiber cereal
3. Banana
4. 1 slice 100% whole-wheat toast with jelly, no margarine or butter
5. 8 ounces skim milk

Lunch
1. Sandwich of tuna or chicken on 100% whole-wheat bread with lettuce or sprouts
2. Carrot and celery sticks
3. Fresh fruit (apple, pear, orange, etc.)
4. 8 ounces skim milk

(Peanut butter could be substituted for meat, and a tossed salad could replace carrots and celery. Yogurt is also good and is easy to make at home without all the added sugar of the ones made commercially.)

Dinner
1. 4-6 ounces baked fish or chicken
2. 1 medium baked potato, sweet potato, or brown rice
3. 1/2-3/4 cup fresh steamed broccoli or spinach salad
4. 1/2-3/4 cup carrots or corn
5. Water
6. Piece of fresh fruit or fruit salad

Snacks and Desserts

Snacks and desserts can have a place in the daily diet. Some suggestions for snacks include raw vegetables, fruit, cold cereals, or popcorn (limit salt and butter). Raw nuts are good but only in limited quantities because they are high in calories. Dried fruits can satisfy a craving for something sweet. Most grocery stores have raisins, dried apples, bananas, prunes, and so on. Here again the amount should be limited because of the high sugar content. Desserts don't have to be eliminated from the diet, only modified or decreased. Cutting a piece of dessert in half may eliminate 100 to 300 calories from the meal and still satisfy the sweet tooth.

Guidelines for Controlling Caloric Intake

1. Sit down to eat at the kitchen or dining room table. Get used to eating in one place. Don't eat in front of the TV, at your desk, at a movie, or at an athletic contest. This alone could eliminate several hundred calories a day.
2. Eat only at specific times. This will cut down on unnecessary snacking.
3. Use a smaller plate when possible. A small plate that is filled can look like it has more food than a large with the same amount of food.
4. Eat slowly. Not only is this better for digestion, but it allows the appestat signals to reach the brain when the stomach is full, before over eating occurs.
5. Carry a Calorie chart to help learn the approximate number of calories in most of the foods a person will be consuming. Small books are available at grocery stores and bookstores that fit into a woman's purse or a man's suit coat pocket.
6. Don't use food as a reward.
7. Make a shopping list when buying food and stick to it. Don't buy on impulse.
8. Don't shop for groceries when hungry.
9. Store food at home out of sight. Don't keep cookies and unhealthy snacks on the counter.
10. Clear the table immediately after a meal.
11. Whenever possible, eat raw, unprocessed fruits and vegetables.
12. Little things mean a lot. One snack or drink every day could add up to 36,500 calories in one year or about 10 pounds. A daily half-hour walk could burn 67,700 calories in one year or 18 pounds. Eliminating toast at breakfast could mean 15 pounds in a year.

Summary

Health is very dependent upon the foods and fluids consumed each day. The seven basic nutrients are carbohydrates, fiber, fats, proteins, vitamins, minerals, and water. Low glycemic complex carbohydrates should be increased in one's diet and simple sugars decreased. The overall dietary intake of carbohydrates should be increased from the present 45 to 60% for good health. Saturated fats and trans fats should be decreased in the diet. High-protein diets are undesirable, and it is possible that a highly varied, semi-vegetarian diet can serve one best in most situations. Adding a daily multivitamin plus mineral supplement to one's diet will create a good insurance policy against nutritional deficiency. Fats, sweets, soft drinks, and alcoholic beverages should to be avoided or limited.

Review Questions

1. What are the two overall functions of nutrients?
2. List the seven basic nutrients needed for maintaining health of the body.
3. What is the primary function of carbohydrates?
4. Which body cells use only carbohydrates for energy?
5. A restricted carbohydrate diet with high energy demands could have what affect on protein in the body?
6. Explain the glycemic index.
7. What is the function of insulin from the pancreas?
8. What is fiber, and what is its function in the body?
9. List the primary sources of fiber and how much fiber one should have a day.
10. What is the function of fats in the body?

11. Compare saturated and unsaturated fats?

12. What is the function of protein in the body?

13. What happens to excess protein in the body?

14. Distinguish between fat-soluble and water-soluble vitamins.

15. Explain the differences between the USDA Food Guide Pyramid and the Healthy Eating Pyramid.

CHAPTER 10

Managing Stress and Back Injuries

Learning Objectives

This chapter examines ways to manage stress and back injuries to improve a person's health fitness. Even those who are physically fit still encounter stressors every day, and how they handle these will increase their health fitness or distract from it. When you complete this chapter you should:

1. Know examples of four groups of stressors (page 121).
2. Understand the role that perception plays in reducing stress (page 121).
3. Recognize the immediate and long-term affects of stress on the body (page 122).
4. Understand the immediate and long-term benefits of physical activity relative to stress page 122).
5. Describe at least six behaviors that can assist with effective stress management (page 125).
6. Know the types of back problems and some recommendations for preventing them (pages 125 - 127).
7. Be able to describe guidelines and exercises that promote a healthy back (page 128).

Key Terms

Back Strain/Sprain
Deep Breathing
Muscle Relaxation Exercises
Meditation
Posture
Ruptured Disc
Slipped Disc
Stress
Stressor

Stress

Hans Selye, who is considered by most experts as the leading authority in the study of *stress*, defines stress as the "response of the body to any demand made upon it." Stress is the body's response to counteract any *stressor*. It is the body's way to maintain homeostasis, or internal environment. Whenever the body's equilibrium is upset, the body attempts to return it to homeostasis.

There are four classifications of stressors:

1. **Social stressors:** relationships with family, friends, and co-workers; financial concerns; changes in one's life; etc.

2. **Environmental stressors:** heat, humidity, cold, noise, heavy traffic, overcrowding, pollution, etc.

3. **Physical stressors:** illnesses, injuries, lack of sleep, caffeine or nicotine, etc.

4. **Psychological stressors:** fear of losing one's job, worry over grades in school, loneliness, anger, guilt, lack of self-esteem, frustration, etc.

Perception of Stressors

The perception of the significance of a stressor often determines the body's response to it. More often than not, stressors are intangible, symbolic, and subject to each person's interpretation. If the mind perceives the stressor as significant or "real", the body's stress response will be set in motion, but this will not occur if the mind perceives the stressor as insignificant.

Perception is influenced by several factors. First, the spiritual dimension of the person influences perception. If the person has a positive belief system, faith, and self-confidence, the person is less likely to perceive the stressor as a serious threat, and the stress response will be minimal. On the other hand, if the person's spiritual dimension is weak and there is fear and worry or a lack of self confidence, the stressor probably will be viewed in a negative light, and the stress response will be greater.

Second, perception is influenced by the intellectual ability. If a person has previous knowledge on how to complete a task, the stress response is usually minimal. On the other hand, if the stressor is not yet been experienced and is a challenge to the intellect, the stress response will be great.

The tendency too often is to think negatively, dwell on problems, and focus on aches and pains. Dwelling too long on negative thoughts can cause the subconscious mind to begin to take control and paralyze the conscious mind. The body will react, and sickness and depression can result. When negative thoughts occur, a healthy response is to capture them, control them, evaluate them, and change them into positive thoughts for meditation. Positive statements should be repeated many times a day until they are driven into the subconscious mind. Then the body will begin to react according to the positive thoughts. Controlling one's thoughts is imperative for good health. Negative thoughts can lead to feelings of defeat, anxiety, distress, and depression; and these emotions can spark many health problems.

Symptoms of Stress

Often the results of poorly handled stress are obvious. Symptoms include feeling tense, having cold and clammy hands, and sleeping difficulties (see Table 10.1). Recognizing when the body is not responding satisfactorily to stress is the first step to overcoming poor stress management.

If a person does not successfully manage the stress and positively adapt to the stressors, the stress response will lead to health problems. Selye believes that when the body is under a chronic state of stress, it is in a constant state of readiness to respond, and almost any disease may develop. Some of these diseases are shown in Table 10.2.

Table 10.1

Immediate Symptoms of Stress

• Pounding of the Heart	• Depression
• Tension	• Trembling
• Insomnia	• Pain in the Neck
• Fatigue	• Irritability
• Dizziness	• Nervous Tic
• Grinding of the Teeth	• Sweating
• Pain in the Low Back	• Lack of Concentration

Table 10.2

Symptoms From Long Term Stress

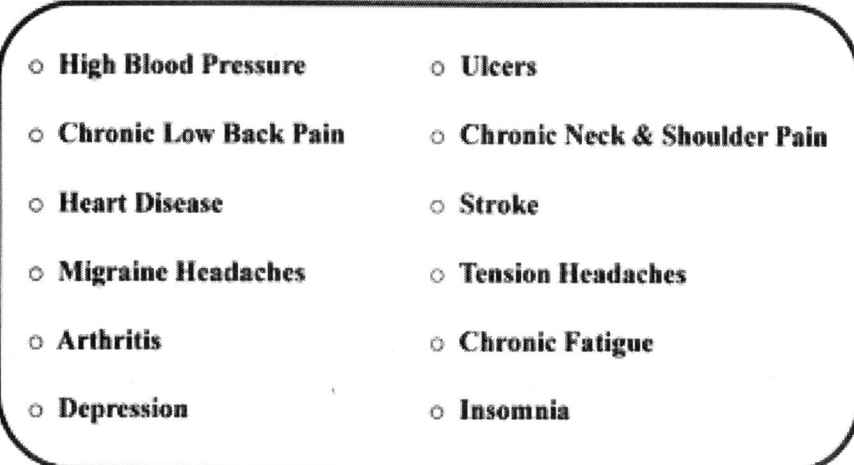

- High Blood Pressure
- Ulcers
- Chronic Low Back Pain
- Chronic Neck & Shoulder Pain
- Heart Disease
- Stroke
- Migraine Headaches
- Tension Headaches
- Arthritis
- Chronic Fatigue
- Depression
- Insomnia

Role of Physical Activity in Stress Management

According to the American National Institute of Mental Health, physical activity has both immediate as well as long term benefits. When engaged in physical activity, immediate benefits include:

1. **Takes the mind off the problem.** It is difficult to worry when focused on a physical activity. When the activity is over, the thought processes become more efficient.

2. **A relaxed feeling when it is over.** Physical activity is invigorating and when it is over reduced anxiety occurs. Muscles tension is relieved, and an improved feeling of self worth occurs.

3. **Breakdown of the chemicals released during the stress response.** Physical activity quickens removal of stress hormones allowing the body to return to homeostasis faster.

4. **Releases endorphins.** Physical activity causes the body's natural tranquilizers to be released.

Many business executives wisely conduct an exercise program at 5:00 or 6:00 P.M., after a busy day of work, to help relieve the tensions of the day. Exercise has been shown to be beneficial in the treatment of depression. Therapists prescribe aerobic exercise as a therapeutic mode to treat depressed patients. However, not all physical activity will necessarily provide the same benefits. Participation in sports activities such as golf, tennis, and racquetball may not assist the body in relieving stress the same way that aerobic activities do such as jogging, walking, and cycling. In competitive sports, where there is pressure to perform well or to win, stress may be increased rather than decreased.

Long-term benefits of physical activity include:

1. **Improves the health and fitness of the body.** Regular exercise helps the body to better withstand day to day stressors.

2. **A positive self-concept.** Regular exercise promotes and improves self-confidence and thus decreasing the number of stressors.

Effective Stress Management

Since stress is inescapable in today's society, it is vital that one learns how to successfully manage it. While it is beyond the scope of this book to thoroughly discuss stress management techniques, the following are some general guidelines:

1. **Plan ahead** - Most stress is due to lack of planning ahead or becoming over committed. Effective planning involves setting realistic goals. Do not plan so much for a day, week, or month that it is impossible to accomplish it all. Also, prioritize tasks to be done so that time will not be wasted on unimportant activities. Develop a list of things to be done, prioritize them, and then set a specific time aside for doing each one.

2. **Replace fear with positive thinking** - Fear of physical danger can be beneficial by inducing the extra physical energy needed to escape. Too often, however, fear is not of a physical danger but of failure. This type of fear is harmful to the body because the common response is lethargy instead of causing an active response. Attempt to replace fears with positive thoughts about oneself and develop a positive self-concept.

3. **Relaxation** - Like aerobic exercise, relaxation techniques can reduce the potential harmful side effects of stress. There are several relaxation procedures.

    Deep Breathing Exercises are simple ways to help reduce stress. Take deep breaths and let the air out slowly. With each breath feel the stress going from the body. Repeat 5 to 10 times.

    Muscle Relaxation is another way to reduce stress. Lie down in a quiet and peaceful place and alternately contract and relax the muscles beginning at the feet and working up to the head.

Meditation is another method to aid in relaxation. Studies demonstrate that, with practice, after 5 to 10 minutes of meditation, heart rate and metabolism have slowed down indicating its effectiveness in stress management. There are several meditation techniques. One method is to sit quietly, eyes closed, and repeat a simple word or phrase. Another is to take a mental vacation and picture yourself at some location that is especially peaceful to you.

4. **Avoid Caffeine and Nicotine** - When feeling under tension or stress, avoid caffeine and nicotine. Both substances are stimulants and add to the stress reactions of the body.

5. **Support Social Groups** - Numerous studies are confirming the need to be a part of a positive social group to reduce stress and related disease. Intimacy, openness, and sharing all help to reduce stress and improve health.

Types of Back Problems

An estimated 80% of the American adult population has suffered from low-back problems at one time or another. Back problems account for more lost man-hours than any other occupational injury and consequently accounts for a significant portion of mounting health costs. Americans spend more than $85 billion a year for tests and treatments from orthopedic physicians, osteopaths, physical therapists, and chiropractors.

Back problems can take several forms. The pain may result from pathological problems such as arthritis, rheumatism, a cancerous tumor growing on the spine, osteoporosis, or infection. It may result from a fall, a blow to the spinal column, or pregnancy. But the vast majorities (over 85%) of back problems are not caused by any of these reasons. Instead, they are due to muscle deficiency caused by an inappropriate lifestyle. Two of the most common back problems are **back strain/sprain** and **slipped disc**.

1. Back Strain/Sprain

The most common back problem is a back strain/sprain which may occur as the result of working hard in the garden, moving the furniture, or undertaking some other physical activity in which the back muscles were required to do more than they were capable of doing at that moment. The injured muscles or tendons cause inflammation, fluid build-up, muscle spasms, and painful pressure on the nerve endings. The muscle spasms constrict the blood vessels and cause further complications by limiting blood flow to the injured area, decreasing the amount of oxygen and nutrients to reach the area and delay the removal of waste products.

The immediate treatment for a back strain/sprain is rest, aspirin or ibuprofen to reduce the inflammation, and perhaps a muscle relaxant prescribed by a physician to relax the muscle spasm. Usually in a few days the pain will be gone, but it will return if a preventive program is not followed.

2. Slipped Disc

Although a slipped disc may be the most talked about back ailment, it accounts for only five percent of back problems. Back strains/sprains account for the other 95%; however, if a back strain/sprain is severe enough, it can mimic a slipped disc.

A slipped disc is technically not slipped. The cartilage that serves as a cushion between the vertebrae is known as a disc. When excess pressure is placed upon the disc, it may herniate (rupture). When this occurs, some of the jelly like center of the disc bulges out of the disc and pushes against the nerves in the spinal cord. These nerves are extremely sensitive, and any amount of pressure against them can trigger excruciating pain.

A long history of repeated attacks of muscle strain/sprain can begin the process of disc deterioration. Initially, the disc deterioration may cause no symptoms and go unnoticed. This process may eventually lead to a **ruptured disc**.

Symptoms of a Ruptured Disc. Although a ruptured disc is often difficult to diagnose, two symptoms are usually present. The first symptom, is pain going down one or both of the legs called sciatica. A ruptured disc is most commonly located in the lower back where it places pressure on the sciatic nerve. If there is no pain down the leg, the problem is probably not from a disc rupture. The second symptom, strongly indicative of a ruptured disc, is pain in the lower back when lifting one straight leg off the floor while lying in a supine position. If the straight leg can be lifted at least 70 to 80 degrees without causing pain in the low back, the chance of a ruptured disc is minimal (this test should never be performed when significant back spasms are occurring). If, on the other hand, the straight leg can be lifted only 20 or 30 degrees before pain is felt; this is an indication of a possible ruptured disc and a physician should be seen.

Treatment for a Ruptured Disc. Very often a ruptured disc requires surgery. However, unless there is a change in lifestyle, the problem will return following the recovery from surgery. It is possible for a ruptured disc to heal in time without surgery and not recur if there is a significant lifestyle change.

Decreasing Back Injuries

Three of the most common reasons for back problems are 1) weak abdominals and spinal muscles with poor hip, spine, and leg flexibility, 2) poor postural habits and body mechanics, and 3) overfatness. By incorporating specific flexibility and strengthening exercises into a regular fitness program, back injuries can be decreased.

Strength Exercises - Four specific muscle groups that support the vertebral column, the pelvis, and the abdomen must have adequate strength to prevent back problems.

1. **Back Muscles** support the entire vertebral column and must be strong. If they are weak, heavy work will strain them and cause back pain.

2. **Abdominal Muscles** must be strong to keep the pelvis tilted up and prevent it from rotating down (giving a potbelly or swayback appearance). When the pelvis is rotated down, undesirable pressure is placed on the vertebrae of the lower back, on the discs, and on the nerves that branch from the spinal cord to the muscles in the low-back area and legs.

3. **Gluteal Muscles** are also important for stabilizing the pelvis and assist in preventing it from rotating down in front. They are attached to the back of the pelvis and the upper part of the back of the thighs.

4. **Iliopsoas Muscles** must be strong and flexible. This muscle group has its upper attachment on the inside of the vertebral column of the lower back. It runs through the pelvic girdle and attaches to the front of the upper thigh. This muscle group is important in hip flexion and also supports and stabilizes the lower part of the back.

Flexibility - Three key muscle groups which keep the body upright are always mildly contracting during sitting, standing, walking, or jogging. These muscle groups are the 1) back, 2) hamstrings, and 3) iliopsoas. Because they are mildly contracting for much of the day, they will develop tightness if specific types of stretching exercises are not performed.

Guidelines for Back Exercise

1. Learn to distinguish between pain and discomfort. Pain while exercising is a signal to stop. Some discomfort is to be expected and will go away shortly after the exercise is finished. Exercise should not be done when pain is present.

2. Progression will be slow if recovering from a back problem, allow three to six months to achieve the strength and flexibility needed for the back to resist strain/sprain. In fact, noticeable improvement for a month or two is not uncommon.

3. Exercise every day when first beginning a back exercise program since the number of repetitions will be so few. After achieving satisfactory levels of strength and flexibility, the exercises need to be performed only three days per week for maintenance.

4. A warm-up should be performed before exercising. If there is back discomfort, taking a short walk, a warm bath, or shower before doing the back exercises will help.

Specific Exercises for Preventing Back Problems

1. **Curl-up** - Lie on the back with knees bent. Raise the head, contract the stomach muscles, and reach up until touching the knees, then lower back down to the starting position. Begin by doing five repetitions, and add one or two repetitions each week. The goal is to do 50 without stopping. After a month of performing 50 curl-ups daily, then gradually replace them with bent knee sit-ups. For example, do 45 curl-ups and five sit-ups for two weeks. Then progress to 40 curl-ups and 10 sit-ups for two weeks. If no pain occurs during the sit-ups, continue to increase them until all 50 are sit-ups. (Sit-ups should be avoided when recovering from a back problem.)

2. **Pelvic raises** - Lie on the back with knees flexed, feet flat on the floor, and arms at the sides resting on the floor. Raise up the pelvis as high as possible by contracting the gluteal muscles, and then lower the pelvis back to the floor. Begin with five and add one or two each week until 50 can be performed without stopping.

3. **Side leg raises** - Lie on one side of the body with the head resting in one hand with the arm bent and elbow on the floor. Raise the upper leg as high as possible keeping the knee straight and hip moving forward. Move the leg slowly up and down. Begin with five on each side the first week and add one or two each week until performing 50 without stopping.

4. **Knees to chest or low-back stretch** - Lie on the back with legs straight. Bend and raise right knee and hug it to the chest with the hands. Repeat using the left knee and then with both knees together. Begin by doing three a day, and then add one per week until able to do 20. When just recovering from a back problem, this exercise will cause some discomfort in the back

muscles. However, as the back heals and flexibility increases, the discomfort will disappear. As flexibility increases, reduce the repetitions to 10, and add the next exercise.

5. **Hamstring stretch** - Sit on the floor with one leg straight and the other bent. Bend forward at the waist over the stretched leg reaching the fingers toward the toes. Switch the legs and repeat. Perform this exercise after mastering the low-back stretch with no discomfort. Start with three repetitions holding for 10 seconds, and add one per week until 10 repetitions can be done.

6. **Quadriceps stretch** - Lay on the side of the body with both legs bent. Grab the top leg at the ankle and gently pull back, stretching the quadriceps. Switch to the other side and repeat with the other leg. Start with three repetitions, hold for 10 seconds, and add one per week up to 10 repetitions.

7. **Back extensions** - Lie face down on the floor with the elbows by the chest, forearms on the floor and hands under the chin. Gently raise the trunk by contracting the back muscles. Once the chest is as far off the ground as possible, slowly return the body to the starting position. Perform this exercise only after back pain has stopped. Begin by doing two, and add one each week until performing 14.

8. **Hanging** - Whether upright or inverted, hang for 30 to 60 seconds each day. Hanging helps the vertebral column to elongate, which reduces the pressure on each vertebral disc. (Do not hang inverted if you have heart disease or high blood pressure).

Other Lifestyle Factors

Several additional factors are crucial in preventing back problems. These include posture, lifting habits, weight reduction, and stress management.

1. Posture

Good *posture* is a habit, and habits are formed by constant repetition. Good posture results from strong muscles; and strong muscles require a strength development exercise program. By developing good positive habits and strong muscles, most back problems can be avoided.

If there was one word that best conveys the mental image of good posture and body alignment, it would be "tall" (Think tall). Adherence to the following three practices will lead to good posture:

1. Hold your head up high and tall. Feel as though you are trying to touch the ceiling with the top of your head.
2. Raise your chest, rib cage, and shoulders.
3. Tilt your pelvis backward by contracting your abdominal muscles and your gluteal muscles.

In addition to practicing the above postural habits, try to remember to place one foot on a stool, chair, or other object when standing for long periods. Also, alternate the feet to allow shifts of weight while keeping the back from excessively swaying (lordosis). When sitting place the feet, with knees bent, on a stool or a footrest. The chair should have a good, firm seat with a cushion. Do not slump. The same advice applies while driving a car. The knees should be bent. Move the seat of the car as close to the steering wheel as feasible to prevent swayback. It is also helpful on long trips to stop at rest areas that furnish tables or benches that may be used for back exercises and stretching.

2. Lifting Habits

Improper lifting of heavy objects or carrying heavy objects can place considerable pressure on the vertebral column and lead to back problems. Thus, proper lifting technique is extremely important. When lifting objects from the floor, the knees should be bent so that the lifting is done with the legs rather than the back. When placing groceries into the trunk of a car, hanging up clothes, or reaching for objects, lift or lower the object as close to the body as possible. When lifting objects while turning, the feet and entire body should be rotated as a unit, since there is less stability and support of the vertebrae in this position.

3. Weight Reduction

Excess body fat places undesirable stress on the vertebral column. An extra 20 or 30 pounds often carried on the abdomen, places considerable strain upon the back and can lead to back pain. Also this additional abdominal fat causes the individual to maintain a poor posture position while sitting and standing.

4. Stress Management

If a person is under constant stress, all the muscles in the body become tense. The slightest movement can cause a strain/sprain in a back muscle. Persons with low-back pain often have a recurrence when they are involved in a stressful situation. It is important to effectively manage stress.

Summary

Stress management involves the total person. Regular physical activity, prioritized time management, positive thinking, relaxation and meditation, avoidance of stimulants, and positive social interaction all contribute to effectively assist in stress management. To overcome or decrease the chance of having back pain, a person needs to increase flexibility and strength in the back, abdomen, hip, and thighs. With 80% of the adult population suffering from back pain during some portion of their life, it is important that appropriate exercises are performed regularly.

Review Questions

1. Define stress and homeostasis.

2. What are four groups of stressors?

3. Discuss the role that perception can have on stress.

4. What are some immediate and long-range symptoms of poor stress management?

5. What are some immediate and long-term benefits of physical activity relative to stress management?

6. List five recommendations in addition to regular aerobic exercise for effective stress management.

7. List four lifestyle factors that are crucial for preventing future back problems.

8. List the exercises that are prescribed for preventing back problems.

9. Distinguish between back sprain/strain and herniated disc.

10. Which muscle groups need to be strengthened for maintaining a healthy back?

CHAPTER

11

Exercise Management for Special Populations

Learning Objectives

This chapter examines the role exercise plays in the management of different disorders. Even those with chronic diseases can improve their quality of life by incorporating appropriate exercise into their lifestyle. When you complete this chapter you should:

1. Know how exercise benefits those with arthritis (page 134).
2. Be able to describe lifestyle changes that need to be made for someone with hypertension (page 141).
3. Know examples of the benefits of exercise for individuals with fibromyalgia (page 140).
4. Understand the three groups that asthmatics fall into concerning exercise (page 135).
5. Recognize the differences between osteoarthritis and rheumatoid arthritis (page 133).
6. Understand how exercise helps with the treatment of cancer (page 136).
7. Describe how exercise and diet can be used to combat obesity (page 143).

Key Terms

Arthritis
Asthma
Cancer
Fibromyalgia
Hyperglycemia
Obesity
Osteoarthritis
Pregnancy
Rheumatoid Arthritis
Type 1 Diabetes
Type 2 Diabetes

Exercising for Special Populations

Over the last decade, physical activity has emerged as one of the key factors in the prevention and management of chronic conditions. Current research clearly demonstrates that regular, moderate-intensity physical activity provides substantial health benefits. Therefore every adult American, including those with chronic disorders, should accumulate 30 minutes or more of moderate-intensity physical activity on most, but preferably all, days of the week. This recommendation is the minimum standard to confer important health benefits but does not represent the optimal amount of physical activity for health.

As it is for all adults, a medical evaluation should be performed before beginning an exercise program. This is especially important for those with chronic disorders. **The following information is designed to be used in conjunction with the physician's recommendations for exercise and is not intended as a substitute.**

Arthritis and Exercise

Arthritis is a condition affecting the joints and is characterized by inflammation, degeneration, and pain. Over 46 million Americans have some form of arthritis with an increasing prevalence as one grows older. The two most common types are **osteoarthritis** and **rheumatoid arthritis**. Osteoarthritis is a degenerative joint disease and is localized to the affected joint. Rheumatoid arthritis is an inflammatory disorder caused by activity of the immune system against joint tissue. This inflammatory response affects many joints and other organs.

Previously, the traditional treatment for arthritis was rest. Current practices have moved toward joint mobility due to the evidence of the beneficial effects of exercise in limiting the symptoms of the disease. Joint protection is of major importance when exercising and should follow the recommendations listed in Table 11.1.

Table 11.1
Recommendations for Exercising with Arthritic Joints

1. Perform low-impact activities
2. Stay away from contact sports and sports with rapid stop-and-go activities
3. Avoid stair climbing and prolong one-legged stances
4. If pain or swelling occur or persist, reduce load on joint
5. Wear insoles and shoes for maximum shock absorption for weight-bearing activities

Exercise benefits for those with arthritis include increased muscular strength, endurance, and flexibility. In addition, the arthritic exerciser may develop an improved sense of well-being, an enhanced quality of sleep, and a healthier body. Aerobic exercise should be performed three to five days per week with an intensity of 60 to 80% of maximum heart rate. The emphasis should be placed on progression of increasing duration over intensity building until 30 minutes of continuous aerobic exercise is reached. Strength training should use pain tolerance to set resistance in affected joints using two to three repetitions initially and building up to 10 – 12 repetitions. Flexibility training is a key exercise component to decrease joint stiffness and should be performed one to two sessions per day. Table 11.2 list exercise recommendations for individuals with arthritis.

Table 11.2
Exercise Program for Arthritis

HEALTH FITNESS CATEGORY	GOALS	OVERLOAD
Cardiorespiratory: Walking & Jogging Treadmill & Stair climbing Cycling & Swimming	Increase time to exhaustion Increase work capacity Improve blood pressure Reduce cardiovascular risk	50 - 80% Max HR 4 - 7 days/week 30 - 60 min/session
Muscular Strength/ Endurance: Circuit weight training	Increase maximal number of repetitions	Low-resistance with high repetitions
Flexibility: Stretching	Maintain or increase range of motion	2 - 3 sessions/week

Asthma and Exercise

Asthma is a chronic illness generally discovered during early childhood and affects over 23 million Americans. Asthma is a reversible condition characterized by airflow obstruction and increased bronchial responsiveness to both allergic and environmental stimuli. There is a wide variability of severity between individuals with asthma. Some mild cases are only noticeable when the asthmatic comes in contact with a trigger stimulus such as allergens or exercise. In severe cases, symptoms are characterized by mostly irreversible airflow obstruction even with medication.

Individuals with asthma notice that this disorder has a large variability in its severity during attacks. With concerns to exercise, the asthmatic population can be grouped into three categories: 1) exercise-induced asthma with no other symptoms; 2) mild asthma where ventilatory restriction does not limit submaximal exercise; and 3) moderate to severe asthma where ventilatory restriction does limit submaximal exercise. Exercise-induced bronchiospasm occurs in 50 to 100% of individuals with asthma. Exercise with appropriate medical regimen is critical in improving the fitness level and quality of life for each asthmatic.

For cardiorespiratory fitness, cardiovascular training should consist of 20 to 60 minutes in duration, three to seven days per week. Any type of aerobic exercise mode is acceptable but exposure to cold air, low humidity, or air pollutants should be avoided. A warm and humid environment is generally best tolerated by asthmatics, such as found at an indoor swimming pool.

Resistance training is also beneficial for the asthmatic. Machine or free weights can be utilized using low resistance and high repetition (15 – 20 RM) two to three days per week. Strength training the respiratory muscles through breathing exercises has been shown to decrease the intensity and number of asthmatic symptoms and cause a reduction in the amount of medical services required. Table 11.3 list exercise recommendations for individuals with asthma.

Table 11.3
Exercise Program for Asthma

HEALTH FITNESS CATEGORY	GOALS	OVERLOAD
Cardiorespiratory: (avoid exercise in cold/dry air) Walking & Treadmill Stair Climbing Swimming & Aquatic Exercise	Develop more efficient breathing patterns Increase work capacity Increase time to exhaustion Be less sensitive to dyspnea	Increase duration over intensity 3 - 7 days/week 30 min/session comortable pace
Muscular Strength/ Endurance: Free & machine weights	Increase number of repetitions	Low-resistance with high repetitions 2 - 3 days/week
Flexibility: Stretching (< 20 sec hold below discomfort point)	Increase range of motion	3 - 4 times/week 3 - 4 sessions/week

Cancer and Exercise

Cancer is a collection of several hundred diseases that possess uncontrolled cellular proliferation with the potential for these cells to spread to other parts of the body (metastasize). It is estimated that 1.4 million new cases of cancer are diagnosed each year in the United States with over 565,000 Americans dying annually. Exercise is an important adjunctive treatment for patients with cancer. People with cancer, as well as those who have survived, may have specific physical limitations because of cancer being multidimensional. These limitations may be due to either the disease itself or from the anticancer treatment (see Table 11.4) which will pose challenges to exercising. The specific effects of cancer on the ability to exercise are determined by the tissue affected and the extent of involvement.

Table 11.4
Effects of Different Anticancer Treatments

CANCER TREATMENT	SHORT TERM EFFECTS	LONG TERM EFFECTS
Chemotherapy	Fatigue Nausea Anemia Muscle pain Weight gain	Fatique Lung Scarring Heart Muscle Disease Leukemia Nerve Damage
Radiation	Fatigue Pain Skin Irritation Pulmonary Inflammation	Fractures Cardiac Scarring Lung Scarring Decreased Flexibility
Surgery	Fatigue Pain Decrease Range of Motion	Pain Nerve Damage Decrease Flexibility
Immunotherapy	Fatigue Flu-like Illness Nerve Damage	Muscle Disease Nerve Damage

Exercise training is safe and beneficial for cancer patients but the goals for exercise vary according to the individual's situation. For those undergoing treatment for cancer, the objective of exercising is to maintain strength, endurance and physiological function. For cancer survivors, exercising should have the goal of returning them to their former level of physical and psychological function. Exercise reduces fatigue and improves functional ability, mood, and quality of life. Before each exercise session, all cancer patients should assess their general health status. This is especially important for those actively receiving chemotherapy. Individuals experiencing vomiting, diarrhea, or a fever should delay their workout session. Cancer patients with low platelet count (< 50,000/mm3) will have an increased risk of bleeding and steps should be taken to prevent falls and elevated blood pressure.

Aerobic exercise should consist of moderate intensity activities performed at least every other day for 15 to 40 minutes per session. Resistance training should be conducted two to three days per week, performing at least six to eight different exercises consisting of both upper and lower body movement. Table 11.5 list exercise recommendations for individuals with cancer.

Table 11.5
Exercise Program for Cancer

HEALTH FITNESS CATEGORY	GOALS	OVERLOAD
Cardiorespiratory: Recumbent Cycling Walking Stair Climbing & Rowing Swimming & Aquatic Exercise	Improve quality of life Reduce fatigue Increase work capacity Control body weight Improve mood	Every other day Symptoms limited, moderate intensity 15 - 40 min/session
Muscular Strength/ Endurance: Circuit weight training Free & machine weights	Increase strength Increase muscular endurance	8 - 12 repetitions 2 - 3 sets/exercise 2 - 3 days/week
Flexibility: Stretching	Increase range of motion	5 - 7 sessions//week

Diabetes and Exercise

Over 21 million people in the United States have diabetes (diabetes mellitus). Diabetes is a group of metabolic diseases characterized by an inability to sufficiently produce or properly use insulin resulting in hyperglycemia. There are two main categories of diabetes. Type 1 diabetes is caused by a deficiency of insulin requiring regular insulin injections or the use of an insulin pump. Type 2 diabetes is the result of the body's insulin receptors become insensitive or resistance to insulin. This is the most common form and affects over 90% of all those suffering from diabetes. Regardless of the type of diabetes, this disease affects the blood vessels and nerves causing several complications to occur. These include vision impairment, kidney disease, peripheral vascular disease, atherosclerosis, and hypertension.

Exercise is an important component of diabetes management and provides several benefits (see Table 11.6). For type 2 diabetes, exercise may be considered a method of treatment. But for type 1 diabetes, exercise is used to minimize the affects of disease and is an important part of a healthy lifestyle. Aerobic, muscular strength/endurance and flexibility training are all appropriate modes for most individuals with diabetes.

Table 11.6
Benefits of Exercise for the Diabetic

- Improved Insulin Sensitivity
- Weight Conrol
- Improved Lipid Profiles
- Lower Risk of Cardiovascular Disease
- Reduction in Blood Pressure
- Better Glucose Tolerance
- Stress Management

Type 1 diabetes requires modification in insulin dosage and carbohydrate ingestion when beginning an exercise program. Often, a reduction of the insulin dosage and/or increase in carbohydrate intake is needed to avoid hypoglycemia that can result from exercise (see Table 11.7). This adjustment is dependent on the intensity and duration of exercise. Supervised exercise or exercising with a workout partner is recommended in case a hypoglycemic event occurs. Symptoms of hypoglycemia include confusion, dizziness, irritability, headache, and nausea.

Aerobic exercise is important to maximize blood glucose control in diabetics. Properly fitting and supportive shoes are required for weight-bearing exercise (e.g. walking and jogging) due to peripheral neuropathy causing feet ulcerations. Those with advance

Table 11.7
Avoiding Exercise-Induced Hypoglycemia

- Measure blood glucose immediately before starting workout and during workout if longer than 30 minutes.
- Consume carbohydrates if glucose < 100 mg/dl.
- Delay workout if glucose is > 300 mg/dl or > 240 mg/dl with Ketone Bodies.
- Avoid exercising during peak insulin action.
- Reduce insulin dose on days of exercise.
- Consume carbohydrates after exercise and monitor closely.
- Avoid exercise late at night to avoid hypoglycemia while sleeping.

peripheral neuropathy should participate in non-impact exercises (e.g. swimming and cycling). Resistance exercises are safe for diabetics, although those with kidney disease or vision impairment should avoid heavy lifting or straining. Table 11.8 list exercise recommendations for individuals with diabetes.

Table 11.8
Exercise Program for Diabetics

HEALTH FITNESS CATEGORY	GOALS	OVERLOAD
Cardiorespiratory: Walking & Jogging Peripheral Neuropath Cycling & Swimming	Increase time to exhaustion Increase work capacity Improve blood pressure Reduce cardiovascular risk	50 - 90% Max HR 4 - 7 days/week 20 - 60 min/session
Muscular Strength/ Endurance: Free weight &/or weight machines	Increase maximal number of repetitions	Low-resistance with high repetitions
Flexibility: Stretching	Maintain or increase range of motion	2 - 3 sessions/week

Fibromyalgia and Exercise

Approximately five million Americans are diagnosed with fibromyalgia. This rheumatological disease affects both men and women. Eighty percent of those affected with fibromyalgia are women between the ages of 20 and 50 years. Fibromyalgia is a multidimensional condition characterized by chronic diffused pain and tenderness at specific anatomical location. Additional symptoms include sleep disturbance, chronic fatigue, depression, anxiety, morning stiffness, and exaggerated perception of physical work.

Individuals with fibromyalgia are typically sedentary and in poor physical condition due to the associated pain and general fatigue. Specific exercises that are poorly tolerated are vigorous or high-impact activities as well as sustained overhead movements. Exercising can produced similar benefits for individuals with fibromyalgia as it does for healthy individuals. However, the primary goal of exercising for those with fibromyalgia is to restore and maintain functional ability. Benefits specific to individuals with fibromyalgia can be found in Table 11.9.

Table 11.9
Benefits of Exercise for Individuals with Fibromyalgia

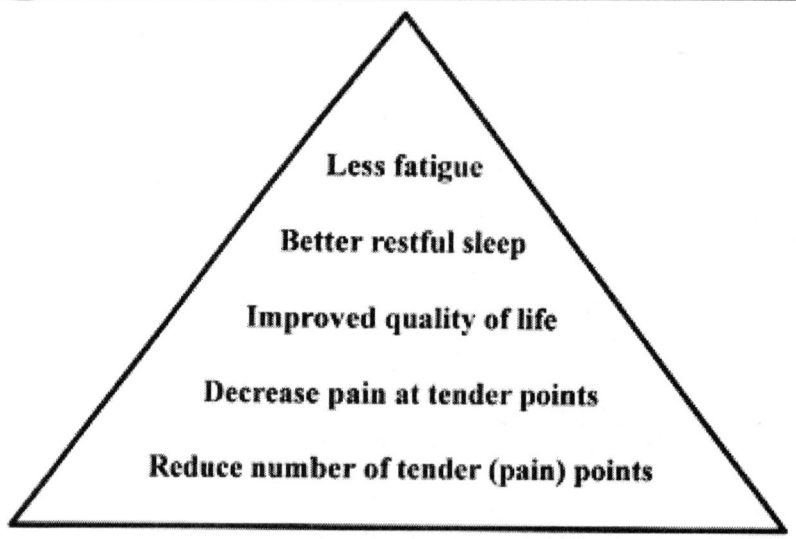

The type of exercises that will benefit fibromyalgia patients should be light to moderate intensity. Some individuals may respond better when exercises are performed in 5 – 10 minutes sessions spaced throughout the day. Developing and maintaining a flexibility program is also essential. Passive and static stretching exercises can reduce the stress and tension in tight muscles. Stretching should be preformed intermittently throughout the training session to enhance training tolerance. Each stretching exercise should not be held longer than 15 – 20 seconds.

Resistance training should be incorporated into the exercise program of individuals with fibromyalgia. Strengthening exercises must focus on muscular endurance using light to moderate resistance for 15 – 20 repetitions. Fibromyalgia individuals should never strength train to the point of muscular failure as this will exacerbate the symptoms of this disorder. Cardiovascular conditioning should consist of low-impact, non-weight-bearing, low-intensity aerobic exercises. When first beginning an exercise program, start out with short exercise bouts and progressively increase the duration as exercise tolerance improves rather than increase intensity. Table 11.10 list exercise recommendations for individuals with fibromyalgia.

Table 11.10
Exercise Program for Fibromyalgia

HEALTH FITNESS CATEGORY	GOALS	OVERLOAD
Cardiorespiratory: Recumbent Cycling Walking & Treadmill Stair Climbing Swimming & Aquatic Exercise	Decrease pain, anxiety and depression Increase work capacity Increase time to exhaustion Reduce cardiovascular risk	Increase duration over intensity 2 - 3 days/week 20 - 40 min/session 50 - 60% Max HR
Muscular Strength/ Endurance: Circuit weight training	Increase number of repetitions	Low-resistance with high repetitions
Flexibility: Stretching (< 20 sec hold below discomfort point)	Increase range of motion	3 - 4 times/sessions 3 - 4 sessions/week

Hypertension and Exercise

Hypertension or high blood pressure affects more than 73 million Americans and is defined as having a systolic blood pressure of 140 mmHg or greater and/or diastolic blood pressure of 90 mmHg or greater. In 1993, the Joint National Committee advocated regular aerobic exercise as an effective treatment for or in combination with medication for decreasing hypertension. To prevent morbidity and mortality from high blood pressure, blood pressure should be lowered and maintained below 140/90 mmHg while concurrently modifying cardiovascular risk factors through lifestyle changes (see Table 11.11).

Table 11.11
Lifestyle Changes for Hypertensive Individuals

1. Decrease weight, if Body Mass Index ov er 25
2. Limit alcohol intake
3. Increase aerobic activity
4. Reduce sodium intake
5. Maintain adequate potassium, calcium & magnesium intake
6. Stop smoking
7. Reduce intake of saurated fat & cholesterol

The benefits of exercise training on hypertension are reduction in both systolic and diastolic blood pressure. Physically active hypertensive individuals also have a lower mortality rates. The conditioning program for hypertensive individuals should include aerobic, muscular endurance, and flexibility exercises. Aerobic exercise guidelines are similar to the recommendations for healthy adults (Chapter 4). However, individuals with blood pressure greater than 180/110 mmHg should only begin aerobic training after initiating drug therapy since untreated hypertension may limit exercise tolerance. Resistance exercises are important for hypertensive individuals but should focus on muscular endurance using 15 – 20 RM (Chapter 5). Increasing the range of motion is needed for most individuals and normal flexibility training guidelines should be followed (Chapter 6). Table 11.12 list exercise recommendations for individuals with hypertension.

Table 11.12
Exercise Program for Hypertension

HEALTH FITNESS CATEGORY	GOALS	OVERLOAD
Cardiorespiratory: Walking & Jogging Treadmill & Stair Climbing Cycling & Swimming	Increase time to exhaustion Increase work capacity Improve blood pressure Reduce cardiovascular risk	50 - 80% Max HR 4 - 7 days/week 30 - 60 min/session
Muscular Strength/ Endurance: Circuit weight training	Increase maximal number of repetitions	Low-resistance with high repetitions
Flexibility: Stretching	Maintain or increase range of motion	2 - 3 sessions/week

Obesity and Exercise

Obesity is a disorder of excess body fat resulting in poor health and quality of life. Currently, 31% of American adults are considered obese, increasing the risk and severity of disease. There are several ways to define obesity as found in Table 11.13. The primary cause for obesity in the United States is diet and physical inactivity. However, environment and heredity may play a role in predisposing an individual to becoming overfat. Years of unhealthy eating and sedentary lifestyle causes unique problems for obese individuals. Besides the typical health problems associated with obesity (Chapter 7), dermatitis, impaired agility, and heat intolerance can cause discomfort during exercise.

Table 11.13
Classification of Obesity by Percentage of Body Fat, Weight and Body Mass Index

	Mildly Obese	Moderately Obese	Severely Obese
Percent Over Ideal Body Weight	21 – 40%	41 – 100%	> 100%
Body Mass Index	30 – 34	35 – 39	> 39
Percent Body Fat Female	32 – 37%	38 – 45%	> 45%
Male	22 – 27%	28 – 35%	> 35%

The primary objective of exercise in the treatment of obesity is to increase energy expenditure while minimizing the potential of injury. Research clearly shows that even a modest weight loss of 10% can dramatically improve obesity related diseases. Exercise alone will not be effective if the obese individual is unmotivated to make additional lifestyle changes. Employing low-intensity aerobic and resistance exercises as well as modifying one's diet is the only method for making significant decreases. For permanent lifestyle changes to occur, behavior therapy will also be required. Table 11.14 list exercise recommendations for obese individuals.

Table 11.14
Exercise Program for Obesity

HEALTH FITNESS CATEGORY	GOALS	OVERLOAD
Cardiorespiratory: 　Stair Climbing & Rowing 　Walking & Treadmill 　Recumbent Cycling 　Swimming & Aquatic 　　Exercise	Reduce cardiovascular risk Increase time to exhaustion Increase work capacity Reduce body weight	40 - 60 min/session 50 - 60% Max HR 5 - 7 days/week Increase duration over intensity
Muscular Strength/ Endurance: 　Circuit weight training 　Free & Machine 　　weights	Increase strength Increase muscular endurance	8 - 12 repetitions 2 - 3 sets/exercise 2 - 3 days/week
Flexibility: 　Stretching	Increase range of motion	5 - 7 sessions/week

Pregnancy and Exercise

Traditionally, pregnancy has been treated similar to an illness because it places enormous demands on a woman's body. This led to the recommendations for pregnant women to be advised to rest and avoid unnecessary physical activity. Today, moderate exercise is encouraged as decades of research has found that physically active mothers-to-be gain positive health benefits without placing the fetus at increased risk. Exercise can be dangerous however if excessive, leading to hypoglycemia, chronic fatigue, and premature labor for the mother. For the fetus, excessive exercise may cause hypoxemia, hyperthermia, hypoglycemia, and low birth weight. In addition, certain conditions require that exercise be considered cautiously. The American College of Obstetricians and Gynecologists has compiled a list of contraindications for exercise during pregnancy and is listed in Table 11.15.

The benefits of regular exercise during pregnancy consist of counteracting the effects of deconditioning and combat fatigue. Muscular strength is maintained with exercise which will improve posture, decrease back pain, speed delivery and hasten recovery from pregnancy. Additional benefits include improved psychological well-being, prevention of type 2 diabetes, and control excessive weight gain. Women who were previously exercising before becoming pregnant can continue with their moderate to even vigorous exercise program. For pregnant women not already involved in an exercise program, they should follow a low intensity program. The type of exercise should be based on comfort and convenience. Non-weight-bearing exercises such as stationary cycling and aquatics may be more comfortable as pregnancy advances. Avoid ballistic exercises, Valsalva maneuver (Chapter 3), and exercising in the supine position. Additional precautions include: avoid exercising in hot, humid environments; consume adequate fluids (Chapter 6); and limit exposure to falling/contact/impact activities (e.g., soccer, boxing, and skydiving). During pregnancy there is an increase chance of joint injury due to the presence of relaxin, a hormone that causes joint laxity in preparation for the deliver of the baby. Also, exercise should stop in the event of vaginal bleeding, feelings of discomfort, abdominal pain/cramping, ruptured membranes, or abnormal/excessive increase in blood pressure or heart rate. Table 11.16 list exercise recommendations for pregnant women.

Table 11.15
Contraindications for Exercise during Pregnancy

1. Pregnancy-induced hypertension
2. Incompetent cervix
3. Intrauterine growth retardation
4. Premature rupture of membranes
5. Persistent second or third trimester bleeding
6. Preterm labor during prior or current pregnancy
7. Preeclampsia or toxemia
8. Valvular or ischemic heart disease
9. Restrictive lung disease
10. Multiple pregnancy at risk for premature labor
11. Low body fat and/or history of anorexia nervosa

Table 11.16
Exercise Program for Pregnancy

HEALTH FITNESS CATEGORY	GOALS	OVERLOAD

Cardiorespiratory:
  Walking & Treadmill
  Recumbent Cycling
  Swimming & Aquatic
    Exercise
	Increase time to exhaustion
	Increase work capacity
	Reduce body weight
		50 - 60% Max HR
		3 - 5 days/week
		30 - 50 min/session
		Increase duration

Muscular Strength/ Endurance:
  Avoid Valsalva maneuver
  Free & Machine
    weights
	Increase muscular endurance	12 - 15 repetitions
		1 - 2 sets/exercise
		2 - 3 days/week

Flexibility: Stretching	Increase range of motion	2 - 3 sessions/week

Summary

Being physically active should be the goal of every American. Even those with chronic conditions can benefit from an appropriate exercise regimen. Before beginning an exercise program with any disorder, proper medical evaluation is required. By following the guidelines for exercise in conjunction with the physician's recommendation, an attenuation of the condition's symptoms will occur along with an improvement in the quality of life.

Review Questions

1. List four lifestyle factors that are crucial for preventing hypoglycemia.

2. List the benefits of aerobic exercise for those with hypertension.

3. What are the main goals of exercise for individuals with fibromyalgia?

4. What type of exercise environment is best tolerated by asthmatics?

5. Distinguish between osteoarthritis and rheumatoid arthritis.

6. Discuss the different goals of exercise for those being treated for cancer compared to cancer survivors.

7. Define obesity in terms of body mass index and percent of body fat.

8. List five contraindications for exercise during pregnancy.

Laboratories

Contents

1. Medical Clearance   149
2. Lifestyle Appraisal   151
3. Measuring One's Heart Rate   155
4. Evaluating Cardiorespiratory Fitness   157
5. Prescribing an Aerobic Exercise Program   161
6. Evaluating Muscular Strength/Endurance   165
7. Prescribing a Muscular Strength/Endurance Exercise Program   169
8. Evaluating Flexibility   171
9. Prescribing a Flexibility and Back Exercise Program   175
10. Body Mass Index   177
11. Estimating Caloric Expenditure   181
12. 24 Hour Caloric Intake Analysis   185
13. Designing a Health Fitness Program and Reevaluation   189

LABORATORY 1
Medical Clearance

Name_____ Section _____ Date _____

There are many health benefits that are associated with regular exercise. However, before increasing your physical activity, medical clearance is the necessary first step to take. While measures will be taken to insure your safety, this class does involve physical activity and you must assume the risk of an injury or accident. While exercise is safe for most apparently healthy individuals, the reaction of the body can't always be totally predicted. Any exercise program can be a risk; but the hazards of sedentary living are far greater than most risks associated with exercise.

Before starting any exercise program, please read carefully the following statements to determine if any situation applies to you that may limit your physical activity. This procedure has been designed to identify contraindications that would warrant the advice of a physician concerning the type of activity most suitable. Therefore, according to the guidelines of the American College of Sports Medicine, before participating in the exercise portion of this class:

1. Each student should notify the instructor if there are any medical problems or physical disability that would limit full participation in class.

2. Students over the age of 40 (males) or 50 (females) should consult with their physician to determine if they are "cleared" to fully participate in the class. If "clearance" is not received, a prescription of exercise modifications is essential for safe participation in an exercise program.

3. Students of any age with any major coronary risk factors and/or symptoms suggestive of cardiopulmonary or other disorder listed below should consult with their physician to determine if they are "cleared" to fully participate in the class.

    1. Diagnosed high blood pressure.
    2. High serum cholesterol.
    3. Cigarette smoking.
    4. Diabetes.
    5. Family history of heart disease in parents or siblings prior to age 55.
    6. Chest pain at rest or during exertion.
    7. Unaccustomed shortness of breath or shortness of breath with mild exertion.

8. Dizziness.
9. Labored breathing.
10. Heart palpitations and/or arrhythmias.
11. Known heart murmur.
12. Joint, muscle, or other orthopedic problems.

I acknowledge that I have read this form in its entirety and that I understand the risks involved in beginning an exercise program. I accept the responsibility of being fully "cleared" to participate in any exercise program and agree to provide information to my instructor concerning any situation that may exist that would prohibit or limit my full participation in this class.

Name (print) _____ ID _____

Signature _____ Date _____

Age _____ Gender (circle one) Male   Female

Class and section _____ Time _____

Instructor _____

LABORATORY **2**

Lifestyle Appraisal

Name_____ Section _____ Date _____

INTRODUCTION

Lifestyle (daily behavior) affects health more than any other factor (e.g. environment and genetics). Research has shown that poor health practices increase the risk of illness and premature death. Self-responsibility is paramount in developing a healthy lifestyle. However, educators and health professionals are important resources for learning and understanding about developing a good lifestyle.

PURPOSE

1. To determine your lifestyle category.
2. To become motivated to improve your health.

PROCEDURE

1. Fill out the Lifestyle Assessment form found on the following two pages.
2. Answer the questions below at the end of the lab.

RESULTS

1. Lifestyle Assessment answers from page 150. ____ ____ ____ ____ ____

   from page 151. ____ ____ ____ ____ ____

   Add each row and column together for a grand total of: _____

TABLE 12.1

Lifestyle Categories for the Results for the Lifestyle Assessment

LIFESTYLE ASSESSMENT SCORE	LIFESTYLE CATEGORY
< 40	Very Healthy
41 - 70	Healthy
71 - 100	Average
101 - 130	Unhealthy
> 131	Very Unhealthy

ANSWERS (check only one)

	almost always	frequently	often	sometimes	almost never
## Personal Health Care					
1. I avoid exposure to tobacco smoke.	___	___	___	___	___
2. When I am sick or injured, I take appropriate action to recover quickly.	___	___	___	___	___
3. I brush my teeth a minimum of twice a day.	___	___	___	___	___
4. I floss my teeth every day.	___	___	___	___	___
5. I get 7 to 8 hours of sleep each night.	___	___	___	___	___
## Drugs and Alcohol					
1. I do not ride in a vehicle in which the operator (this includes me) is under the influence of drugs or alcohol.	___	___	___	___	___
2. I avoid the use of all tobacco products.	___	___	___	___	___
3. I limit my alcohol consumption to less than one drink per day.	___	___	___	___	___
4. I only use drugs or medications when prescribed by a physician.	___	___	___	___	___
5. I read and follow the instructions provided with any drug or medication I take.	___	___	___	___	___
## Fitness Physical					
1. I do some light stretching before exercising and gradually increase my intensity during the work-out.	___	___	___	___	___
2. I increase my daily activity level by climbing stairs or walking/cycling instead of riding.	___	___	___	___	___
3. I drink plenty of water (or sport drink) before, during, and after a work-out.	___	___	___	___	___
4. I exercise aerobically (continuous jogging, walking, cycling, & etc.) for a minimum of 20 minutes 6 to 7 days per week.	___	___	___	___	___
5. I stretch to improve flexibility five days per week.	___	___	___	___	___
TOTAL NUMBER OF CHECKS IN EACH ROW	___	___	___	___	___
TIMES CONSTANT	X 1	X 2	X 3	X 4	X 5
(TRANSFER THESE NUMBERS TO PAGE)	=___	=___	=___	=___	=___

	almost always	frequently	often	sometimes	almost never

Psychological
1. I feel good about myself and the way I act.
2. I find it easy to get along with others without compromising my beliefs or morals.
3. I go to sleep quickly and wake up rested.
4. I enjoy life and the challenges it brings.
5. I have control over my emotions.

Spiritual
1. I am happy with my spiritual life.
2. Prayer is an important part of my life.
3. I read the Bible everyday.
4. I look for opportunities to share my beliefs with others.
5. People can tell I'm a Christian by the way I lead my life.

Personal Behavior
1. I worry about making decisions.
2. I accept responsibility for my actions.
3. I set realistic goals for myself.
4. Developing close, personal relationships is easy.
5. I feel at ease when placed in an unfamiliar environment.

Nutrition
1. At each meal I try to consume food that is high in fiber.
2. I try to consume foods with low levels of fats and oils.
3. I don't add salt to my food.
4. I eat several servings of fruits and vegetables each day.
5. I eat a variety of foods each day and limit my sweets.

TOTAL NUMBER OF CHECKS IN EACH ROW	____	____	____	____	____
TIMES CONSTANT	X 1	X 2	X 3	X 4	X 5
(TRANSFER THESE NUMBERS TO PAGE)	=____	=____	=____	=____	=____

DISCUSSION

1. What is your present lifestyle category?

2. What lifestyle changes can you make today to improve your overall health?

3. What lifestyle changes will take you several weeks to change? Why?

LABORATORY **3**

Measuring One's Heart Rate

Name_____ Section_____ Date_____

INTRODUCTION

The amount of oxygen consumed by the body is proportionate to heart rate. For this reason, heart rate gives a simple and readily available index of cardiac stress.

PURPOSE

1. Become accurate in detecting and counting heart rate.
2. To demonstrate the effect of participating in various activities on heart rate.

PROCEDURE

1. Students will find their heart rate (Chapter 4, page 44) after each activity and count for 10 seconds and multiply by 6 for calculating heart rate for one minute.
2. Students record the results and answer the questions.

RESULTS

1. Measure your resting heart rate. To get a valid resting measure, record your heart rate three days in a row in the morning before you get out of bed and record the lowest value. A less accurate method is to lay still with eyes closed for 10 minutes and then measure heart rate.

    a. Resting heart rate _____

2. Measure your heart response to physical activity.

    a. Standing at attention _____
    b. Casual walk (3-4 min.) _____
    c. Jog in place (3 min.) _____

DISCUSSION

1. Compare your heart rate at rest to the various forms of physical activity. Did your heart rate increase or decrease? Why this change?

2. Would persons sometimes feel faint if they were jogging hard and suddenly stopped and stood still? Why?

3. Why is a lower resting heart rate considered healthier than a higher one?

LABORATORY 4

Evaluating Cardiorespiratory Fitness

Name_____ Section _____ Date _____

INTRODUCTION

Understanding one's cardiorespiratory fitness level is important in developing an exercise program. It is the foundation of determining the beginning intensity of an aerobic exercise program as well as charting progression throughout the phases of conditioning. It also allows the students to rate their level of aerobic capacity in relation to health fitness standards.

PURPOSE

1. To help the students evaluate and rate their own level of cardiorespiratory fitness.
2. To understand the relationship between maximal oxygen uptake (consumption) and cardiorespiratory fitness.
3. To develop an awareness of satisfactory standards for cardiorespiratory fitness.

PROCEDURES

1. Warm-up and stretch properly (Chapter 6, pages 65 - 69).
2. Accurately time a 1.5 mile Run/Walk at the fastest possible pace for this distance on a track or other precisely marked course.
3. Record time to the nearest second.
4. Cool down properly.
5. Using the tables provided, determine one's level of fitness and the correlating estimated maximal oxygen consumption

Note: This test should not be taken by anyone who has any health or medical problem that may be worsened by taking this test. Student should be "medically cleared" before taking this test.

RESULTS

1. Determine your level of cardiorespiratory fitness and oxygen consumption. Use the appropriate tables (12.2 and 12.3).

    1.5 mile run time _____ min : sec

    Maximal Oxygen Consumption _____ ml/kg/min

    Cardiorespiratory Fitness Level _____

TABLE 12.2

1.5 Mile Time and Maximal Oxygen Uptake (VO$_2$ max ml/kg/min)

1.5-Mile Time min	VO$_2$ max	1.5-Mile Time min	VO$_2$ max
<7:30	>72	13:00	38
7:30	72	13:30	36
8:00	67	14:00	34
8:30	62	14:30	32
9:00	58	15:00	31
9:30	55	15:30	30
10:00	52	16:00	29
10:30	49	16:30	28
11:00	46	17:00	27
11:30	44	17:30	26
12:00	42	18:00	25
12:30	40	>18:00	<25

Adapted from Wilmore, Jack and Costill, David. Training for Sport and Activity. Third Edition. Dubuque: W. C. Brown. 1988. p. 368

TABLE 12.3

Cardiorespiratory and Health Fitness Standards According to Maximal Oxygen Uptake (ml/kg/min)

FITNESS LEVEL	AGE									
	18 - 29		30 - 39		40 - 49		50 - 59		60 - 69	
	Male	Female	Male	Female	Male	Female	Male	Female	Male	Female
Excellent	60	53	56	50	53	47	50	44	48	42
Very Good	53	46	49	43	45	39	43	37	41	35
Good	43	37	40	34	39	33	34	28	31	26
Fair	36	30	34	28	33	27	30	25	26	21
Poor	31	26	30	24	29	23	26	21	21	17
Very Poor	<31	<26	<30	<24	<29	<23	<26	<21	<21	<17

Adapted from Cooper, Ken. The Aerobics Way. New York: M. Evans & Company, 1977, pp. 280-281, and Hoeger, Werner and Hoeger, Sharon. Fitness and Wellness. Englewood: Morton Publishing Company, 1990, p. 15.

DISCUSSION

1. What is the relationship between maximal oxygen consumption and cardiorespiratory fitness?

2. Discuss your cardiorespiratory fitness relative to health fitness standards. How does your cardiorespiratory fitness relate to your own health?

3. If your fitness standard was below the good level for health, why?

LABORATORY **5**

Prescribing an Aerobic Exercise Program

Name _____ Section _____ Date _____

INTRODUCTION

Most beginning exercisers either workout too intensely having to stop before they receive a sufficient benefit, or they do not workout at a great enough overload to obtain cardiorespiratory improvement. Students should target their exercise heart rate to be between 70 and 85 percent of their maximum exercise heart rate. The emphasis on an aerobic exercise program should be on extending the duration time of the exercise without tiring.

PURPOSE

1. To practice taking exercise heart rate.
2. To learn what happens to your heart rate when walking/jogging at different paces.
3. To determine the walking/jogging pace that will produce an exercise heart rate that will give you the training effect.
4. To figure your heart rate training zone.
5. To select an appropriate progression rate for an aerobic exercise program.

PROCEDURE

1. Calculate your predicted maximal heart rate and your 60%, 70%, 80%, and 90% heart rate intensities.
2. Do general warm-up exercise for five minutes.
3. Walk/Jog for about two minutes at a specific pace (casual walk, brisk walk, fast walk, slow jog, and fast jog).
4. Immediately after completing the two minutes, take heart rate for 10 seconds and multiply by six to get exercise heart rate per minute.
5. Plot heart rate for each pace on the graph.
6. Rest 2-3 minutes before going at next faster pace.
7. From graph, determine pace at which to exercise aerobically between 70 and 80% of your maximum heart rate.
8. Prescribe a personal aerobic exercise program.

RESULTS

1. Calculate your Maximal Heart Rate (MHR)

   220 - age = _____ MHR

2. Calculate your Exercise Heart Rate at the following intensities:

   MHR x .60 = _____ 60% Intensity

   MHR x .70 = _____ 70% Intensitiy

   MHR x .80 = _____ 80% Intensity

   MHR x .90 = _____ 90% Intensity

3. Plot heart rate for the following paces:

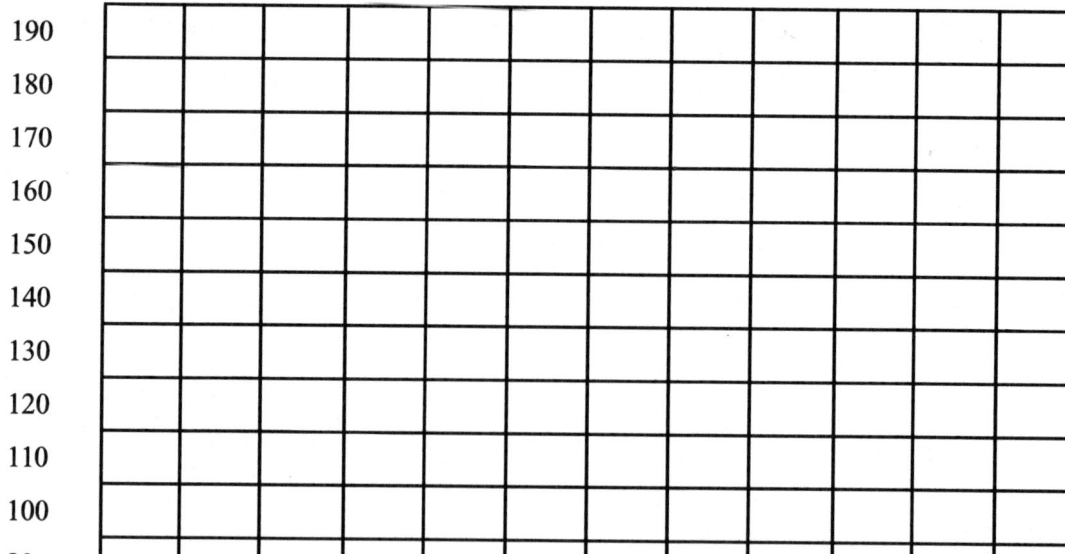

DISCUSSION

1. What pace do you need to walk/jog to be in your heart rate training zone? What percent of maximum heart rate do you feel is appropriate for you as you begin your exercise program? Why?

2. Following the principles of conditioning (overload, specificity, and individuality), prescribe yourself an aerobic exercise program to improve or maintain your cardiorespiratory fitness. Your goal for the future should be to exercise by walking, jogging, swimming, cycling, or a comparable aerobic activity three to five days per week for 60 minutes at 60-65%, or 45 minutes at 70-75%, or 30 minutes at 80-85%.

    What days of the week will you exercise? _____

    What time of the day will you exercise? _____

    Starting level: _____ (from Table 6.4 and Figures 6.10 and 6.11).

3. Considering your need, interests, and the availability of the activity, what will be the best aerobic exercise for you to do and why?

LABORATORY **6**

Evaluating Muscular Strength Endurance

Name_____ Section _____ Date _____

INTRODUCTION

Developing muscular strength/endurance can enhance an individual's ability to resist fatigue and the ability to perform physical movement for extended periods of time without getting tired. In the absence of fatigue, there is greater success and enjoyment in daily work and recreational activities. Increasing one's strength can aid in the prevention of injuries, low back pain, poor posture , and other hypokinetic diseases as well as improve physical performance. In this lab, the students will be able to see how their level of muscular strength/endurance compares to health fitness standards.

PURPOSE

1. To evaluate the student's muscular strength/endurance.
2. To understand the importance of muscular strength/endurance in an exercise program.

PROCEDURE

1. Warm-up and stretch properly.
2. Students will find a partner to help with the test.

SIT-UP TEST

1. Perform as many bent-leg sit-ups as possible within 60 seconds with your arms crossed in front of your chest touching your elbows to your thighs.
2. Appointed testers will time each test.
3. Partners will repeat the same procedure.

PUSH-UP TEST

1. Support the body in a push-up position from the toes (men) or knees (women).
2. Keeping the body rigid, lower the body until the chest touches the floor. Repeat as many times as possible in 60 seconds with no more than 2 seconds rest between each push up.

PULL-UP TEST

1. Gripping a horizontal chinning bar with an over grip, pull you body up until the chin is above the bar, then lower yourself until the arms are fully extended. Repeat as many times as possible.

2. Females perform a flexed arm hang. Gripping a horizontal chinning bar with an over grip. Time begins when chin is placed over the bar with the arms flexed and stops when the chin drops below the bar.

RESULTS

1. Record the number of sit-ups, pull-ups or seconds for flex arm hang, and push-ups completed and your fitness level for muscular strength/endurance (Refer to Table 12.4).

Number of sit-ups: _____   Fitness Level: _____

Number of pull-ups or seconds
   for Flex arm hang: _____   Fitness Level: _____

Number of push-ups: _____   Fitness Level: _____

TABLE 12.4

Fitness Standards For Sit-ups, Push-ps, and Pull-ups/Flexed Arm Hang Tests

SIT-UPS STANDARDS

FITNESS LEVEL	15 - 19 Years Male	15 - 19 Years Female	20 - 29 Years Male	20 - 29 Years Female	30 - 39 Years Male	30 - 39 Years Female	40 - 49 Years Male	40 - 49 Years Female	50 - 59 Years Male	50 - 59 Years Female	60 - 69 Years Male	60 - 69 Years Female
Excellent	>48	>41	>42	>35	>35	>28	>30	>24	>25	>18	>22	>15
Good	42-47	36-41	37-42	31-35	31-35	24-28	26-30	20-24	22-25	12-18	17-22	12-15
Average	38-41	32-35	33-36	25-30	27-30	20-23	22-25	15-19	18-21	5-11	12-16	4-11
Fair	33-37	27-31	29-32	21-24	22-26	15-19	17-21	7-14	13-17	3-4	7-11	2-3
Poor	<31	<27	<29	<21	<22	<15	<17	<7	<13	<3	<7	<2

PUSH-UPS STANDARDS

FITNESS LEVEL	15 - 19 Years		20 - 29 Years		30 - 39 Years		40 - 49 Years		50 - 59 Years		60 - 69 Years	
	Male	Female	Male	Female	Male	Female	Male	Female	Male	Female	Male	Female
Excellent	>38	>32	>35	>29	>29	>26	>23	>21	>20	>19	>17	>15
Good	29-38	25-32	29-35	21-29	22-29	20-26	17-23	15-21	13-20	11-19	11-17	12-15
Average	23-28	18-24	22-28	15-20	17-21	13-19	13-16	11-14	10-12	7-10	8-10	4-11
Fair	18-22	12-17	17-21	10-14	12-16	8-12	10-12	5-10	7-9	2-6	5-7	2-3
Poor	<18	<12	<17	<10	<12	<8	<10	<5	<7	<2	<5	<2

PULL-UPS / FLEX ARM HANG IN SECONDS STANDARDS

FITNESS LEVEL	15 - 19 Years		20 - 29 Years		30 - 39 Years		40 - 49 Years		50 - 59 Years		60 - 69 Years	
	Male	Female	Male	Female	Male	Female	Male	Female	Male	Female	Male	Female
Excellent	>14	>33	>13	>27	>11	>21	>8	>17	>6	>15	>4	>13
Good	12-14	20-33	10-13	18-27	8-11	15-21	5-8	11-17	4-6	8-15	3-4	6-13
Average	8-11	10-19	6-9	8-17	4-8	7-14	2-4	4-10	2-3	1-7	1-2	1-5
Fair	5-7	3-9	2-5	2-7	1-3	1-6	1	1-3	1	0	0	0
Poor	0-4	0-2	0-2	0-1	0	0	0	0	0	0	0	0

DISCUSSION

1. What is the relationship between muscular strength and endurance?

2. Discuss your muscular strength/endurance fitness in regards to fitness standards. How does your muscular strength/endurance fitness relate to your own health?

3. If your fitness standard was below the good level for health, why?

LABORATORY **7**

Prescribing a Muscular Strength/Endurance Exercise Program

Name_____ Section _____ Date _____

INTRODUCTION

Weight training is probably the best exercise method for increasing strength/muscular endurance. Other benefits of weight training include the prevention of injury, the strengthening of bones, and aid in controlling body composition. This lab provides some basic resistance training exercises that can be implemented into a health fitness program.

PURPOSE

1. To provide the student instruction in safe techniques for weight training.
2. To learn basic resistance training exercises for the major muscle groups.
3. To prescribe an exercise program for the improvement or maintenance of muscular strength/endurance.

PROCEDURE

1. Warm-up and stretch properly.
2. Instructor will demonstrate correct techniques in selected weight training exercises.
3. Students will experiment and perform each exercise.
4. Prescribe a personal muscular strength/endurance exercise program.

RESULTS

1. Set up a weight training program and experiment to determine the appropriate weight for set 1 and set 2. Use a three-quarters 10 RM (repetition maximum) weight for set 1 and a 10 RM weight for set 2.

Exercise	Weight for set 1	Weight for set 2
Bench Press	_____	_____
Lat Pull	_____	_____
Elbow Extension	_____	_____
Arm Curls	_____	_____
Knee Extensions	_____	_____
Knee Curls	_____	_____

DISCUSSION

1. Following the principles of conditioning (overload, specificity, and individuality), prescribe yourself a weight training program to improve or maintain your muscular strength/endurance fitness.

    What days of the week will you resistance train: _____

    What time of the day: _____

2. Which area of the body do you feel you have below average strength? Why?

3. Why is it important to develop or have good muscular strength/endurance?

LABORATORY **8**

Evaluating Flexibility

Name_____ Section _____ Date _____

INTRODUCTION

Flexibility has traditionally been the most neglected of the health fitness components of physical fitness. Today, however, it is recognized as an integral part of any proper exercise program. Increased range of motion is thought to aid in the prevention of injuries associated with loss of mobility. The importance of this lab is to develop an awareness of one's level of flexibility.

PURPOSE

1. To evaluate and rate the student's level of flexibility.
2. To understand what is an acceptable range of motion.

PROCEDURE

1. Warm-up and stretch properly.
2. Students will find a partner to help with the three flexibility tests.
3. Follow the directions below to complete all three tests.

SIT-AND-REACH TEST

DIRECTIONS: The sit-and-reach test measures the flexibility of the lower back and hamstrings.

1. Sit on the floor with shoes removed and facing the flexibility box.
2. With knees fully extended and feet four inches apart, place the box against the flat bottom of the feet.
3. Extend arms straight forward with one hand placed on top of the other, palms down.
4. Reach forward as far as possible and hold the position until measured to the nearest half inch.
5. The best of three trials is recorded. The partner makes sure the legs remain straight by placing a hand on the knees and both hands remain even.

SHOULDER LIFT TEST

DIRECTIONS: The shoulder lift test measures the flexibility of the shoulders.

1. Lie on your stomach with arms extended and holding a straight edge.
2. With the forehead maintaining contact with the floor, raise the arms as high as possible.
3. The greatest distance achieved between the floor and the straight edge is recorded of the three trials.

ACHILLES STRETCH TEST

DIRECTIONS: The Achilles stretch test measures the flexibility of the ankles.

1. Stand facing the wall with extended arms and legs straight with toes facing forward.
2. Lean against the wall with the hands and press the hips to the wall while maintaining straight legs.
3. Your partner will measure the ankle angle with a goniometer and record the best of three trials.

TABLE 12.5

Flexibility Standards for Sit-and-Reach, Shoulder Lift, and Achilles Stretch

FLEXIBILITY STANDARDS

Fitness Level	Sit-and-Reach	Shoulder Lift	Achilles Stretch
Excellent	> 23 inches	> 26 inches	< 60 derees
Very Good	21.5 - 23 inches	24.5 - 26 inches	60 - 69 degrees
Good	18.5 - 21 inches	21.5 - 24 inches	70 - 79 degrees
Average	16.5 - 18 inches	18.5 - 21 inches	80 - 89 degrees
Fair	13.5 - 16 inches	14.5 - 18 inches	90 - 99 degrees
Poor	11.5 - 13 inches	10.5 - 14 inches	100 - 110 degrees
Very Poor	< 11 inches	< 10 inches	> 110 degrees

RESULTS

1. Record your results below from the flexibility tests and determine your level of fitness.

   Sit-and-Reach Score: _____   Fitness Level: _____

   Shoulder Lift Score: _____   Fitness Level: _____

   Achilles Stretch Score: _____   Fitness Level: _____

DISCUSSION

1. Discuss your flexibility relative to fitness level. How does your flexibility relate to your own health?

2. If your fitness standard was below the good level for health, why?

3. Which areas of your body that were tested are the least flexible and why?

LABORATORY 9

Prescribing a Flexibility and Back Exercise Program

Name _____ Section _____ Date _____

INTRODUCTION

Flexibility or range of motion is the amount of movement in a joint. Flexibility allows joints to move with greater ease and efficiency, as well as with quicker responsiveness and coordination. The benefits of increased flexibility are a decrease in injuries and muscle soreness. Flexibility is an integral part of an exercise program. The best time to perform flexibility training is after your workout during the cool-down (Chapter 6). However, stretching may be executed any time the joint and muscles involved are warm with good blood flow.

Included in this laboratory are also several back exercises. At some point in their lives, approximately 80 percent of all adults will experience back pain that limits their ability to function normally. An estimated 75 million Americans have recurring back problems, and two million cannot hold jobs as a result of low back pain causing 93 million days of lost work per year and $10 billion in worker's compensation. Proper care of the back is essential to good health and the addition of back exercises to an exercise program can be a preventive measure to one's future health.

PURPOSE

1. To provide the student with safe range of motion exercises that can be incorporated into their health fitness program.
2. To learn the importance of and understand techniques for a warm-up and cool-down in an exercise program.
3. To provide the student with safe exercises for preventing or alleviating low back pain.
4. To learn proper methods for strengthening the lower back.
5. To learn the importance of proper lower back care.

PROCEDURE

1. Students will walk or jog slowly for three to five minutes as a general warm up.
2. Instructor will provide instruction and explanation for proper utilization of flexibility and back exercises.

Flexibility Exercises (see Chapter 6)	**Back Exercises (see Chapter 10)**
Shoulder stretch across	Curl-up
Shoulder stretch behind	Pelvic raises
Shoulder stretch side	Side leg raises
Trunk stretch to side	Knees to chest
Hip & trunk stretch	Back extensions
Hamstring stretch	
Groin stretch	
Thighs stretch (quadriceps)	
Achilles stretch (Calf)	

RESULTS

1. Following the principles of conditioning (overload, specificity, and individuality), prescribe yourself a program to improve or maintain your flexibility and strength of your back.

   When will you perform your stretching and back exercises?

   Days/week: _____ Time of day: _____

DISCUSSION

1. Why should you perform flexibility and back exercises weekly?

2. Have you ever had low back pain? If so, how did you get rid of it?

3. Which flexibility and back exercises do you feel would be best for you to incorporate into a health fitness program?

LABORATORY **10**

Body Mass Index

Name_____ Section _____ Date _____

INTRODUCTION

Poor body composition is one result of a sedentary lifestyle. Excess body weight in the form of fat is associated with a number of specific health risks that include an increase in hypertension, strokes, type 2 diabetes, cancers, and osteoarthritis. One simple technique used to determine excess body fat and its associated health risks is the body mass index (BMI).

PURPOSE

1. To determine your health risk associated with your BMI.
2. To become motivated to improve your health.

PROCEDURE

1. Have your height and weight measured.
2. Use the Body Mass Index chart on page 178 to determine BMI.
3. Check the risk of disease based upon your BMI (see Table 12.6).

RESULTS

1. Record your weight without shoes on to the nearest pound. _____

2. Record your height without shoes on to the nearest inch. _____

3. Record your BMI after locating it on the Body Mass Index Chart. _____

TABLE 12.6

Disease Risk and Fitness Category Associated with Body Mass Index

Fitness Level	Body Mass Index	Risk of Disease
Underweight	< 19	High
Normal	19 - 24	Low
Overweight	25 - 29	Moderate
Obesity	30 - 34	High
Obesity II	35 - 39	Very High
Extreme Obesity	> 39	Extremely High

BODY MASS INDEX (BMI) CHART

Weight (Lbs)	59	60	61	62	63	64	65	66	67	68	69	70	71	72	73	74	75	76	77	78
100	20	20	19	18	18															
105	21	21	20	19	19	18	18													
110	22	22	21	20	20	19	18	18												
115	23	23	22	21	20	20	19	19	18	18										
120	24	23	23	22	21	21	20	19	19	18	18									
125	25	24	24	23	22	22	21	21	20	19	19	18								
130	26	25	25	24	23	22	22	21	20	20	19	19	18	18						
135	27	26	26	25	24	23	22	22	21	21	20	19	19	18	18					
140	28	27	26	26	25	24	23	23	22	21	21	20	20	19	18	18				
145	29	28	27	27	26	25	24	23	23	22	21	21	20	20	19	19	18	18		
150	30	29	28	27	27	26	25	24	23	23	22	22	21	20	20	19	19	18	18	
155	31	30	29	28	27	27	26	25	24	24	23	22	22	21	20	20	19	19	18	18
160	32	31	30	29	28	27	27	26	25	24	24	23	22	22	21	21	20	19	19	19
165	33	32	31	30	29	28	27	27	26	25	24	24	23	22	22	21	21	20	19	19
170	34	33	32	31	30	29	28	27	27	26	25	24	24	23	22	22	21	21	20	20
175	35	34	33	32	31	30	29	28	27	27	26	25	24	24	23	22	22	21	20	20
180	36	35	34	33	32	31	30	29	28	27	27	26	25	24	24	23	22	22	21	21
185	37	36	35	34	33	32	31	30	29	28	27	27	26	25	24	24	23	23	22	21
190	38	37	36	35	34	33	32	31	30	29	28	27	26	26	25	24	24	23	23	22
195	39	38	37	36	35	34	33	32	31	30	29	28	27	26	26	25	24	24	23	23
200	40	39	38	37	35	34	33	32	31	30	30	29	28	27	26	26	25	24	24	23
205		40	39	38	36	35	34	33	32	31	30	29	29	28	27	26	26	25	24	24
210			40	39	37	36	35	34	33	32	31	30	29	29	28	27	26	26	25	24
215			40	39	38	37	36	35	34	33	32	31	30	29	28	28	27	26	26	25
220				40	39	38	37	36	35	34	33	32	31	30	29	28	28	27	26	25
225					40	39	38	36	35	34	33	32	31	31	30	29	28	27	27	26
230						40	38	37	36	35	34	33	32	31	30	30	29	28	27	27
235						40	39	38	37	36	35	34	33	32	31	30	29	29	28	27
240							40	39	38	37	36	35	34	33	32	31	30	29	29	28
245								40	38	37	36	35	34	33	32	32	31	30	29	28
250								40	39	38	37	36	35	34	33	32	31	31	30	29
255									40	39	38	37	36	35	34	33	32	31	30	30
260										40	39	37	36	35	34	33	33	32	31	30
265										40	39	38	37	36	35	34	33	32	32	31
270											40	39	38	37	36	35	34	33	32	31
275												40	38	37	36	35	34	34	33	32
280												40	39	38	37	36	35	34	33	32
285													40	39	38	37	36	35	34	33
290													40	39	38	37	36	35	34	34
295														40	39	38	37	36	35	34
300															40	39	38	37	36	35

Height Inches

DISCUSSION

1. What is the disease risk for your BMI (see Table 12.6)?

2. Are you satisfied with your BMI? Why?

3. What lifestyle changes can you make to improve your BMI?

LABORATORY **11**

Estimating Caloric Expenditure

Name _____ Section _____ Date _____

INTRODUCTION

Controlling one's weight and body fat can be accomplished best through diet and exercise. To minimize the loss of fat free weight (muscle), a weight reduction of no more than 1 – 2 pounds a week is recommended. Although the elimination of extra calories in the amount of food consumed per day can be achieved quite easily, the caloric expenditure during exercise is more difficult. However, weight lost through aerobic activities will insure a greater loss of fat and a more permanent fat loss. By monitoring intensity of exercise, caloric expenditure can be estimated. A negative caloric balance of 3500 calories is equal to one pound of fat.

PURPOSE

1. To learn how to calculate the estimated caloric expenditure of aerobic activities.
2. To understand the relationship between intensity and caloric expenditure.
3. To determine the amount of exercise per week needed to lose a pound of fat.

PROCEDURE

1. Calculate your Basal Metabolic Rate (BMR) using the equations in Table 12.7.
2. Determine your daily physical exertion level (DPEL) using Table 12.9.
3. Calculate the caloric expenditure of your fitness activities using Table 12.10.
4. Using the following equations, determine your daily total caloric expenditure (DTCE).

RESULTS

1. Calculate your BMR from Table 12.7. _____

TABLE 12.7
Estimation of Basal Metabolic Rate (BMR) in Calories per Day

Males: BMR (Calories/day) = 66.47 + (13.75 x body weight in kg) + (5 x height in cm) - (6.76 x age) - (BMI Adjustment see Table 12.8)

Females: BMR (Calories/day) = 655.1 + (9.56 x body weight in kg) + (1.85 x height in cm) - (4.68 x age) - (BMI Adjustment see Table 12.8)

MULTIPLY POUNDS BY .4536 FOR KILOGRAMS (kg)
MULTIPLY INCHES BY 2.54 FOR CENTIMETERS (cm)

TABLE 12.8
Body Mass Index (BMI) Adjustment

If your BMI is < 19   multiply it by .5 = BMI Adjustment
                19 - 24 multiply it by 1   = BMI Adjustment
                25 - 29 multiply it by 5   = BMI Adjustment
                30 - 34 multiply it by 10 = BMI Adjustment
                35 - 39 multiply it by 15 = BMI Adjustment
                > 39   multiply it by 20 = BMI Adjustment

2. Multiply your BMR by your daily physical exertion level (DPEL) activity factor (see Table 12.9).

$$\underline{\hspace{2cm}} \times \underline{\hspace{2cm}} = \underline{\hspace{3cm}}$$
BMR   Activity Factor   Daily Caloric Expenditure (DCE)

TABLE 12.9
Classification of Daily Physical Exertion Level (DPEL) Including Work but Excluding Exercise

DPEL Classification	Activity Factor	Most of Your Day Consists of
Sedentary	1.3	Office/Computer Work, Watching TV, Driving, Studying, Reading, Cooking, and etc.
Moderate	1.5	House Cleaning, Walking, Yard Work, Climbing stairs, Building Trades Occupation, and etc.
Active	1.7	Military on Active Duty, Manual Laborer, Lumberjack, and etc.

3. Calculate the number of calories expended (CE) per fitness activity (see Table 12.10).

Fitness Activity	Cal/min/Kg	Body Wt (Kg)	Time (min)	CE
_____	_____ X	_____ X	_____ =	_____
_____	_____ X	_____ X	_____ =	_____
_____	_____ X	_____ X	_____ =	_____
_____	_____ X	_____ X	_____ =	_____

Total Fitness Activities Caloric Expenditure (TFACE) _____

TABLE 12.10

Common Fitness Activities and Caloric Expenditure Per Minute Per Body Weight in Kilograms

Fitness Activities	Cal/min/Kg	Fitness Activities	Cal/min/Kg
Basketball		Music Aerobics	
1/2 court	.13	Moderate	.10
Full court	.15	Intense	.13
Cycling		Racquetball	
Leisure < 10 mph	.06	Singles	.15
Intense 10-20 mph	.11	Doubles	.10
Racing > 20 mph	.17	Resistance Training	.08
Golf		Swimming (Fitness)	.15
Walking	.08	Tennis	
Riding	.04	Singles	.14
Jogging (on level)		Doubles	.10
6 min/mile	.25	Walking (on level)	
7 min/mile	.22	14 min/mile	.11
8 min/mile	.21	15 min/mile	.095
9 min/mile	.19	16 min/mile	.09
10 min/mile	.17	17 min/mile	.085
11 min/mile	.15	18 min/mile	.08
12 min/mile	.14	19 min/mile	.075
13 min/mile	.12	20 min/mile	.07

4. Add DCE and TFACE together plus Calories expended during Thermogenesis (200 for males and 150 for females) to determine the daily total caloric expenditure (DTCE).

DCE	_____
+ TFACE	_____
+ Thermo	200 or 150
DTCE	_____

DISCUSSION

1. How is exercise intensity related to caloric expenditure?

2. Which type of fitness activities use the most Calories per minute?

3. How does physical activity affect your caloric expenditure while at rest?

LABORATORY **12**

24 Hour Caloric Intake Analysis

Name_____ Section _____ Date _____

INTRODUCTION

Body weight fluctuates according to hydration levels and the balance between daily caloric intake and expenditure. In order for an individual to decrease, increase, or maintain his or her body weight, he or she must follow the energy balance equations (Chapter 7). To decrease body weight caloric intake must be below expenditures. For an increase in weight, additional caloric consumption above expenditure is required. By matching daily caloric intake to expenditure, an individual will maintain a stable body weight.

Consuming food and fluids without regard to nutritional value will lead the body to a diseased state, as well as limits physiological and cognitive development. By learning the nutritional and caloric value of foods/fluids, an individual will be able to make appropriate choices to improve his or her health.

The calories consumed each day are converted into energy that will be either stored (e.g. fat) or used to perform work (e.g. exercise). The body expends energy in three ways: (1) basal/resting metabolic rate, (2) digesting and assimilating, and (3) physical activity.

PURPOSE

1. To become aware of your personal dietary habits and nutritional needs.
2. To determine daily caloric intake.

PROCEDURE

1. Record the amount of food and fluid you consumed during a 24 hour period on Table 12.11.
2. Calculate your total calories consumed for the 24 hour period.

TABLE 12.11

Food Serving Record for a 24 Hour Period

Using the amount per servings found in Chapter 9, pages 113-114, list the number of actual servings you had for each food group. Record the total number of servings on page 187 to calculate caloric intake.

FOOD GROUP	BREAKFAST Food #Servings	LUNCH Food #Servings	DINNER Food #Servings	SNACKS Food #Servings
Breads, cereals and other grain products: Whole grain or enriched				
Fruit: Citrus, melons, berries, all other fruit				
Vegetables: Dark green leafy, deep yellow, all other vegetales				
Protein Group 1: Lean meat, poultry, fish, or Eggs Beans, nuts, and peas				
Protein Group 2: Low fat milk, cheese, yogurt				

Food Group	Suggested Daily Servings	Number of Actual Servings		Calories per Serving		Total Calories
Bread and Cereals	6-11	_____	X	80	=	_____
Fruit	2-4	_____	X	60	=	_____
Vegetables	3-5	_____	X	25	=	_____
Protein Group 1	2-3	_____	X	150	=	_____
Protein Group 2	2-4	_____	X	120	=	_____
Oils/Salad Dressing/Spreads (Tablespoons)		_____	X	50	=	_____
Sweets/Sodas/Alcohol (Items)		_____	X	150	=	_____

TOTAL CALORIC INTAKE FOR 24 HOURS _____

DISCUSSION

1. Are you meeting the recommended daily servings of each food group? Explain why?

2. Is your daily caloric intake equal to your daily caloric expenditure (Laboratory 11)? Explain why?

3. What lifestyle changes in your daily nutritional and exercise habits must you make to decrease your chance of developing excess body fat?

LABORATORY **13**

Designing a Health Fitness Program and Reevaluation

Name_____ Section _____ Date _____

INTRODUCTION

To have health fitness and enjoy all of the benefits associated with it, one must first be self motivated and believe this is an important goal to achieve. If this is the desire, then the individual must also realize that reaching the goal of health fitness will take time and that ones lifestyle must also change. When designing a health fitness program, the individual needs to assess present fitness level, create a program to improve weak areas, and then reassess to determine if the program is meeting the desired goals. Once health fitness is reached, then a maintenance program is established and followed throughout ones life.

PURPOSE

1. To examine your present fitness level of the five health fitness components.
2. To design a program to help you achieve health fitness.
3. To develop a healthy lifestyle.

PROCEDURE

1. Student will record the evaluating of health fitness results from Laboratories 4, 6, 8, and 10.
2. Create a weekly physical activity plan.
3. Record six weeks of health fitness activities.
4. Reevaluate the health fitness components and adjust weekly physical activity plan to achieve health fitness goals.
5. Retake the Lifestyle Appraisal to determine lifestyle category and if any adjustments need to be made.

RESULTS

1. Evaluation of Health Fitness

    Cardiorespiratory Fitness (Laboratory 4)

          1.5 mile run time _____   Fitness Level _____

Muscular Strength/Endurance (MS/ME) Fitness (Laboratory 6)

  Number of sit-ups _____ Fitness Level _____

  Number of pull-ups/
  Flex Arm Hang (sec) _____ Fitness Level _____

  Number of push-ups _____ Fitness Level _____

Flexibility Fitness (Laboratory 8)

  Sit-and-Reach _____ Fitness Level _____

  Shoulder Left _____ Fitness Level _____

  Achilles Stretch _____ Fitness Level _____

Body Mass Index (Laboratory 10)

  BMI _____ Fitness Level _____

2. Health Fitness Goals

 Cardiorespiratory Fitness Fitness Level _____

 Muscular Strength/Endurance Fitness Fitness Level _____

 Flexibility Fitness Fitness Level _____

 Body Mass Index Fitness Level _____

3. Weekly Physical Activity Plan

In order to improve in health fitness, a weekly physical activity schedule needs to be planned. If not planned into one's day, exercise often is neglected.

Activity	Monday	Tuesday	Wednesday	Thursday	Friday	Saturday	Sunday
Aerobic							
MS/ME							
Flexibility							
Sports							

4. Six Week Exercise Logs

AEROBIC ACTIVITY LOG

Week		Sun	Mon	Tues	Wed	Thurs	Fri	Sat
One	Activity							
	Intensity*							
	Time							
Two	Activity							
	Intensity							
	Time							
Three	Activity							
	Intensity							
	Time							
Four	Activity							
	Intensity							
	Time							
Five	Activity							
	Intensity							
	Time							
Six	Activity							
	Intensity							
	Time							

*Record average heart rate for the entire time of the activity.

MUSCULAR STRENGTH/ENDURANCE WEIGHT TRAINING LOG

EXERCISE	Week / Day											
	WT											
	REPS											
	SETS											
	WT											
	REPS											
	SETS											
	WT											
	REPS											
	SETS											
	WT											
	REPS											
	SETS											
	WT											
	REPS											
	SETS											
	WT											
	REPS											
	SETS											
	WT											
	REPS											
	SETS											
	WT											
	REPS											
	SETS											

FLEXIBILITY LOG

Exercise	Week One Days			Week Two Days			Week Three Days			Week Four Days			Week Five Days			Week Six Days		

5. Reassessment of Health Fitness (after 6 weeks of exercise)

    Cardiorespiratory Fitness (Laboratory 4)

        1.5 mile run time _____ Fitness Level _____

    Muscular Strength/Endurance Fitness (Laboratory 6)

        Number of sit-ups _____ Fitness Level _____

        Number of pull-ups/
        Flex Arm Hang (sec) _____ Fitness Level _____

        Number of push-ups _____ Fitness Level _____

    Flexibility Fitness (Laboratory 8)

        Sit-and-Reach _____ Fitness Level _____

        Shoulder Lift _____ Fitness Level _____

        Achilles Stretch _____ Fitness Level _____

    Body Mass Index (Laboratory 10)

        BMI _____ Fitness Level _____

6. Lifestyle appraisal Retake

ANSWERS (check only one)

	almost always	frequently	often	sometimes	almost never

Personal Health Care

1. I avoid exposure to tobacco smoke.

2. When I am sick or injured, I take appropriate action to recover quickly.

3. I brush my teeth a minimum of twice a day.

4. I floss my teeth every day.

5. I get 7 to 8 hours of sleep each night.

Drugs and Alcohol

1. I do not ride in a vehicle in which the operator (this includes me) is under the influence of drugs or alcohol.

2. I avoid the use of all tobacco products.

3. I limit my alcohol consumption to less than one drink per day.

4. I only use drugs or medications when prescribed by a physician.

5. I read and follow the instructions provided with any drug or medication I take.

Fitness Physical

1. I do some light stretching before exercising and gradually increase my intensity during the work-out.

2. I increase my daily activity level by climbing stairs or walking/cycling instead of riding.

3. I drink plenty of water (or sport drink) before, during, and after a work-out.

4. I exercise aerobically (continuous jogging, walking, cycling, & etc.) for a minimum of 20 minutes 6 to 7 days per week.

5. I stretch to improve flexibility five days per week.

TOTAL NUMBER OF CHECKS IN EACH ROW	___	___	___	___	___
TIMES CONSTANT	X 1	X 2	X 3	X 4	X 5
(TRANSFER THESE NUMBERS TO PAGE)	=___	=___	=___	=___	=___

	almost always	frequently	often	sometimes	almost never

Psychological
1. I feel good about myself and the way I act.

2. I find it easy to get along with others without compromising my beliefs or morals.

3. I go to sleep quickly and wake up rested.

4. I enjoy life and the challenges it brings.

5. I have control over my emotions.

Spiritual
1. I am happy with my spiritual life.

2. Prayer is an important part of my life.

3. I read the Bible everyday.

4. I look for opportunities to share my beliefs with others.

5. People can tell I'm a Christian by the way I lead my life.

Personal Behavior
1. I worry about making decisions.

2. I accept responsibility for my actions.

3. I set realistic goals for myself.

4. Developing close, personal relationships is easy.

5. I feel at ease when placed in an unfamiliar environment.

Nutrition
1. At each meal I try to consume food that is high in fiber.

2. I try to consume foods with low levels of fats and oils.

3. I don't add salt to my food.

4. I eat several servings of fruits and vegetables each day.

5. I eat a variety of foods each day and limit my sweets.

TOTAL NUMBER OF CHECKS IN EACH ROW	____	____	____	____	____
TIMES CONSTANT	X 1	X 2	X 3	X 4	X 5
(TRANSFER THESE NUMBERS TO PAGE)	=____	=____	=____	=____	=____

Lifestyle Assessment answers from page 192. _____ _____ _____ _____ _____

from page 193. _____ _____ _____ _____ _____

Add each row and column together for a grand total of: _____

LIFESTYLE CATEGORIES

LIFESTYLE ASSESSMENT SCORE	LIFESTYLE CATEGORY
< 40	Very Healthy
41 - 70	Healthy
71 - 100	Average
101 - 130	Unhealthy
> 131	Very Unhealthy

DISCUSSION

1. Did you meet your health fitness goal for cardiorespiratory, muscular strength/endurance, and flexibility fitness? If not, why?

2. Did you improve on your lifestyle category? If not, why?

3. What do you attribute to the success or failure of your health fitness program? What changes need to be made to improve your current fitness level?

Bibliography

Chapter 1

Alters, S. & Schiff, W. (2003) *Essential Concepts for Healthy Living* (3rd Ed). Boston: Jones and Bartlett.

Berkel, N. & De Waard, P. (1983) Mortality pattern and life expectancy of seventh-day Adventists in the Netherlands. *International Journal of Epidemiology*, 12, 455-459.

Booth, F. & Chakravarthy, M. (2002) Cost and consequences of sedentary living: New battleground for an old enemy. *President's Council on Physical Fitness and Sports, Research Digest*, 3(16).

Caspersen, C., Pereira, M., & Curran, K. (2000) Changes in physical activity patterns in the United States, by sex and cross-sectional age. *Medicine and Science in Sports and Exercise*, 32(9), 1601-1609.

Centers for Medicare and Medicaid Services, Office of the Actuary, National Health Statistics Group (2009) *National Health Care Expenditures Data*, March.

Chenoweth, D. & Leutzinger, J. (2006) The economic cost of physical inactivity and excess weight in American adults. *Journal of Physical Activity and Health*, 3, 148-163.

Conn, V., Minor, A., Burks, K., Rantz, M., & Pomeroy, S. (2003) Integrative review of physical activity intervention research with aging adults. *Journal of the American Geriatrics Society*, 51(8), 1159-1168.

Council on Foreign Relations (2009) *Healthcare Cost and U.S. Competitiveness*.

Dorn, J., Vena, J., Brasure, J., Freudenheim, J., & Graham, S. (2003) Lifetime physical activity and breast cancer risk in pre- and postmenopausal women. *Medicine and Science in Sports and Exercise*, 35(2), 278-285.

Edlin, G., & Golanty, E. (2007) *Health and Wellness* (9th Ed). Sudbury, MA: Jones and Bartlett Publishers.

Enstrom, J. (1980) Cancer mortality among Mormons in California during 1968 – 1975. *Journal of Clinical Investigation*, 65, 1073 – 1082.

Enstrom, J. & Breslow, L. (2007) Lifestyle and reduced mortality among active california morons, 1980 – 2004. *Preventive Medicine*, 46, 133-136.

Hamann, B. (2001) *Disease Identification, Prevention, & Control* (2nd Ed). Boston: McGraw Hill.

Healy, G., Dunstan, D., Salmon, J., Shaw, J., Zimmet, P., & Owen, N. (2008) Television time and continuous metabolic risk in physically active adults. *Medicine and Science in Sports and Exercise*, 40(4), 639-645.

Hu, F., Manson, J., Stampfer, M., Colditz, G., Liu, S., Solomon, C., & Willet, W. (2001) Diet, Lifestyle, and the risk of type 2 diabetes mellitus in women. *New England Journal of Medicine*, 345, 790-797.

Insel, P. & Roth, W. (2004) *Core Concepts in Health* (9th Ed). Boston: McGraw Hill.

Khaw, K., Wareham, N., Bingham, S., Welch, A., Luben, R., & Day, N. (2008) Combined inpact of health behaviours and mortality in men and women: the EPIC-Norfolk prospective population study. *Public Library of Science*, 5(1), 12 – 28.

Lee, I-M. (2003) Physical activity and cancer prevention- data from epidemiologic studies. *Medicine and Science in Sports and Exercise*, 35(11), 1823-1827.

Masoro, E. (1987) Biology of aging. *Archives of Internal Medicine*, 147, 166-190.

National Health Statistics Group (2009) 2007 national health care expenditures data. *Center for Medicate and Medicaid Services*.

National Sporting Goods Association (2008) *The Sporting Goods Market in 2008*. Mount Prospect, IL:NSGA Press.

Olshansky, S. Passaro, D., Hershow, R., Hershow, R., Layden, J., Carnes, B., Brody, J., Hayflick, L., Butler, R., Allison, D., & Ludwig, D. (2005) A potential decline in life expentancy in the united states in the 21st century. *The New England Journal of Medicine*, 352(11), 1138-1145.

Phillips, R., Kuzma, J., Beeson, W., & Lotz, T. (1980) Influence of selection versus lifestyle on risk of fatal cancer and cardiovascular disease among Seventh-Day Adventists. *American Journal of Epidemiology*, 112, 269-314.

Phillips, R., Kuzma, J., Beeson, W., & Lotz, T. (1980) Mortality among California Seventh-Day Adventists for selected cancer sites. *Journal of Clinical Investigation*, 65, 1097-1107.

Putnam, S., Cerhan, J., Parker, A., Bianchi, G., Wallace, R., Cantor, K., & Lynch, C. (2000) Lifestyle and anthropometric risk factors for prostate cancer in a cohort of Iowa men. *Annals of Epidemiology*, 10(6), 361-369.

Rippe, J. (1999) *Lifestyle Medicine*. Malden, MA: Blackwell Science.

Rowland, D. (2009) Health care and Medicaid: Weathering the recession. *New England Journal of Medicine*, 360(13), 1273-1276.

Spain, C. & Franks, B. (2001) Healthy people 2010: Physical activity and fitness. *President's Council on Physical Fitness and Sports Research Digest*, 3(13), 1-16.

U. S. Department of Health and Human Services (2009) Deaths: Final data for 2006. National Vital Statistics Reports, 57(14), 1-20.

West, D. (1980) Cancer risk factors: An analysis of Utah Mormons and non-Mormons. *Journal of Clinical Investigation*, 65, 1083-1095.

Chapter 2

Autenrieth, C., Schneider, A., Doring, A., Meisinger, C., Herder, C., Koenig, W., Huber, G., & Thorand, B. (2009) Association between different domains of physical activity and markers of inflammation. *Medicine and Science in Sports and Exercise*, 41(9), 1706-1713.

Bird, S., Theakston, S., Owen, A., & Nevill, A. (2003) Characteristics associated with 10-km running performance among a group of highly trained male endurance runners age 21-63 years. *Journal of Aging and Physical Activity*, 11, 333-350.

Carroll, S., Cooke, B., & Butterly, R. (2000) Metabolic clustering, physical activity and fitness in nonsmoking, middle-aged men. *Medicine and Science in Sports and Exercise*, 32(12), 2079-2086.

Chan, J., Knutsen, S., Blix, G., Lee, J., & Fraser, G. (2002) Water, other fluids, and fatal coronary heart disease: the Adventist Health Study. *American Journal of Epidemiology*, 155(9), 827-833.

Corbin, C. & Pangrazi, R. (2000) Definitions: Health, fitness, and physical activity. *President's Council on Physical Fitness and Sports Research Digest*, 3(9), 1-8.

Cotman, C. & Engesser-Cesar, C. (2002) Exercise enhances and protects brain function. *Exercise and Sport Sciences Review*, 30(2), 75-79.

Cottreau, C., Ness, R., & Kriska, A. (2000) Physical activity and reduced risk of ovarian cancer. *Obstetrics and Gynecology*, 96(4), 609-614.

Evenson, K., Stevens, J., Cai, J., Thomas, R., & Thomas, O. (2003) The effect of cardiorespiratory fitness and obesity on cancer mortality in women and men. *Medicine and Science in Sports and Exercise*, 35(2), 270-277.

Friedenreich, C., Courneya, K., & Brayant, H. (2001) Relation between intensity of physical activity and breast cancer risk reduction. *Medicine and Science in Sports and Exercise*, 33(9), 1538-1545.

Haskel, W., Lee, I., Pate, R., Powell, K., Blair, S., Franklin, B., Macera, C., Heath, G., Thompson, P., & Bauman, A. (2007) Physical activity and public health: Updated recommendation for adults from the american college of sports medicine and the American heart association. *Medicine and Science in Sports and Exercise*, 39(8), 1423-1434.

Hutchinson, K., Alessio, H., Hoppes, S., Gruner, A., Sanker, A., Ambrose, J., & Rudge, A. (2000) Effects of cardiovascular fitness and muscle strength on hearing sensitivity. *Journal of Strength and Conditioning Research*, 14(3), 302-309.

Johnson, C., Murray, D., Elder, J., Jobe, J., Dunn, A., Kubik, M., Voorhees, C., & Schachter, K. (2008) Depressive symptoms and physical activity in adolescent girls. *Medicine and Science in Sports and Exercise*, 40(5), 818-826.

Knudson, D., Magnusson, P., & McHugh, M. (2000) Current issues in flexibility fitness. *President's Council on Physical Fitness and Sports Research Digest*, 3(10), 1-8.

Lakka, T., Laaksonen, D., Lakka, H-M., Mannikko, N., Niskanen, L. Rauramaa, R. & Salonen, J. (2003) Sedentary lifestyle, poor cardiorespiratory fitness, and the metabolic syndrome. *Medicine and Science in Sports and Exercise*, 35(8), 1279-1286.

Larew, K., Hunter, G., Larson-Meyer, D., Newcomer, B., McCarthy, J., & Weinsier, R. (2003) Muscle metabolic function, exercise performance, and weight gain. *Medicine and Science in Sports and Exercise*, 35(2), 230-236.

Lee, I-M. & Buchner, D. (2008) The importance of walking to public health. *Medicine and Science in Sports and Exercise*, 40(7S), S512-S518.

Lee, I-M., Rexrode, K., Cook, N., Hennekens, C., & Buring, J. (2001) Physical activity and breast cancer risk: The Women's Health Study. *Cancer Causes and Control*, 12, 137-145.

Lee, I-M. & Paffenbarger, R. (2001) Preventing coronary heart disease: The role of physical activity. *Physician and Sportsmedicine*, 29(2), 37-52.

Mansfield, E. (2006) Designing exercise programs to lower fracture risk in mature women. *Strength and Conditioning Journal*, 28(1), 24-29.

Martin, K. Sinden, A., & Fleming, J. (2000) Inactivity may be hazardous to your image: The effects of exercise participation on impression formation. *Journal of Sports and Exercise Psychology*, 22, 283-291.

Martin, S., Pence, B., & Woods, J. (2009) Exercise and respiratory tract viral infections. *Exercise and Sport Science Review*, 37(4), 157-164.

Matthews, C., Ockene, I., Freedson, P., Rosal, M., Merriam, P., & Hebert, J. (2002) Moderate to vigorous physical activity and risk of upper-respiratory tract infection. *Medicine and Science in Sports and Exercise*, 34(8), 1242-1248.

McArdle, W., Katch, F., & Katch, V. (2001) *Exercise Physiology: Energy, Nutrition, and Human Performance* (5th Ed). Philadelphia, PA: Lippincott Williams & Wilkins.

McGuire, D., Levine, B., Williamson, J., Snell, P., Blomqvist, C., Saltin, B., & Mitchell, J. (2001) A 30-year follow-up of the Dallas Bed Rest and Training Study II: Effect of age on cardiovascular adaptation to exercise training. *Circulation*, 104, 1358-1361.

McLean, J., Barr, S., & Prior, J. (2001) Dietary restraint, exercise, and bone density in young women: are they related? *Medicine and Science in Sports and Exercise*, 33(8), 1292-1296.

Meyer, H., Sogaard, A., Tverdal, A., & Selmer, R. (2002) Body mass index and mortality: The influence of physical activity and smoking. *Medicine and Science in Sports and Exercise*, 34(7), 1065-1070.

National Institute of Health. (2001) *Osteoporosis and Related Bone Disease*. National Resource Center Newsletter: Washington, D.C.

Nieman, D., Henson, D., Austin, M., & Brown, V. (2005) Immune response to a 30-minute walk. *Medicine and Science in Sports and Exercise*, 37(1), 57-62.

Office of the Assistant Secretary for Planning and Evaluation (2002) *Physical activity fundamental to preventing disease*. U.S. Department of Health and Human Services.

Ozkan, A. & Kin-isler, A. (2007) The reliability and validity of regulating exercise intensity by ratings of perceived exertion in step dance sessions. *Journal of Strength and Conditioning Research*, 21(1), 296-300.

Rognmo, O., Bjornstad, T., Kahrs, C., Tjonna, A., Bye, A., Haram, P., Stolen, T., Slordahl, S. & Wisloff, U. (2008) Endothelial function in highly endurance-trained men: Effects of acute exercise. *Journal of Strength and Conditioning Research*, 22(2), 535-542.

Sanchez-Villegas, A., Ara, I., Cuillen-Grima, F., Bes-Rastrollo, M., Varo-Cenarruzabettia, J. & Martinez-Gozalez, M. (2008) Physical activity, sedentary index, and mental disorders in the SUN cohort study. *Medicine and Science in Sports and Exercise*, 40(5), 827-834.

Sorichter, S., Martin, M., Julius, P., Schwirtz, A., Huonker, M., Luttmann, W., Walterspacher, S., & Berg, A. (2006) Effects of unaccustomed and accustomed exercise on the immune response in runners. *Medicine and Science in Sports and Exercise*, 38(10), 1739-1745.

Steene-Johannessen, J., Anderssen, S., Kolle, E., & Andersen, L. (2009) Low muscle fitness is associated with metabolic risk in youth. *Medicine and Science in Sports and Exercise*, 41(7), 1361-1367.

Steffen, P., Sherwood, A., Gullette, E., Georgiades, A., Hinderliter, A., & Blumenthal, J. (2001) Effects of exercise and weight loss on blood pressure during daily life. *Medicine and Science in Sports and Exercise*, 33(10), 1635-1640.

Talbot, L., Metter, E., & Fleg, J. (2000) Leisure-time physical activities and their relationship to cardiorespiratory fitness in healthy men and women 18-95 years old. *Medicine and Science in Sports and Exercise*, 32(3), 417-425.

Welk, G. & Blair, S. (2000) Physical activity protects against the health risks of obesity. *President's Council on Physical Fitness and Sports Research Digest*, 3(12), 1-8.

Chapter 3

American Heart Association. (2004) *Heart Disease and Stroke Statistical Update 2004*. Dallas, TX: American Heart Association.

Axen, K. & Axen, K. (2001) *Illustrated Principles of Exercise Physiology*. Upper Saddle River, NJ: Prentice Hall.

Mackinnon, L. (1999) *Advances in Exercise Immunology*. Champaign, IL: Human Kinetics.

McArdle, W., Katch, F., & Katch, V. (2007) *Exercise Physiology: Energy, Nutrition, & Human Performance* (6th Ed). Baltimore: Lippincott Williams & Wilkins.

Powers, S. & Howley, E. (2007) *Exercise Physiology: Theory and Application to Fitness and Performance* (6th Ed). Boston: McGraw Hill

Robergs, R. & Keteyian, S. (2003) *Fundamentals of Exercise Physiology for Fitness, Performance, and Health* (2nd Ed). Boston: McGraw Hill.

Smekal, g., Von Duvillard, S., Frigo, P., Tegelhofer, T., Pokan, R., Hofmann, P., Tschan, H., Baron, R., Wonisch, M., Renezeder, K., & Bachl, N. (2007) Menstrual cycle: No effect on exercise cardiorespiratory variables or blood lactate concentration. *Medicine and Science in Sports and Exercise*, 39(7), 1098-1106.

Chapter 4

Achten, J., Gleeson, M., & Jeukendrup, A. (2002) Determination of the exercise intensity that elicits maximal fat oxidation. *Medicine and Science in Sports and Exercise*, 34(1), 92-97.

American College of Sports Medicine (2007) Exercise and acute cardiovascular events: Placing the risks into perspective. *Medicine and Science in Sports and Exercise*, 39(5), 886-898.

American Heart Association (2008) Heart disease and stroke statistics – 2008 update. *Circulation*, 117, e25 – c146.

Bassuk, S. & Manson, J. (2003) Physical activity and cardiovascular disease prevention in women: How much is good enough? *Exercise and Sport Sciences Reviews*, 31(4), 176-181.

Braith, R. (2002) Exercise for those with chronic hearth failure. *The Physician and Sportsmedicine*, 30(9), 29-34.

Campbell, P., Campbell, K., Wener, M., Wood, B., Potter, J., McTiernan, A., & Ulrich, C. (2009) A yearlong exercise intervention decreases CRP among obese postmenopausal women. *Medicine and Science in Sports and Exercise*, 41(8), 1533-1539.

Chintanadilok, J. & Lowenthal, D. (2002) Exercise in treating hypertension. *The Physician and Sportsmedicine*, 30(3), 11-23.

Conroy, M., Cook, N., Manson, J., Buring, J., & Lee, I-M. (2005) Past physical activity, current physical activity, and risk of coronary heart disease. *Medicine and Science in Sports and Exercise*, 37(8), 1251-1256.

Dowling, E. (2001) How exercise affects lipid profiles in women. *The Physician and Sportsmedicine*, 29(9), 45-49.

Dvorak, R., Tchernof, A., & Starling, R. (2000) Respiratory fitness, free living physical activity, and cardiovascular disease risk in older individuals: A doubly labeled water study. *Journal Clinical Endocrinology and Metabolism*, 85(3), 957-963.

Dwyer, J., Navab, M., Dwyer, K., Hassan, K., Sun, P., Shircore, A., Hama-Levy, S., Hough, G., Wang, X., Drake, T., Merz, C., & Fogelman, A. (2001) Oxygenated carotenoid lutein and progression of early atherosclerosis: The Los Angeles atherosclerosis study. *Circulation*, 103(24), 2922-2927.

Eisenmann, J., Womack, C., Reeves, M., Pivarnik, J., & Malina, R. (2001) Blood lipids in young distance runners. *Medicine and Science in Sports and Exercise*, 33(10), 1661-1666.

Field, A., Coakley, E., Must, A., Spadano, J., Laird, N., Dietz, W., Rimm, E., & Colditz, G. (2001) Impact of overweight on the risk of developing common chronic diseases during a 10-year period. *Archives of Internal Medicine*, 161(13), 1581-1586.

Forman, J., Stampfer, M., & Curhan, G. (2009) Diet and lifestyle risk factors associated with incident hypertension in women. *Journal of the American Medical Association*, 302, 401-411.

Freimann, S., Kessler-icekson, G., Shahar, I., Radon-Aizik, S., Yitzhaky, A., Eldar, M., & scheinowitz, M. (2009) Exercise training alters the molecular response to myocardial infarction. *Medicine and Science in Sports and Exercise*, 41(4), 757-765.

Green, D. (2009) Exercise training as vascular medicine: direct inpacts on the vasculature in humans. *Exercise and Sport Science Review*, 37(4), 196-202.

Hamier, M. & Stamatakis, E. (2009) Physical activity and risk of cardiovascular disease events: inflammatory and metabolic mechanisms. *Medicine and Science in Sports and Exercise*, 41(6), 1206-1211.

Jakicic, J. & Gallagher, K. (2003) Exercise considerations for the sedentary, overweight adult. *Medicine and Science in Sports and Exercise*, 31(2), 91-95.

Jensen, M., Chiuve, S., & Rimm, E. (2008) Obesity, behavioral lifestyle factors, and risk of acute coronary events. *Circulation*, 117, 3062-3069.

Kamphuis, M., Geerlings, M., Tijhuis, M., Giampaoli, S., Nissinen, A., Grobbee, D., & Kromhout, D. (2007) Physical inactivity, depression, and risk of cardiovascular mortality. *Medicine and Science in Sports and Exercise*, 39(10), 1693-1699.

Kantomaa, M., Tammelin, T. Ebeling, H., & Taanila, A. (2008) Emotional and behavioral problems in relation to physical activity in youth. *Medicine and Science in Sports and Exercise*, 40(10),1749-1756.

Katzmarzyk, P., Church, T., Craig, C., & Bouchard, C. (2009) Sitting time and mortality from all causes, cardiovascular disease, and cancer. *Medicine and Science in Sports and Exercise*, 41(5), 998-1005.

Katzmarzyk, P., Gagnon, J., Leon, A., Skinner, J., Wilmore, J., Rao, D., & Bouchard, C. (2001) Fitness, fatness, and estimated coronary heart disease risk: The HERITAGE Family Study. *Medicine and Science in Sports and Exercise*, 33(4), 585-590.

Kronenberg, F., Pereira, M., Schmitz, M., Arnett, D., Evenson, K., Crapo, R., Jensen, R., Burke, G., Sholinsky, P., Ellison, R., & Hunt, S. (2000) Influence of leisure time physical activity and television watching on atherosclerosis risk factors in the NHLBI Family Heart Study. *Atherosclerosis*, 153(2), 433-443.

Lachance, D., Champetier, S., Plante, E., Bouchard-Thomassin, A., Roussel, E., Couet, J., & Arsenault, M. (2009) Effects of exercise in volume overload: insights from a model of aortic regurgitation. *Medicine and Science in Sports and Exercise*, 41(6), 1230-1238.

Laughlin, M. (2004) Physical activity in prevention and treatment of coronary disease: The battle line is in exercise vascular cell biology. *Medicine and Science in Sports and Exercise*, 36(3), 352-362.

Laukkanen, J., Lakka, T., Rauramaa, R., Kuhanen, R., Venalainen, J., Salonen, R., & Salonen, J. (2001) Cardiovascular fitness as a predictor of mortality in men. *Archive of Internal Medicine*, 26(6), 825-831.

Lee, C & Blair, S. (2002) Cardiorespiratory fitness and stroke mortality in men. *Medicine and Science in Sports and Exercise*, 34(4), 592-595.

Lee, C & Blair, S. (2002) Cardiorespiratory fitness and smoking-related and total mortality in men. *Medicine and Science in Sports and Exercise*, 34(5), 735-739.

Lee, I., Rexrode, K., Cook, N., Manson, J., & Buring, J. (2001) Physical activity and coronary heart disease in women: Is "no pain, no gain" passé? *Journal of the American Medical Association*, 285, 1447-1454.

Lee, I-M., Sesso, H., & Paffenbarger, R. (2000) Physical activity and coronary heart disease risk in men: Does the duration of exercise episodes predict risk? *Circulation*, 102(9), 981-986.

Libonati, J. (2007) Aerobic run training improves brachial artery flow-mediated dilation. *Journal of Strength and Conditioning Research*, 21(4), 1291-1295.

Ludwig, D., Pereira, M., Kroenke, C., Hilner, J., Van Horn, L., Slattery, M., & Jacobs, D. (1999) Dietary fiber, weight gain, and cardiovascular disease: Risk factors in young adults. *Journal of the American Medical Association*, 282, 1539-1546.

Marzolini, S. Oh, P., Thoman, S., & Goodman, J. (2008) Aerobic and resistance training in coronary disease: Single versus multiple sets. *Medicine and Science in Sports and Exercise*, 40(9), 1557-1564.

Milne, K. & Noble, E. (2008) Response of the myocardium to exercise: Sex-specific regulation of Hsp70. *Medicine and Science in Sports and Exercise*, 40(4), 655-662.

Mota, M., Pardono, E., Lima, L., Arsa, G., Bottaro, M., Campbell, C., & Simoes, H. (2009) Effects of treadmill running and resistance exercises on lowering blood pressure during the daily work of hypertensive subjects. *Journal of Strength and Conditioning Research*, 23(8), 2331-2338.

Pate, R., O'Neill, J., & Lobelo, F. (2008) The evolving definition of "sedentary". *Exercise and Sport Science Review*, 36(4), 173-178.

Pescatello, L., Franklin, B., Fagard, R., Farquhar, W., Kelley, G., & Ray, C. (2004) Exercise and hypertension. *Medicine and Science in Sports and Exercise*, 36(3), 533-553.

Rankinen, T., Church, T., Rice, T., Bouchard, C., & Blair, S. (2007) Cardiorespiratory fitness, BMI, and risk of hypertension: The HYPGENE study. *Medicine and Science in Sports and Exercise*, 39(10), 1687-1692.

Reifenberger, M., Turk, J., Newcomer, S., Booth, F., & Laughlin, M. (2007) Perivascular fat alters reactivity of coronary artery: Effects of diet and exercise. *Medicine and Science in Sports and Exercise*, 39(12), 2125-2134.

Richardson, C., Kriska, A., Lantz, P. & Hayward, R. (2004) Physical activity and mortality across cardiovascular disease risk groups. *Medicine and Science in Sports and Exercise*, 36(11), 1923-1929.

Roetert, E. (2006) Lifelong physical fitness to prevent heart disease. *Strength and Conditioning Journal*, 28(3), 75-76.

Roger, V. (2009) Lifestyle and cardiovascular health individual and societal choices. *Journal of the American Medical Association*, 302, 437-439.

Slentz, C., Hournard, J., & Kraus, W. (2007) Modest exercise prevents the progressive disease associated with physical inactivity. *Exercise and Sport Science Reviews*, 35(1), 18-23.

Smith, J. (2001) Exercise and Atherogenesis. *Exercise and Sport Sciences Reviews*, 29(2) 49-53.

Sorace, P. (2006) Exercise, physical activity, and dyslipidemia. *Strength and Conditioning Journal*, 28(4), 57-59.

Telford, R. (2007) Low physical activity and obesity: Causes of chronic disease or simply predictors? *Medicine and Science in Sports and Exercise*, 39(8), 1233-1240.

Thompson, P. (2001) Exercise rehabilitation for cardiac patients: A beneficial but underused therapy. *Physician and Sportsmedicine*, 29(1), 69-75.

Tuomilehto, J., Lindstrom, J., Eriksson, J., Valle, T., Hamalainen, H., Ilanne-Parikka, P., Keinanen-Kiukaanniemi, S., Laakso, M., Louheranta, A., Rastas, M., Salminen, V., & Uusitupa, M. (2001) Prevention of type 2 diabetes mellitus by changes in lifestyle among subjects with impaired glucose tolerance. *New England Journal of Medicine*, 344(18), 1343-1350.

Twisk, J., Kemper, H., & Van Mechelen, W. (2000) Tracking of activity and fitness and the relationship with cardiovascular disease risk factors. *Medicine and Science in Sports and Exercise*, 32(8), 1455-1461.

Vainionpaa, A., Korpelainen, R., Kaikkonen, H., Knip, M., Leppaluoto, J., & Jamsa, T. (2007) Effect of impact exercise on physical performance and cardiovascular risk factors. *Medicine and Science in Sports and Exercise*, 39(5), 756-736.

Wannamethee, S., Shaper, A., & Walker, M. (2000) Physical activity and mortality in older men with diagnosed coronary heart disease. *Circulation*, 102(12), 1358-1363.

Williams, P. (2001) Physical fitness and activity as separate heart disease risk factors: A meta-analysis. *Medicine and Science in Sports and Exercise*, 33(5), 754-761.

Williams, P. (2008) relationship of running intensity to hypertension, hypercholesterolemia, and diabetes. *Medicine and Science in Sports and Exercise*, 40(10), 1740-1748.

Williams, P. (2009) Incident hypercholesterolemia in relation to changes in vigorous physical activity. *Medicine and Science in Sports and Exercise*, 41(1), 73-80.

Williams, P. (2009) Lower prevalence of hypertension, hypercholesterolemia, and diabetes in marathoners. *Medicine and Science in Sports and Exercise*, 41(3), 523-529.

Wing, R., Jakicic, J., Neiberg, Lang, W., Blair, S., Cooper, L., Hill, J., Johnson, K., Lewis, C., & the Look Ahead Research Group (2007) fitness, fatness, and cardiovascular risk factors in type 2 diabetes: Look AHEAD study. *Medicine and Science in Sports and Exercise*, 39(12), 2107-2116.

Wu, T., Trevisan, M., Genco, R., Dorn, J., Falkner, K., & Sempos, C. (2000) Periodontal disease and risk of cerebrovascular disease: The first national health and nutrition examination survey and its follow-up study. *Archives of Internal Medicine*, 160(18), 2749-2755.

Chapter 5

American College of Sports Medicine. (2009) Position stand: Progression models in resistance training for healthy adults. *Medicine and Science in Sports and Exercise*, 41(3), 687-694.

Andreoli, A., Monteleone, M., Van Loan, M., Promenzio, L., Tarantino, U., & De Lorenzo, A. (2001) Effects of different sports on bone density and muscle mass in highly trained athletes. *Medicine and Science in Sports and Exercise*, 33(4), 507-511.

Beck, T., Housh, T., Johnson, G., Weir, J., Cramer, J., Coburn, J., Malek, M., & Mielke, M. (2007) Effects of two days of isokinetic training on strength and electromyographic amplitude in the agonist and antagonist muscles. *Journal of Strength and Conditioning Research*, 21(3), 757-762.

Binzen, C., Swan, P., & Manore, M. (2001) Post exercise oxygen consumption and substrate use after resistance exercise in women. *Medicine and Science in Sports and Exercise*, 33(6), 932-938.

Buresh, R., Berg, K., & French, J. (2009) The effect of resistive exercise rest interval on hormonal response, strength, and hypertrophy with training. *Journal of Strength and Conditioning Research*, 23(1), 62-71.

Coffey, V., Reeder, D., Lancaster, G., Yeo. W., Febbraio, M., Yaspelkis, B. & Hawley, J. (2007) Effect of high-frequency resistance exercise on adaptive responses in skeletal muscle. *Medicine and Science in Sports and Exercise*, 39(12), 2135-2144.

Cormie, P., McCaulley, G., & McBride, J. (2007) Power versus strength-power jump squat training: Influence on the load-power relationship. *Medicine and Science in Sports and Exercise*, 39(6), 996-1003.

Craig, B. & Judge, L. (2009) The basics of resistance training program design: Where do I start! *Strength and conditioning Journal*, 31(6), 75-77.

Creighton, D., Morgan, A., & Boardley, D. (2001) Weight-bearing exercise and markers of bone turnover in female athletes. *Journal of Applied Physiology*, 90(2), 565-570.

Dorgo, S., King, G., & Rice, C. (2009) The effects of manual resistance training on improving muscular strength and endurance. *Journal of Strength and Conditioning Research*, 23(1), 293-303.

Ebben, W. & Leigh, D. (2006) The effects of resistance training on cardiovascular patients. *Strength and Conditioning Journal*, 28(2), 54-58.

Fahey, T. (2003) *Basic Weight Training for Men and Women* (5th Ed). Boston: McGraw Hill.

Franco, B., Signorelli, G., trajano, G., & De Oliveira, C. (2008) acute effects of different stretching exercise on muscular endurance. *Journal of Strength and Conditioning Research*, 22(6), 1832-1837.

Garcia-Lopez, D., De Paz, J., Moneo, E., Jimenez-Jimenez, R., Bresciani, G., & Izquierdi, M. (2007) Effects of short vs. long rest period between sets on elbow-flexor muscular endurance during resistance training to failure. *Journal of Strength and Conditioning Research*, 21(4), 1320-1324.

Hass, C., Garzarella, L., De Hoyos, D., & Pollock, M. (2000) Single versus multiple sets in long-term recreational weightlifters. *Medicine and Science in Sports and Exercise*, 32(1), 235-242.

Humburg, H., Baars, H., Schroder, J., Reer, R., & Braumann, K. (2007) 1-set vs. 3-set resistance training: A crossover study. *Journal of Strength and Conditioning Research*, 21(2), 578-582.

Hunter, G., Wetzstein, C., & Fields, D. (2000) Resistance training increases total energy expenditure and free-living physical activity in older adults. *Journal of Applied Physiology*, 89(3), 977-984.

Ikeda, E., Borg, A., Brown, D., Malouf, J., Showers, K., & Li, S. (2009) The Valsalva maneuver revisited: The influence of voluntary breathing on isometric muscle strength. *Journal of Strength and Conditioning Research*, 23(1), 127-132.

Katzmarzyk, P. & Craig, C. (2002) Musculoskeletal fitness and risk of mortality. *Medicine and Science in Sports and Exercise*, 34(5), 740-744.

Kelly, S., brown, L., Coburn, J., Zinder, S., Gardner, L., & Nguyen, D. (2007) The effect of single versus multiple sets on strength. *Journal of Strength and Conditioning Research*, 21(4), 1003-1006.

Khike, K. & Greenwood, M. (2006) Resistance exercise for post-myocardial infarction patients: Current guidelines and future considerations. *Strength and Conditioning Journal*, 28(6), 56-62.

Krieger, J. (2009) Single versus multiple sets of resistance exercise: a meta-regression. *Journal of Strength and Conditioning Research*, 23(6), 1890-1901.

Kraemer, W., Adams, K., Cafarelli, E., Dudly, G., Dooly, C., Feigerbaum, M. Fleck, S., Franklin, B., Fry, A., Hoffman, J., Newton, R., Potteiger, J., Stone, M., Ratamess, N., & Triplett-McBride, T. (2002) Progression models in resistance training for healthy adults. *Medicine and Science in Sports and Exercise*, 34(2), 364-380.

Kraemer, W., Keuning, M., Ratamess, N., Volek, J., McCormick, M., Bush, J., Nindl, B., Gordon, S., Mazzetti, S., Newton, R., Gomex, A., Wickham, R., Rubin, M., & Hakkinen, K. (2001) Resistance training combined with bench-step aerobics enhances women's health profile. *Medicine and Science in Sports and Exercise*, 33(2), 259-269.

Lagally, K., Cordero, J., Good, J., brown, D., & McCaw, S. (2009) Physiologic and metabolic responses to a continuous functional resistance exercise workout. *Journal of Strength and Conditioning Research*, 23(2), 373-379.

LaFontaine, T. (2001) Strength and conditioning in the prevention and management of cerebrovascular accident (stroke). *Strength and Conditioning Journal*, 23(6), 49-52.

Lowndes, J., Carpenter, R., Zoeller, R., Seip, R., Moyna, N., Price, T., Clardson, P., Gordon, P., Pescatello, L., Visich, P., Devaney, J., Gordish-Dressman, H., Hoffman, E., Thompson, P., & Angelopoulos, T. (2009) *Journal of Strength and Conditioning Research*, 23(7), 1915-1920.

Mejia, S. & Sorace, P. (2008) Strength and conditioning for frail persons. *Strength and Conditioning Journal*, 30(6), 36-40.

Mirand, H., fleck, S., simao, R., barreto, A., dantas, E., & Novaes, J. (2007) effect of two different rest period lengths on the number of repetitions performed during resistance training. *Journal of Strength and Conditioning Research*, 21(4), 1032-1036.

Musa, D., Adeniran, S., Dikko, A., & Sayers, S. (2009) the effect of a high-intensity interval training program on high-density lipoprotein cholesterol in young men. *Journal of Strength and Conditioning Research*, 23(2), 587-592.

National Strength and Conditioning Association (2000) *Essentials of Strength Training and Conditioning* (2nd Ed). Champaign, IL: Human Kinetics.

Nguyen, V., Loethen, J., & Lafontaine, T. (2008) Resistance training and dietary supplementation for persons with reduced bone mineral density. *Strength and Conditioning Research*, 30(5), 28-31.

O'Connor, B., Simmons, J., & O'Shea, P. (2000) *Strength Training Today* (2nd Ed). Belmont, CA: Wadsworth Thomson Learning.

Queiroz, A., Gagliardi, J., Fobjaz, C., & Rezk, C. (2009) Clinic and ambulatory blood pressure responses after resistance exercise. *Journal of Strength and Conditioning Research*, 23(2), 571-578.

Ross, M. & Denegar, C. (2001) Effect of exercise on bone mineral density in postmenopausal women. *Strength and Conditioning Journal*, 23(4), 30-35.

Sewright, K., Hubal, M., Kearns, A., Holbrook, M., & Clarkson, P. (2008) Sex differences in response to maximal eccentric exercise. *Medicine and Science in Sports and Exercise*, 40(2), 242-251.

Sorace, P., Mahady, T., & Brignola, N. (2009) Hypertension and resistance training. *Strength and Conditioning Journal*, 31(1), 33-35.

Vaile, J., Gill, N., & Blazevich, A. (2007) The effect of contrast water therapy on symptoms of delayed onset muscle soreness. *Journal of Strength and Conditioning Research*, 21(3), 697-702.

Walts, C., Hanson, E., Delmonico, M., Yao, L., Wang, M., & Hurley, B. (2008) Do sex or race differences influence strength training effects on muscle or fat? *Medicine and Science in Sports and Exercise*, 40(4), 669-676.

Willardson, J. & Burkett, L. (2008) The effect of different rest intervals between sets on volume components and strength gains. *Journal of Strength and Conditioning Research*, 22(1), 146-152.

Chapter 6

Ali, A., Williams, C., Nicholas, C., & Foskett, A. (2007) The influence of carbohydrate- electrolyte ingestion on soccer skill performance. *Medicine and Science in Sports and Exercise*, 39(11), 1969-1976.

Alter, M. (1996) *Science of Flexibility* (2nd Ed). Champaign, IL: Human Kinetics.

American College of Sports Medicine. (2006) *ACSM's Guidelines for Exercise Testing and Prescription* (7th Ed). Philadelphia: Lippincott Williams and Wilkins.

American College of Sports Medicine. (2006) Prevention of cold injuries during exercise. *Medicine and Science in Sports and Exercise*, 38(12), 2012-2020.

American College of Sports Medicine, (2007) Exercise and fluid replacement. *Medicine and Science in Sports and Exercise*, 39(2), 377-387.

American College of Sports Medicine. (2007) Exertional heat illness during training and competition. *Medicine and Science in Sports and Exercise*, 39(3), 556-566.

Andersen, J. (2006) Flexibility in performance: foundational concepts and practical issues, *Athletic Therapy Today*, 11(3), 9-12.

Armstrong, L., Casa, D., Maresh, C., & Ganio, M. (2007) Caffeine, fluid-electrolyte balance, temperature regulation, and exercise-heat tolerance. *Exercise and Sport Science Review*, 35(3), 135-140.

Bacurau, R., Monteiro, G., Ugrinowitsch, C., Tricoli, V., Cabral, F., & Aoki, M. (2009) Acute effect of a ballistic and a static stretching exercise bout on flexibility and maximal strength. *Journal of Strength and Conditioning Research*, 23(1), 304-308.

Bazett-Jones, D., Gibson, M., & McBride, J. (2008) Sprint and vertical jump performances are not affected by six weeks of static hamstring stretching. *Journal of Strength and Conditioning Research*, 22(1), 25-31.

Beckett, J., Schneiker, K., Wallman, K., Dawson, B., & Guelfi, K. (2009) Effects of static stretching on repeated sprint and change of direction performance. *Medicine and Science in Sports and Exercise*, 41(2), 444-450.

Beedle, B. & Mann, C. (2007) A comparison of two warm-ups on joint range of motion. *Journal of Strength and Conditioning Research*, 21(3), 776-779.

Bradley, P. Olsen, P., & Portas, M. (2007) The effect of static, ballistic, and proprioceptive neuromuscular facilitation stretching on vertical jump performance. *Journal of Strength and Conditioning Research*, 21(1), 223-226.

Brooks, G., Fahey, T., White, T. & Baldwin, K. (2000) *Exercise Physiology: Human Bioenergetics and Its Applications* (3rd Ed). Mountain View, CA: Mayfield Publishing.

Caplan, N., Rogers, R., Parr, M., & Haves, P. (2009) The effect of proprioceptive neuromuscular facilitation and static stretch training on running mechanics. *Journal of Strength and Conditioning Research*, 23(4), 1175-1180.

Chinevere, T., Kenefick, R., cheuvront, S., Lukaski, H., & Sawka, M. (2008) Effect of heat acclimation on sweat minerals. *Medicine and Science in Sports and Exercise*, 40(5), 886-891.

Coso, J., Estevez, E., & Mora-Rodriguez, R. (2009) Caffeine during exercise in the heat: Thermoregulation and fluid-electrolyte balance. *Medicine and Science in Sports and Exercise*, 41(1), 164-173.

Dalleck, L., borresen, E., wallenta, J., Zahler, K., & Boyd, E. (2008) A moderate-intensity exercise program fulfilling the America college of sports medicine net energy expenditure recommendation improves health outcomes in premenopausal women. *Journal of Strength and Conditioning Research*, 22(1), 256-262.

Doriot, N. & Wangh, X. (2006) Effects of age and gender on maximum voluntary range of motion of the upper body joints. *Ergonomics*, 49(3), 269-81.

Dougherty, K., Chow, M., & Kenney, W. (2009) Responses of lean and obese boys to repeated summer exercise in the heat bouts. *Medicine and Science in Sports and Exercise*, 41(2), 279-289.

Hawkins, J. & Hawkins, S. (2001) *Walking for Fun and Fitness* (3rd Ed). Belmont, CA: Wadsworth/Thomson Learning.

Hough, P., Ross, E., & Howatson, G. (2009) Effects of dynamic and static stretching on vertical jump performance and electromyographic activity. *Journal of Strength and Conditioning Research*, 23(2), 507-512.

Huber, F. (2006) *Essentials of Physical Activity Laboratory Manual* (6th Ed). Peosta, IL: Eddie Bowers Publishing.

Johannsen, N., Lind, E., King, D., & Sharp, R. (2009) Effect of Preexercise electrolyte ingestion on fluid balance in men and women. *Medicine and Science in Sports and Exercise*, 41(11), 2017-2025.

Jones, L., Cleary, M., Lopez, R., Zuri, R., & Lopez, R. (2008) Active dehydration impairs upper and lower body anaerobic muscular power. *Journal of Strength and Conditioning Research*, 22(2), 455-463.

Judelson, D., Maresh, C., Farrell, M., Yamamoto, L., Armstrong, L., Kraemier, W., Volek, J., Spiering, B., Casa, D., & Anderson, J. (2007) Effect of hydration state on strength, power, and resistance exercise performance. *Medicine and Science in Sports and Exercise*, 39(10), 1817-1824.

Kenefick, R., Ely, B., Cheuvront, S., Palombo, L., Goodman, D., & Sawka, M. (2009) Prior heat stress: Effect on subsequent 15-min time trial performance in the heat. *Medicine and Science in Sports and Exercise*, 41(6), 1311-1316.

Kilpatrick, M., Robertson, R., Powers, J., Mears, J., & Ferrer, N. (2009) Comparisons of RPE before, during, and after self-regulated aerobic exercise. *Medicine and Science in Sports and Exercise*, 41(3), 681-686.

Kirwan, J. & Jing, M. (2002) Modulation of insulin signaling in human skeletal muscle in response to exercise. *Exercise and Sport Sciences Reviews*, 30(2), 85-95.

Kokkonen, J., Nelson, A., Eldredge, C., & Winchester, J. (2007) Chronic static stretching improves exercise performance. *Medicine and Science in Sports and Exercise*, 39(10), 1825-1831.

LaRoche, D., Lussier, M., & Roy, S. (2008) Chronic stretching and voluntary muscle force. *Journal of Strength and Conditioning Research*, 22(2), 5890-596.

Lee, J., Shirreffs, S., & Maughan, R. (2008) Cold drink ingestion improves exercise endurance capacity in the heat. *Medicine and Science in Sports and Exercise*, 40(9), 1637-1644.

Mahieu, N., McNair, P., De Muynck, M., Stevens, V., blanckaert, I., Smits, N., & Witvrouw, E. (2007) Effect of static and ballistic stretching on the muscle-tendon tissue properties. *Medicine and Science in Sports and Exercise*, 39(3), 494-501.

Magal, M. (2005) Hyperhydration strategies: Are they effective? *Strength and Conditioning Journal*, 27(5), 86-90.

Martin, S., Morrow, J., Jackson, A., & Dunn, A. (2000) Variables related to meeting the CDC/ACSM physical activity guidelines. *Medicine and Science in Sports and Exercise*, 32(12), 2087-2092.

Nelson, R. & Bandy, W. (2005) An update on flexibility. *Strength and conditioning Journal*, 27(1), 10-16.

Potteiger, J., Schroeder, J., & Goff, K. (2000) Influence of music on ratings of perceived exertion during 20 minutes of moderate intensity exercise. *Perceptual and Motor Skills*, 91(3), 848-854.

Rafferty, A., Reeves, M., McGee, H., & Pivarnik, J. (2002) Physical activity patterns among walkers and compliance with public health recommendations. *Medicine and Science in Sports and Exercise*, 34(8), 1255-1261.

Rancour, J., Holmes, C., & Cipriant, D. (2009) The effects of intermittent stretching following a 4-week static stretching protocol: a randomized trial. *Journal of Strength and Conditioning Research*, 23(8), 2217-2222.

Rector, R., Rogers, R., Ruebel, M., Widzer, M., & Hinton, P. (2009) Lean body mass and weight-bearing activity in the prediction of bone mineral density in physically active men. *Journal of Strength and Conditioning Research*, 23(2), 427-435.

Riewald, S. (2008) Changes in sweat mineral concentrations after heat acclimatization. *Strength and Conditioning Journal*, 30(6), 45-46.

Rodriguez, R., Coso, J., & Estevez, E. (2008) Thermoregulatory responses to constant versus variable-intensity exercise in the heat. *Medicine and Science in Sports and Exercise*, 40(11), 1945-1952.

Rosato, F. (2000) *Jogging and Walking for Health & Fitness* (4th Ed). Englewood, CO: Morton Publishing.

Ross, C. (2000) Walking, exercising, and smoking: Does neighborhood matter? *Social Science and Medicine*, 51, 265-274.

Roland, T., Hagenbuch, S., Pober, D., & Garrison, A. (2008) Exercise tolerance and thermoregulatory responses during cycling in boys and men. *Medicine and Science in Sports and Exercise*, 40(2), 282-287.

Sexton, P. & Chambers, J. (2006) The importance of flexibility for functional range of motion. *Athletic Therapy Today*, 11(3), 13-17.

Sharman, M., Cresswell, A., & Riek, S. (2006) Proprioceptive neuromuscular facilitation stretching: Mechanisms and clinical implication. *Sports Medicine*, 36(11), 929-939.

Shrier, I. (2004) Does stretching improve performance? A systematic and critical review of the literature. *Clinical Journal of Sports Medicine*, 14(5), 267-273.

Sim, A., Dawson, B., Guelfi, K., Wallman, K., & Young, W. (2009) Effects of static stretching in warm-up on repeated sprint performance. *Journal of Strength and Conditioning Research*, 23(7), 2155-2162.

Stewart, R., Duhamel, T., Rich, S. Tupling, A., & green, H. (2008) Effects of consecutive days of exercise and recovery on muscle mechanical function. *Medicine and Science in Sports and Exercise*, 40(2), 316-325.

Stone, M., O'Bryant, H., Ayers, C., & Sands, W. (2006) Stretching: Acute and chronic? The potential consequences. *Strength and Conditioning Journal*, 28(6), 66-74.

Swanson, J. (2006) A functional approach to warm-up and flexibility. *Strength and Conditioning Journal*, 28(5), 30-36.

Thacker, S., Gilchrist, J., Stroup, D., & Kimsey, JR., C. (2004) The impact of stretching on sports injury risk: A systematic review of the literature. *Medicine and Science in Sports and Exercise*, 36(3), 371-378.

Thomas, D., Lewis, H., McCaw, S., & Adams, M. (2001) The effects of continuous and discontinuous walking on physiologic response in college-age subjects. *Journal of Strength and Conditioning Research*, 15(2), 264-265.

Vandervoort, A. (2009) Potential benefits of warm-up for neuromuscular performance of older athletes. *Exercise and Sport Science Review*, 37(2), 60-65.

Vetter R. (2007) Effects of six warm-up protocols on sprint and jump performance. *Journal of Strength and Conditioning Research*, 21(3), 819-823.

Wisleff, U., Ellingsen, O., & Kemi, O. (2009) High-intensity interval training to maximize cardiac benefits of exercise training? *Exercise and Sport Science Review*, 37(3), 139-146.

Woods, K., Bishop, P., & Jones, E. (2007) Warm-up and stretching in the prevention of muscular injury. *Sports Medicine*, 37(12), 1089-1099.

Wyon, M., Felton, L., & Galloway, S. (2009) A comparison of 2 stretching modalities on lower-limb range of motion measurements in recreational dancers. *Journal of Strength and Conditioning Research*, 23(7), 2144-2148.

Chapter 7

Abdel-Hamid, T. (2003) Exercise and diet in obesity treatment: An integrative system dynamics perspective. *Medicine and Science in Sports and Exercise*, 35(3), 400-414.

Alexander, J. (2002) The role of resistance exercise in weight loss. *Strength and Conditioning Journal*, 24(1), 65-69.

American College of Sports Medicine. (2009) Position stand: Appropriate physical activity intervention strategies for weight loss and prevention of weight regain for adults. *Medicine and Science in Sports and Exercise*, 41(2), 459-469.

Basterra-Gortari, F., Bes-Rastrollo, M., Pardo-fernandez, M., Forga, I., Martinez, J., & Martinez-Gonzalez, M. (2009) Changes in weight and physical activity over two years in Spanish alumni. *Medicine and Science in Sports and Exercise*, 41(3), 516-522.

Brown, S., Norris, J., Torgan, C., Duscha, B., Bales, C., Slentz, C., & Kraus, W. (2000) Effects of moderate exercise training in the absence of weight loss on cardiovascular risk factors in mildly obese subjects. *Clinical Exercise Physiology*, 2(1), 27-33.

Carey, D. (2009) Quantifying differences in the "fat burning" zone and the aerobic zone: implications for training. *Journal of Strength and Conditioning Research*, 23(7), 2090-2095.

Carroll, J. & Kyser, C. (2002) Exercise training in obesity lowers blood pressure independent of weight change. *Medicine and Science in Sports and Exercise*, 34(4), 596-601.

Davis, J., Tung, A., Chak, S., Ventura, E., Byrd-Williams, C., Alexander, K., Lane, C., Weigensberg, M., Sprulit-Metz, D., & Goran, M. (2009) Aerobic and strength training reduces adiposity in overweight latina adolescents. *Medicine and Science in Sports and Exercise*, 71(7), 1494-1503.

Dietz, W. (2004) The effects of physical activity on obesity. *Quest*, 56, 1-11.

Dixon, C. & Andreacct, J. (2009) Effect of resistance exercise on percent body fat using leg-to-leg and segmental bioelectrical impedance analysis in adult. *Journal of Strength and Conditioning Research*, 23(7), 2025-2032.

Donnelly, J. & smith, B. (2005) Is exercise effective for weight loss with ad libitum diet? Energy balance, compensation, and gender difference. *Exercise and Sport Sciences Reviews*, 33(4), 169-174.

Erichman, J., Kerbey, A., & James, W. (2002) Physical activity and its impact on health outcomes. Paper 2: Prevention of unhealthy weight gain and obesity by physical activity: An analysis of the evidence. *International Association for the Study of Obesity*, 3, 273-287.

Finkelstein, B., Fiebelkorn, F., & Wang, T. (2004) State-level estimates of annual medical expenditures attributable to obesity. *Obesity Research*, 12, 18-24.

Hollowell, R., Willis, L., Slentz, C., Topping, J., Bhakpar, M., & Kraus, W. (2009) Effects of exercise training amount on physical activity energy expenditure. *Medicine and Science in Sports and Exercise*, 41(8), 1640-1644.

Jakicic, J., Clark, K., Coleman, E., Donnelly, J., Foreyt, J., Melanson, E., Volek, J., & Volpe, S. (2001) Appropriate intervention strategies for weight loss and prevention of weight regain for adults. *Medicine and Science in Sports and Exercise*, 33(12), 2145-2156.

Jonas, S. (2001) Weighing in on the obesity epidemic: What do we do now? *ACSM's Health and Fitness Journal*, 5(5), 7-11.

Joyner, M. (2003) Obesity update. *Exercise and Sport Sciences Reviews*, 31(1), 1-2.

Kavouras, S., Panagiotakos, D., Pitsavos, C., Chrysohoou, C., Anastasiou, C., Lentzas, Y., & Stefanadis, C. (2007) Physical activity, obesity status, and Glycemic control: The ATTICA study. *Medicine and Science in Sports and Exercise*, 39(4), 606-611.

Kemmler, W., Stengel, S., Engelke, K., & Kalender, W. (2009) Exercise decreases the risk of metabolic syndrome in elderly females. *Medicine and Science in Sports and Exercise*, 41(2), 297-305.

Kondo, D. & Sokol, M. (2006) Eating disorders in primary care. *Postgraduate Medicine*, 119(3), 59-65.

Koutsari, C., Karpe, F., Humphreys, S., Frayn, K., & Hardman, A. (2001) Exercise prevents the accumulation of triglyceride-rich lipoproteins and their remnants seen when changing to a high-carbohydrate diet. *Arteriosclerosis, Thrombosis, and Vascular Biology*, 21(9), 1520-1525.

Lee, M., Sedlock, D., Flynn, M., & Kanimori, G. (2009) Resting metabolic rate after endurance exercise training. *Medicine and Science in Sports and Exercise*, 41(7), 1444-1451.

LeMura, L., Von Duvillard, S., Andreacci, J., Klebez, J., Chelland, S., & Russo, J. (2000) Lipid and lipoprotein profiles, cardiovascular fitness, body composition, and diet during and after resistance, aerobic and combination training in young women. *European Journal of Applied Physiology*, 82(5), 451-458.

Malatesta, D., Werlen, C., Bulfaro, S., Cheneviere, X., & Borrani, F. (2009) Effect of high-intensity interval exercise on lipid oxidation during postexercise recovery. *Medicine and Science in Sports and Exercise*, 41(2), 364-374.

Mayo, M., Grantham, J., & Balasekaran, G. (2003) Exercise-induced weight loss preferentially reduces abdominal fat. *Medicine and Science in Sports and Exercise*, 35(2), 207-213.

McGuigan, M., Tatasciore, M., Newton, R., & Pettigrew, S. (2009) Eight weeks of resistance training can significantly alter body composition in children who are overweight or obese. *Journal of Strength and Conditioning Research*, 23(1), 80-85.

Melanson, E., Maclean, P., & Hill, J. (2009) Exercise improves fat metabolism in muscle but does not increase 24-h oxidation. *Exercise and Sport Science Review*, 37(2) 93-101.

Mestek, M., Plaisance, E., Ratcliff, L., Taylor, J., Wee, S., & Grandjean, P. (2008) Aerobic exercise and postprandial lipemia in men with the metabolic syndrome. *Medicine and Science in Sports and Exercise*, 40(12), 2105-2111.

Mudd, L., Rafferty, A., Reeves, M., & Pivarnik, J. (2008) Physical activity recommendations: An alternative approach using energy expenditure. *Medicine and Science in Sports and Exercise*, 40(10), 1757-1763.

Plowman, S. & Smith, D. (2002) *Exercise Physiology for Health, Fitness, and Performance* (2nd Ed). San Francisco: Bejamin Cummings.

Poston, W. & Foreyt, J. (2002) Body mass index: Uses and limitations. *Strength and Conditioning Journal*, 24(4), 15-17.

Riewald, S. (2007) what is the cost of being inactive or overweight? *Strength and Conditioning Journal*, 29(6), 23-24.

Rolls, B. & Bell, E. (2000) Dietary approaches to the treatment of obesity. *Medical Clinics of North America*, 84(2), 401-418.

Ross, R., Dagnone, D., Jones, P., Smith, H., Paddags, A., Hudson, R., & Janssen, I.(2000) Reduction in obesity and related comorbid conditions after diet-induced weight loss or exercise-induced weight loss in men. A randomized, controlled trial. *Annals of Internal Medicine*, 133(2), 92-103.

Ross, R., Freeman, J., & Janssen, I. (2000) Exercise alone is an effective strategy for reducing obesity and related comorbidities. *Exercise and Sport Sciences Reviews*, 28(4), 165-170.

Sundgot-Borgen, J., Rosenvinge, J., Bahr, R., & Schneider, L. (2002) The effect of exercise, cognitive therapy, and nutritional counseling in treating bulimia nervosa. *Medicine and Science in Sports and Exercise*, 34(2), 190-195.

Trichopoulou, A., Gnardellis, C., Benetou, V., Lagiou, P., Bamia, C., & Trichopoulos, D. (2002) Lipid, protein, and carbohydrate intake in relation to body mass index. *European Journal of Clinical Nutrition*, 56(1), 37-43.

U.S. Department of Health and Human Services. (2001) *The Surgeon General's Call to Action to Prevent and Decrease Overweight and Obesity*. Rockville, MD: U.S. Government Printing Office.

Williams, P. (2007) Maintaining vigorous activity attenuates 7-yr weight gain in 8340 runners. *Medicine and Science in Sports and Exercise*, 39(5), 801-809.

Williams, P. (2008) Asymmetric weight gain and loss from increasing and decreasing exercise. *Medicine and Science in Sports and Exercise*, 40(2), 296-302.

Willis, G., Smith, F., & Willis, A. (2009) Frequency of exercise for body fat loss: a controlled cohort study. *Journal of Strength and Conditioning Research*, 23(8), 2377-2380.

Chapter 8

Aagaard, P., Magnusson, P., Larsson, B., Kjer, M., & Krustrup, P. (2007) Mechanical muscle function, morphology, and fiber type in lifelong training elderly. *Medicine and Science in Sports and Exercise*, 39(11), 1989-1996.

Adams, K., O'Shea, P., & O'Shea, K. (1999) Aging: Its effects on strength, power, flexibility, and bone density. *Strength and Conditioning Journal*, 21(2), 65-77.

American College of Sports Medicine (2004) Physical activity programs and behavior counseling in older adult populations. *Medicine and Science in Sports and Exercise*, 36(11), 1997-2005.

American College of Sports Medicine (2009) Position stand: Exercise and physical activity for older adults. *Medicine and Science in Sports and Exercise*, 41(7), 1510-1530.

Anaya, S., Church, T., Blair, S., Myers, J., & Earnest, C. (2009) Exercise dose-response of the Ve/VCO2 slope in postmenopausal women in the DREW study. *Medicine and Science in Sports and Exercise*, 41(5), 971-976.

Arent, S., Landers, D., & Etnier, J. (2000) The effects of exercise on mood in older adults: A meta-analytic review. *Journal of Aging and Physical Activity*, 8, 407-430.

Ashe, M., Eng, J., Miller, W., & Soon, J. (2007) Disparity between physical capacity and participation in seniors with chronic disease. *Medicine and Science in Sports and Exercise*, 39(7), 1139-1146.

Beck, B. & Snow, C. (2003) Bone health across the lifespan – Exercising our options. *Exercise and Sport Sciences Reviews*, 31(3), 117-122.

Bellew, J., Symons, T., & Vandervoort, A. (2005) Geriatric fitness: Effects of aging and recommendations for exercise in older adults. *Cardiopulmonary Physical Therapy Journal*, 16(1), 20-31.

Besson, H., Ekelund, U., Brage, S., Luben, R., Bingham, S., Khaw, K., & Wareham, N. (2008) Relationship between subdomains of total physical activity and mortality. *Medicine and Science in Sports and Exercise*, 40(11), 1909-1915.

Bischoff, H., Conzelmann, M., & Lindemann, D. (2001) Self-reported exercise before age 40: Influence on quantitative skeletal ultrasound and fall risk in the elderly. *Archive of Physical Medicine Rehabilitation*, 82, 801-806.

Boon, H., Jonkers, R., Koopman, R., Blaak, E., saris, W., Wagenmakers, A., & Van Loon, L. (2007) substrate source use in older, trained males after decades of endurance training. *Medicine and Science in Sports and Exercise*, 39(12), 2160-2170.

Boreham, C., Wallace, W., & Nevill, A. (2000) Training effects of accumulated daily stair-climbing exercise in previously sedentary young women. *Preventive Medicine*, 30(4), 277-281.

Brentano, M., Cadore, E., Da Silva, I., Ambrosini, A. Coertjens, M. Perkowicz, R., Viero, I., & Kruel, L. (2008) Physiological adaptations to strength and circuit training in postmenopausal women with bone loss. *Journal of Strength and Conditioning Research*, 22(6), 1816-1825.

Cassilhas, R., Viana, V., Grassmann, V., Santos, R., Santos, R., Tufik, S., Mello, M. (2007) The impact of resistance exercise on the cognitive function of the elderly. *Medicine and Science in Sports and Exercise*, 39(8), 1401-1407.

Chevan, J. (2008) Demographic determinants of participation in strength training activities among U.S. adults. *Journal of Strength and Conditioning Research*, 22(2), 553-558.

Chin A Paw, M., De Jong, N., Pallast, E., Kloek, G., Schouten, E., & Kok, F. (2000) Immunity in frail elderly: A randomized controlled trial of exercise and enriched foods. *Medicine and Science in Sports and Exercise*, 32(12), 2005-2011.

Colado, J. & Triplett, N. (2008) Effects of a short-term resistance program using elastic bands versus weight machines for sedentary middle-aged women. *Journal of Strength and Conditioning Research*, 22(5), 1441-1448.

Conroy, M., Simkin-Silverman, L., Pettee, K., Hess, R., Kuller, L., & Kriska, A. (2007) Lapses and psychosocial factors related to physical activity in early postmenopause. *Medicine and Science in Sports and Exercise*, 39(10), 1858-1866.

Craig, B. (2002) Resistance training and bone growth in the elderly. *Strength and Conditioning Journal*, 24(3), 63-64.

Delvaux, K., Lefevre, J., Philippaerts, R., Dequeker, J., Thomis, M., Vanreusel, B., Claessens, A., Vanden, E., Beunen, G., & Lysens R. (2001) Bone mass and lifetime physical activity in Flemish males: A 27-year follow-up study. *Medicine and Science in Sports and Exercise*, 33(11), 1868-1875.

Dimeo, F., Bauer, M., & Varahram, I. (2001) Benefits from aerobic exercise in patients with major depression. *British Journal of Sports Medicine*, 35(2), 114-117.

Fielding, R., Katula, J., Miller, M., Abbott-Pillola, K., Jordan, A., Glynn, N., Goodpaster, B., Walkup, M., King, A., Rejeski, W., & for the Life Study Investigators (2007) Activity adherence and physical function in older adults with functional limitations. *Medicine and Science in Sports and Exercise*, 39(11), 1997-2004.

Fulton, J., Masse, L., Tortolero, S., Watson, K., Heesch, K., Kohl, H., Blair, S., & Caspersen, C. (2001) Field evaluation of energy expenditure from continuous and intermittent walking in women. *Medicine and Science in Sports and Exercise*, 33(1), 163-170.

Gordon, S., Lake, J., Westerkamp, C., & Thomson, D. (2008) Does AMP-activated protein kniase negatively mediate aged fast-twitch skeletal muscle mass? *Exercise and Sports Science Review*, 36(4), 179-186.

Harris, C., DeBeliso, M., Adams, K., Irmischer, B., & Gibson, T. (2007) detraining in the older adult: Effects of prior training intensity on strength retention. *Journal of Strength and Conditioning Research*, 21(3), 813-818.

Janssen, I. & Jolliffe, C. (2006) Influence of physical activity on mortality in elderly with coronary artery disease. *Medicine and Science in Sports and Exercise*, 38(3), 418-423.

Karavirta, L., Tulppo, M., Laaksonen, D., Nyman, K., Laukkanen, R., Kinnunen, H., Hakkinen, A., & Hakkinen, K. (2009) Heart rate dynamics after combined endurance and strength training in older men. *Medicine and Science in Sports and Exercise*, 41(7), 1436-1443.

Keogh, J. (2003) Improving the functional ability of the elderly with resistance training. *Strength and Conditioning Journal*, 25(1) 26-28.

Kritz-Silverstein, D., Barrett-Connor, E., & Corbeau, C. (2001) Cross-sectional and prospective study of exercise and depressed mood in the elderly: The Rancho Bernardo Study. *American Journal of Epidemiology*, 153(6) 596-603.

Laroche, D., Knight, C., Dickie, J., Lussier, M., & Roy, S. (2007) Explosive force and fractionated reaction time in elderly low- and high-active women. *Medicine and Science in Sports and Exercise*, 39(9), 1659-1665.

Lockard, M., Gopinathannair, R., Paton, C., Phares, D., & Hagberg, J. (2007) Exercise training-induced changes in coagulation factors in older adults. *Medicine and Science in Sports and Exercise*, 39(4), 587-592.

Malatesta, D., Vismara, L., Menegoni, F., Galli, M., Romei, M., & Capodaglio, P. (2009) Mechanical external work and recovery at preferred walking speed in obese subjects. *Medicine and Science in Sports and Exercise*, 41(2), 426-434.

Micklas, B. & Brinkley, T. (2009) Exercise training as a treatment for chronic inflammation in the elderly. *Exercise and Sport Science Review*, 37(4), 165-170.

Nelson, M., Rejeski, W., blair, S., Duncan, P., Judge, J., King, A., Macera, C., & Castaneda-Sceppa, C. (2007) Physical activity and public health in older adults: Recommendation from the American college of sports medicine and the american heart association. *Medicine and Science in Sports and Exercise*, 39(8), 1435-1445.

Opdenacker, J., Delecluse, C., & Boen, F. (2009) The longitudinal effects of a lifestyle physical activity intervention and a structured exercise intervention on physical self-perceptions and self-esteem in older adults. *Journal of Sport and Exercise Psychology*, 31, 743-760.

Pontifex, M., Hillman, C., Fernhall, B., Thompson, K., & Valentini, T. (2009) The effect of acute aerobic and resistance exercise on working memory. *Medicine and Science in Sports and Exercise*, 41(4), 927-934.

Paalanne, N., Korpelainen, R., Taimela, S., Auvinen, J., Tammtlin, T., Hietikko, T., Kaikkonen, H., Kaikkonen, K., & Karppinen, J. (2009) Muscular fitness in relation to physical activity and television viewing among young adults. *Medicine and Science in Sports and Exercise*, 41(11), 1997-2002.

Paw, M., De Jong, N., Pallast, E., Kloek, G., Schouten, E., & Kok,F. (2000) Immunity in frail elderly: A randomized controlled trial of exercise and enriched foods. *Medicine and Science in Sports and Exercise*, 32(12), 2005-2011.

Riewald, S. (2009) Exercise for improved cognitive function in the elderly. Strength and Conditioning Journal, 31(5), 89-94.

Ronai, P. & Sorace, P. (2009) Peripheral arterial disease and exercise. *Strength and Conditioning Journal*, 31(5), 50-54.

Satariano, W., Haight, T., & Tager, I. (2000) Reasons given by older people for limitation or avoidance of leisure time physical activity. *Journal of American Geriatrics Society*, 48, 505-512.

Scott, D., Blizzard, L., Fell, J., & Jones, G. (2009) Ambulatory activity, body composition, and lower-limb muscle strength in older adults. *Medicine and Science in Sports and Exercise*, 41(2), 383-389.

Seo, D. & Torabi, M. (2007) Differences in vigorous and moderate physical activity by gender, race/ethnicity, age, education, and income among U.S. adults. *American Journal of Health Education*, 38(3), 122-130.

Sillanpaa, E., Hakkinen, A., Nyman, K., Mattila, M., Cheng, S. Karavirta, L., Laaksonen, D., Huuhka, N., Kraemer, W., & Hakkinen, K. (2008) Body composition and fitness during strength and/or endurance training in older men. *Medicine and Science in Sports and Exercise*, 40(5), 950-958.

Sisson, S., Katzmarzyk, P., Earnest, C., Bouchard, C., Blair, S., & Church, T. (2009) Volume of exercise and fitness nonresponse in sedentary, postmenopausal women. *Medicine and Science in Sports and Exercise*, 41(3), 539-545.

Siu, P. (2009) Muscle apoptotic response to denervation, disuse, and aging. *Medicine and Science in Sports and Exercise*, 41(10) 1876-1886.

Takeshima, N., Rogers, N., Rogers, M., Islam, M., Koizumi, D., & Lee, S. (2007) functional fitness gain varies in older adults depending on exercise mode. *Medicine and Science in Sports and Exercise*, 39(11), 2036-2043.

Urso, M. (2009) Disuse atrophy of human skeletal muscle: cell signaling and potential interventions. *Medicine and Science in Sports and Exercise*, 41(10), 1860-1868.

Van Cauter, E., Leproult, R., & Plat, L. (2000) Age-related changes in slow wave sleep and REM sleep and relationship with growth hormone and cortisol levels in healthy men. *Journal of the American Medical Association*, 284(7), 861-868.

Van Dam, R., Schuit, A., Feskens, E., Seidell, J., & Kromhout, D. (2002) Physical activity and glucose tolerance in elderly men: The Zutphen Elderly study. *Medicine and Science in Sports and Exercise*, 34(7), 1132-1136.

Vincent, K. & Braith, R. (2002) Resistance exercise and bone turnover in elderly men and women. *Medicine and Science in Sports and Exercise*, 34(1), 17-23.

Yaffe, K., Barnes, D., Nevitt, M., Lui, L., & Covinsky, K. (2001) A prospective study of physical activity and cognitive decline in elderly women who walk. *Archives of Internal Medicine*, 161(14), 1703-1708.

Williams, P (2009) Incident diverticular disease is inversely related to vigorous physical activity. *Medicine and Science in Sports and Exercise, 41(5), 1042-1047.*

Williams, P. (2009) Relationship of incident glaucoma versus physical activity and fitness in male runners. *Medicine and Science in Sports and Exercise*, 41(8), 1566-1572.

Chapter 9

Adams, A. & Best, T. (2002) The role of antioxidants in exercise and disease prevention. *Physician and Sportsmedicine*, 30(5), 37-44.

American College of Sports Medicine, American Dietetic Association, & Dietitians of Canada (2009) Joint position statement: nutrition and athletic performance. *Medicine and Science in Sports and Exercise*, 41(3), 709-720.

Awad, A., Chan, K., Downie, A., & Fink, C. (2000) Peanuts as a source of beta-sitosterol, a sterol with anticancer properties. *Nutrition and Cancer*, 36(2), 238-241.

Barr, S. & Broughton, T. (2000) Relative weight, weight loss efforts and nutrient intakes among health-conscious vegetarian, past vegetarian and nonvegetarian women ages 18 to 50. *Journal of the American College of Nutrition*, 19(6), 781-788.

Davies, K., Heaney, R., Recker, R., Lappe, J., Barger-Lux, M., Rafferty, K., & Hinders, S. (2000) Calcium intake and body weight. *Journal of Clinical Endocrinology and Metabolism*, 85(12), 4635-4638.

Dawson, M. (2000) The importance of vitamin A in nutrition. *Current Pharmaceutical Design*, 6(3), 311-325.

De Roos, N., Bots, M., & Katan, M. (2001) Replacement of dietary saturated fatty acids by trans fatty acids lowers serum HDL cholesterol and impairs endothelial function in healthy men and women. *Thrombosis and Vascular Biology*, 21(7), 1233-1237.

Evans, W. (2000) Vitamin E, vitamin C, and exercise. *American Journal of Clinical Nutrition*, 72(2 Suppl), 647-652.

Food and Nutrition Board and Institute of Medicine. (2000) *Dietary Reference Intakes for Vitamin A, Vitamin K, Arsenic, Boron, Chromium, Copper, Iodine, Iron, Manganese, Molybdenum, Nickel, Silicon, Vanadium, and Zinc.* Washington, D.C.: National Academy Press.

Food and Nutrition Board and Institute of Medicine. (2000) *Dietary Reference Intakes for Vitamin C, Vitamin E, Selenium, and Carotenoids.* Washington, D.C.: National Academy Press.

Food and Nutrition Board and Institute of Medicine. (2004) *Dietary Reference Intakes for Water, potassium, Sodium, Chloride, and Sulfate.* Washington, D.C.: National Academy Press.

Grandjean, A. (2002) Dietary supplements: Consumers' views. *Strength and Conditioning Journal*, 24(6), 19-20.

Hajjar, I., Grim, C., George, V., & Kotchen, T. (2001) Impact of diet on blood pressure and age-related changes in blood pressure in the US population: Analysis of NHANES III. *Archive of Internal Medicine*, 161(4), 589-593.

Hamilton, K (2007) Antioxidants and cardioprotection. *Medicine and Science in Sports and Exercise*, 39(9), 1544-1553.

Heber, D. & Bowerman, S. (2001) Applying science to changing dietary patterns. *Journal of Nutrition*, 131(11), 3078-3081.

Henriksen, E. & Saengsirisuwan, V. (2002) Exercise training and antioxidants: Relief from oxidative stress and insulin resistance. *Exercise and Sport Sciences Reviews*, 31(2), 79-84.

Hodson, L., Skeaff, C., & Chisholm, W. (2001) The effect of replacing dietary saturated fat with polyunsaturated or monounsaturated fat on plasma lipids in free-living young adults. *European Journal of Clinical Nutrition*, 55(10), 908-915.

Hu, G. & Gassano, P. (2000) Antioxidant nutrients and pulmonary function: the Third National Health and Nutrition Examination Survey (NHANES III). *American Journal of Epidemiology*, 151(10), 975-981.

Hudson, E., Dinh, P., Kokubun, T., Simmonds, M., & Gescher, A. (2000) Characterization of potentially chemopreventive phenols in extracts of brown rice that inhibit the growth of human breast and colon cancer cells. *Cancer Epidemiology, Biomarkers and Prevention*, 9(11), 1163-1170.

Iso, H., Pexrode, K., Stampfer, M., Manson, J., Colditz, G., Speizer, F., Hennekens, C., & Willett, W. (2001) Intake of fish and omega-3 fatty acids and risk of stroke in women. *Journal of the American Medical Association*, 285, 304-312.

Jacobs, D. Pereira, M., Meyer, K., & Kushi, L. (2000) Fiber from whole grains, but not refined grains, in inversely associated with all-cause mortality in older women: The Iowa women's health study, *Journal of the American College of Nutrition*, 19(3), 326S-330S.

Joshipura, K., Hu, F., Manson, J., Stampfer, M., Rimm, E., Speizer, F., Colditz, G., Ascherio, A., Rosner, B., Spiegelman, D., & Willett, W. (2001) The effect of fruit and vegetable intake on risk for coronary heart disease. *Annals of Internal Medicine*, 134(12), 1106-1114.

Karlsson, J. (1997) *Antioxidants and Exercise*. Champaign, IL: Human Kinetics.

Kolasa, K. (2000) Alphabet soup. *Strength and Conditioning Journal*, 22(1), 30-31.

Krauss, R., Eckel, R., & Howard, B. (2001) Revision 2000: A statement for healthcare professionals from the Nutrition Committee of the American Heart Association. *Journal of Nutrition*, 131, 132-146.

Kurowska, E., Spence, J., Jordan, J., Wetmore, S., Freeman, D., Piche, L., & Seratore, P. (2000) HDL-cholesterol-raising effect of orange juice in subjects with hypercholesterolemia. *American Journal of Clinical Nutrition*, 72(5), 1095-1100.

Laursen, P. (2001) Free radicals and antioxidant vitamins: Optimizing the health of the athlete. *Strength and Conditioning Journal*, 23(2), 17-25.

Lin, Y., Lyle, R., McCabe, L., McCabe, G., & Weaver, C. (2000) Dairy calcium is related to changes in body composition during a two-year exercise intervention in young women. *Journal of the American College of Nutrition*, 19(6), 754-760.

Ludwig, D., Majzoub, J., Al-Zahrani, A., Dallal, G., Blanco, I., & Roberts, S. (1999) High glycemic index foods, overeating, and obesity. *Pediatrics*, 103(3), 26.

MacDonald, R. (2009) Nutrition and cancer prevention. *ACSM Fit Society Page*, spring, 1-2.

McDermott, J. (2000) Antioxidant nutrients: Current dietary recommendations and research update. *Journal of the American Pharmaceutical Association*, 40(6), 785-799.

Nestle, M. & Dixon, L. (2004) *Taking Sides: Clashing Views on Controversial Issues in Food and Nutrition*. Guiford, CT: McGraw-Hill/Dushkin.

Roodenburg, A., Leenen, R., Van Het Hof, K., Westrate, J., & Tijburg, L. (2000) Amount of fat in the diet affects bioavailability of lutein esters but not of alpha-carotene, beta-carotene, and vitamin E in humans. *American Journal of Clinical Nutrition*, 71(5), 1187-1193.

Slattery, M., Benson, J., Ma, K., Schaffer, D., & Potter, J. (2001) Trans-fatty acids and colon cancer. *Nutrition and Cancer*, 39(2), 170-175.

Terry, P., Giovannucci, E., Michels, K., Bergkvist, L., Hansen, H., Holmberg, L., & Wolk, A. (2001) Fruit, vegetables, dietary fiber, and risk of colorectal cancer. *Journal of the National Cancer Institute*, 93(7), 525-533.

Weisburger, J. (2000) Eat to live, not live to eat. *Nutrition*, 16(9), 767-773.

Chapter 10

Bartholomew, J., Morrison, D., & Ciccolo, J. (2005) Effects of acute exercise on mood and well-being in patients with major depressive disorder. *Medicine and Science in Sports and Exercise*, 37(12), 2032-2037.

Carter, J., Beam, W., McMahan, S., Barr, M., & Brown, L. (2006) The effects of stability ball training on spinal stability in sedentary individuals. *Journal of Strength and Conditioning Research*, 20(2), 429-435.

Cheng, Y., Macera, C., Davis, D., & Blair, S. (2000) Physical activity and peptic ulcers. Does physical activity reduce the risk of developing peptic ulcers? *The Western Journal of Medicine*, 173(2), 101-107.

Ebenbichler, G., Oddsson, L., Kollmitzer, J., & Erim, Z. (2001) Sensory-motor control of the lower back: Implications for rehabilitation. *Medicine and Science in Sports and Exercise*, 33(11) 1889-1898.

Ehrman, J., Gordon, P., Visich, P., & Keteyian, S. (2003) *Clinical Exercise Physiology*. Champaign, IL: Human Kinetics.

Epel, E., McEwen, B., Seeman, T., Matthews, K., Castellazzo, G., Brownell, K., Bell, J., Lckovics, J. (2000) Stress and body shape: Stress-induced cortisol secretion is consistently greater among women with central fat. *Psychosomatic Medicine*, 62(5), 623-632.

Garg, A., Chren, M., Sands, L., Matsui, M., Marenus, K., Feingold, K., & Elias, P. (2001) Psychological stress perturbs epidermal permeability barrier homeostasis: Implications for the pathogenesis of stress-associated shin disorders. *Archives of Dermatology*, 137(1), 53-59.

Gavrieli, R. Ashlagi-amiri, T., Eliakim, A., Nemet, D., Zigel, L., Berger, S., Falk, B., & Wolach, B. (2008) The effect of aerobic exercise on neutrophil functions. *Medicine and Science in Sports and Exercise*, 40(9), 1623-1628.

Hales, D. (2004) *An Invitation to Health* (3rd Ed). Belmont, CA: Wadsworth/Thomson Learning.

Hansen, C., Stevens, L., & Coast, J. (2001) Exercise duration and mood state: How much is enough to feel better? *Health Psychology*, 20(4), 267-275.

Hassmen, P., Koivula, N., & Uutela, A. (2000) Physical exercise and psychological well-being: A population study in Finland. *Preventive Medicine*, 30(1), 17-25.

Hides, J., Jull, G., & Richardson, C. (2001) Long-term effects of specific stabilizing exercises for first-episode low back pain. *Spine*, 26(11), 243-248.

Kell, R. & Asmundson G. (2009) A comparison of two forms of periodized exercise rehabilitation programs in the management of chronic nonspecific low-back pain. *Journal of Strength and Conditioning Research*, 23(2), 513-523.

Kolber, M. & Beekhuizen, K. (2007) Lumbar stabilization: An evidence-based approach for the athlete with low back pain. *Strength and Conditioning Journal*, 29(2), 26-37.

Kolber, M. & Fiebert, I. (2005) Addressing flexibility of the rectus femoris in the athlete with low back pain. *Strength and Conditioning Journal*, 27(5), 66-73.

Phillips, A., burns, V., & Lord, J. (2007) Stress and exercise: Getting the balance right for aging immunity. *Exercise and Sport Science Reviews*, 35(1), 35-39.

Riewald, S. (2007) Regular exercise: Good for the body, good for the mind? *Strength and Conditioning Journal*, 29(3), 41-42.

Rogers, R. (2006) Research-based rehabilitation of the lower back. *Strength and Conditioning Journal,* 28(1), 30-35.

Ross, M. (2007) Preventing low back pain with athlete education and the prone press-up exercise. *Strength and Conditioning Journal*, 29(6), 78-80.

Staum, M. & Brotons, M. (2000) The effect of music amplitude on the relaxation response. *Journal of Music Therapy*, 37(1), 22-39.

Stoney, C. & Engebretson, T. (2000) Plasma homocysteine concentrations are positively associated with hostility and anger. *Life Science*, 66(23), 2267-2275.

Wassell, J., Gardner, L., Landsittel, D., Johnston, J., & Johnston, J. (2000) A prospective study of back belts for prevention of back pain and injury. *Journal of the American Medical Association*, 284(21), 2727-2732.

Chapter 11

Albright, A., Franz, M., Hornsby, G., Kriska, A., Marrero, D., Ulrich, I. & Verity, L. (2000) Exercise and type 2 diabetes. *Medicine and Science in Sports and Exercise*, 32(7), 1345-1360.

American College of Sports Medicine. (2006) Impact of physical activity during pregnancy and postpartum on chronic disease risk. *Medicine and Science in Sports and Exercise*, 38(5), 989-1000.

Barnes, J., & Pujol, T. (2001) Exercise considerations for patients with Osteoarthritis. *Strength and Conditioning Journal*, 23(3), 74-76.

Barnes, J., Pujol, T., & Elder, C. (2002) Exercise considerations for patients with rheumatoid arthritis. *Strength and Conditioning Journal*, 24(3), 46-50.

Beck, K., Joyner, M., & Scanlon, P. (2002) Exercise-induced asthma: Diagnosis, treatment, and regulatory issues. *Exercise and Sport Sciences Reviews*, 30(1), 1-3.

Bell, R. (2002) The effects of vigorous exercise during pregnancy on birth weight. *Journal of Science and Medicine in Sport*, 5, 32-36.

Borodulin, K., Evenson, K., Wen, F., Herring, A., & Benson, A. (2008) Physical activity patterns during pregnancy. *Medicine and Science in Sports and Exercise*, 40(11), 1901-1908.

Brassard, P., Legault, S., Garneau, C., Bogaty, P., Dumesnil, J., & Poirier, P. (2007) Normalization of diastolic dysfunction type 2 diabetics after exercise training. *Medicine and Science in Sports and Exercise*, 39(11), 1896-1901.

Brown, W. (2002) The benefits of physical activity during pregnancy. *Journal of Science and Medicine in Sports*, 5, 37-45.

Burnham, T. & Wilcox, A. (2002) Effects of exercise on physiological and psychological variables in cancer survivors. *Medicine and Science in Sports and Exercise*, 34(12), 1863-1867.

Caspersen, C. & Fulton, J. (2008) Epidemiology of walking and type 2 diabetes. *Medicine and Science in Sports and Exercise*, 40(7S), S519-S528.

Clapp, J. (2001) Early pregnancy exercise benefits babies. *Australian Nursing Journal*, 8, 22-25.

Clapp, J., Hyungjin, K., Burciu, B., & Lopez, B. (2000) Beginning regular exercise in early pregnancy: Effect on fetoplacental growth. *American Journal of Obstetrics and Gynecology*, 183, 1484-1489.

Clapp, J., Hyungjin, K., Burciu, B., Schmidt, S., Petry, K., & Lopez, B. (2002) Continuing regular exercise during pregnancy: Effect on exercise volume on fetoplacental growth. *American Journal of Obstetrics and Gynecology*, 186, 142-147.

Colberg, S. & Walsh, J. (2002) Pumping insulin during exercise. *The Physician and Sportsmedicine*, 30(4), 33-38.

Courneya, K. (2001) Exercise intervention during cancer treatment: Biopsychosocial outcomes. *Exercise and Sport Sciences Reviews*, 29(2), 60-64.

Courneya, K., Mackey, J., & Jones, L. (2000) Coping with cancer. *The Physician and Sportsmedicine*, 28(5), 49-56.

Courneya, K., Mackey, J., & McKenzie, D. (2002) Exercise for breast cancer survivors. *The Physician and Sportsmedicine*, 30(8), 33-38.

Davis, J. & Green, J. (2007) Resistance training and type-2 diabetes. *Strength and Conditioning Journal*, 29(1), 42-48.

Dempsey, J., Butler, C., & Williams, M. (2005) No need for a pregnant pause: Physical activity may reduce the occurrence of gestational diabetes mellitus and preeclampsia. *Exercise and Sport Sciences Reviews*, 33(3), 141-149.

Dengel, D., Brown, M., Reynolds, T., & Supiano, M. (2006) Effect of aerobic exercise training on renal responses to sodium in hypertensive. *Medicine and Science in Sports and Exercise*, 38(2), 217-222.

Dishuck, J., Harrelson, G., & Harrelson, L. (2001) Educating the asthmatic athlete. *Athletic Therapy Today*, 6(5), 26-32.

Durstine, J. & Moore, G. (2003) *Exercise Management for Persons with Chronic Disease and Disabilities* (2nd Ed). Champaign, IL: Human Kinetics.

Feairheller, D., Brown, M., Park, J., Brinkley, T., Basu, S., Hagberg, J., Ferrell, R., & Fenty-Stewart, N. (2009) Exercise training, NADPH oxidase p22phox gene polymorphisms, and hypertension. *Medicine and Science in Sport and Exercise*, 41(7), 1421-1428.

Galvao, D., Nosaka, K., Taaffe, D., Spry, N., Kristjanson, L., McGuigan, M., Suzuki, K., Yamay, K., & Newton, R. (2006) Resistance training and reduction of treatment side effects in prostate cancer patients. *Medicine and Science in Sports and Exercise*, 38(12), 2045-2052.

Griffin, T. & Guilak, F. (2005) The role of mechanical loading in the onset and progression of osteoarthritis. *Exercise and Sport Sciences Reviews*, 33(4), 195-200.

Hartman, C., Manos, T., Winter, C., Hartman, D., Li, B., & Smith, J. (2000) Effects of T'ai Chi training on function and quality of life indicators in older adults with osteoarthritis. *Journal of the American Geriatrics Society*, 48(12), 1553-1559.

Horowitz, J. (2007) Exercise-induced alterations in muscle lipid metabolism improve insulin sensitivity. *Exercise and Sport Sciences Reviews*, 35(4), 192-196.

Herrero, f., Balmer, J., San Juan, A., Foster, C., Fleck, S., Perez, M., Canete, S., Earnest, C., & Lucia, A. (2006) Is cardiorespiratory fitness related to quality of life in survivors of breast cancer? *Journal of Strength and Conditioning Research*, 20(3), 535-540.

Hurley, M., Mitchell, H., & Walsh, N. (2002) In osteoarthritis, the psychosocial benefits of exercise are as important as physiological improvements. *Exercise and Sport Sciences Reviews*, 31(3), 138-143.

Irwin, M. (2006) Randomized controlled trials of physical activity and breast cancer prevention. *Exercise and Sport Science Reviews*, 34(4), 182-193.

Kirk, E., Donnelly, J., Smith, B., Honas, J., Lecheminant, J., Bailey, B., Jacobsen, D., & Washburn, R. (2009) Minimal resistance training improves daily energy expenditure and fat oxidation. *Medicine and Science in Sports and Exercise*, 41(5), 1122-1129.

Kovan, J. & Mackowiak, T. (2001) Exercise-induced asthma. *Athletic Therapy Today*, 6(5), 22-25.

LaFontaine, T. (2000) Strength and conditioning in fibromyalgia patients. *Strength and Conditioning Journal*, 22(5), 42-44.

Lalande, S., Gusso, S., Hofman, P., & Baldi, J. (2008) Reduced leg blood flow during submaximal exercise in type 2 diabetes. *Medicine and Science in Sports and Exercise*, 40(4), 612-617.

Levinger, I., Goodman, C., Hare, D., Jerums, G., Morris, T., & selig, S. (2009) Psychological responses to acute resistance exercise in men and women who are obese. *Journal of Strength and Conditioning Research*, 23(5), 1548-1552.

Magann, E., Evans, F., & Weitz, B. (2002) Antepartum, intrapartum, and neonatal significance of exercise on healthy low-risk pregnant working women. *Obstetrics and Gynecology*, 99, 466-472.

McTiernan, A. (2003) Physical activity, exercise, and cancer: Prevention to treatment-symposium overview. *Medicine and Science in Sports and Exercise*, 35(11), 1821-1826.

Meyer, B & Lemley, K. (2000) Utilizing exercise to affect the symptomology of fibromyalgia: A pilot study. *Medicine and Science in Sports and Exercise*, 32(10), 1691-1697.

Mickleborough, T. (2008) A nutritional approach to managing exercise-induced asthma. *Exercise and Sport Science Reviews*, 36(3), 135-144.

Mickleborough, T., Lindley, M., & Ray, S. (2005) Dietary salt, airway inflammation, and diffusion capacity in exercise-induced asthma. *Medicine and Science in Sports and Exercise*, 37(6), 904-914.

Painter, P. (2008) Exercise in chronic disease: Physiological research needed. *Exercise and Sport Science Reviews*, 36(20), 83-90.

Paleville, D., Topp, R., & Swank, A. (2007) Effects of aerobic training prior to and during chemotherapy in a breast cancer patient: A case study. *Journal of Strength and Conditioning Research*, 21(2), 635-637.

Padilla, J., Wallace, J., & Park, S. (2005) Accumulation of physical activity reduces blood pressure in pre- and hypertension. *Medicine and Science in Sports and Exercise*, 37(8), 1264-1275.

Patzan, J. & Sorace, P. (2007) Exercise-induced broncho-constriction in athletes and recreational athletes. *Strength and Conditioning Journal*, 29(3), 21-23.

Peel, J., Sui, X., Adams, S., Hebert, J., Hardin, J., & Blair, S. (2009) A prospective study of cardiorespiratory fitness and breast cancer mortality. *Medicine and Science in Sports and Exercise*, 41(4), 742-748.

Poidevigne, M. & O'Connor, P. (2005) Physical activity and mood during pregnancy. *Medicine and Science in Sports and Exercise*, 37(8), 1374-1380.

Praet, S., Manders, R., Lieverse, A., Kuipers, H., Stehouwer, C., Keizer, H., & Loon, L. (2006) Influence of acute exercise on hyperglycemia in insulin-treated type 2 diabetes. *Medicine and Science in Sports and Exercise*, 38(12), 2037-2044.

Pujol, T., Barnes, J., & Elder, C. (2007) Resistance training during pregnancy. *Strength and Conditioning Journal*, 29(2), 44-46.

Ribeiro, I., Iborra, R., Neves, M., Lottenberg, S., Charf, A., Nunes, V., Negrao, C., Nakandakare, E., Quintao, E., & Passarelli, M. (2008) HDL atheroprotection ay aerobic exercise training in type 2 diabetes mellitus. *Medicine and Science in Sports and Exercise*, 40(5), 779-786.

Ronai, P., sorace, P., & LaFontaine, T. (2008) Resistance training for persons with osteoarthritis and rheumatoid arthritis. *Strength and Conditioning Journal*, 30(2), 32-36.

Schwartz, A., Mori, M., Gao, R. Nail, L., & King, M. (2001) Exercise reduces daily fatigue in women with breast cancer receiving chemotherapy. *Medicine and Science in Sports and Exercise*, 33(5), 718-723.

Shephard, R. (1990) *Fitness in Special Populations*. Champaign, IL: Human Kinetics.

Taylor, J. (2007) The impact of a supervised strength and aerobic training program on muscular strength and aerobic capacity in individuals with type 2 diabetes. *Journal of Strength and Conditioning Research*, 21(3), 824-830.

Tomas-Carus, P., Hakkinen, A., Gusi, N., Leal, A., Hakkinen, K., & Ortega-Alonso, A. (2007) Aquatic training and detraining on fitness and quality of life in fibromyalgia. *Medicine and Science in Sports and Exercise*, 39(7), 1044-1050.

Vallance, J., Courneya, K., Plotnikoff, R., Dinu, I., & Mackey, J. (2008) Maintenance of physical activity in breast cancer survivors after a randomized trial. *Medicine and Science in Sports and Exercise*, 40(1), 173-180.

Wang, J., Chung, Y., & Chow, S. (2009) Exercise affects platelet-impeded antitumor cytotoxicity of natural killer cell. *Medicine and Science in Sports and Exercise*, 41(1), 115-122.

Ward, S. (2005) Diabetes, exercise, and foot care. *The Physician and Sportsmedicine*, 33(8), 33-40.

Williams, P. (2008) Vigorous exercise, fitness and incident hypertension, high cholesterol, and diabetes. *Medicine and Science in Sports and Exercise*, 40(6), 998-1006.

Williams, P. & Franklin, B. (2007) Vigorous exercise and diabetic, hypertensive, and hypercholesterolemia medication use. *Medicine and Science in Sports and Exercise*, 39(11), 1933-1941.

Wyatt, F., Milam, S., Manske, R., & Deere, R. (2001) The effects of aquatic and traditional exercise programs on persons with knee osteoarthritis. *Journal of Strength and Conditioning Research*, 15(3), 337-340.

Laboratories

Adams, G. (2002) *Exercise Physiology Laboratory Manual* (4th Ed). Boston: McGraw Hill.

American College of Sports Medicine. (1998) *ACSM's Resource Manual for Guidelines for Exercise Testing and Prescription* (3rd Ed). Baltimore: Williams and Wilkins.

Heyward, V.H. (2002) *Advanced Fitness Assessment & Exercise Prescription*. (4th Ed). Champaign, IL: Human Kinetics.

Hoeger, W. & Hoeger, S. (2006) *Principles & Labs for Physical Fitness*. (5th Ed). Belmont, CA: Thomson/Wadsworth.

Howley, E. & Franks B. (2003) *Health Fitness Instructor's Handbook* (4th Ed). Champaign, IL:Human Kinetics.

Huber, F. & Techanchuk, P. (2003) *Essentials of Physical Activity: Laboratory Manual*. (5th Ed.) Peosta, IL: Eddie Bowers Publishing.

Kravitz, L. (1998) *Anybody's Guide to Total Fitness* (5th Ed). Dubuque, IA: Kendall/Hunt.

Roberts, S., Robergs, R., & Hanson, P. (1997) *Clinical Exercise Testing and Prescription: Theory and Application*. Boca Raton, FL: CRC Press.

Glossary of Terms

A

Acclimatization - The process of chronic adaptation to a given environmental stress.

Adipocyte - A fat cell that has the ability to increase in size and number.

Aerobic Exercise - A continuous exercise required oxygen that last longer than three minutes and involves using major muscle groups in a repetitive motion.

Aging Process - A progressive loss of physical and mental capacities that eventually culminates in death.

Anaerobic Exercise - An activity requiring quick burst of speed or large amount of strength using the stored energy within the muscle cells and last less than two minutes.

Anaerobic Metabolism - The chemical process by which energy is made available for the body without the utilization of oxygen.

Anemia - A reduction below normal in the number of red blood cells or in the quantity of hemoglobin in the blood.

Anorexia Nervosa - An eating disorder involving self-starvation.

Antioxidant - A substance that prevents the formation of free radicals in the body that are a natural by-product of oxidation and are thought to cause the development of chronic diseases.

Arteries - The vessels that carry blood away from the heart to various parts of the body.

Arterioles - The small branches of arteries.

Arthritis - A general term referring to an inflammation of the joints causing pain, swelling, and restricted motion.

Asthma - A chronic condition often of allergic origin marked by labored breathing and constriction of the chest.

Atrium - The upper chamber on either side of the heart which transmits blood it receives to the same side ventricle.

B

Back Strain/Sprain - A dull and continuous pain in the back often due to a sudden action using fatigued or out of conditioned muscles and usually resolves itself with rest and time.

Ballistic Stretching - An exercise designed to increase the range of motion of a joint by utilizing bouncing movements.

Basal Metabolic Rate (BMR) - The amount of calories the body needs to maintain normal bodily functions in a resting state.

Binge Eating Disorder - An illness characterized by episodes of consuming large amounts of food in a short period of time brought on by an emotional or psychological event.

Bioelectrical Impedance - A method of determining body fat percentage by measuring the resistance to a low-level current passed through the body.

Blood Pressure - The force exerted by the blood against the artery walls.

Body Composition - The ratio of fat tissue mass to lean tissue mass in the body and has a direct affect on an individual's health.

Body Mass Index (BMI) - A measurement to estimate the risk of disease from excess body weight and is determined by dividing a person's weight in kilograms by the square of their height in meters.

Bulimia Nervosa - An eating disorder consisting of recurring binge-eating followed by purging.

C

Calories - A unit by which energy is measured.

Cancer - A collection of diseases characterized by the presence of malignant tumors of potentially unlimited growth that expand locally by invasion and throughout the body by metastasis.

Capillaries - A microscopic blood vessel between an artery and a vein where the interchange of various substances between the blood and tissues take place.

Carbohydrate - A group of chemical substances composed of carbon, hydrogen, and oxygen that can be used efficiently as an energy source.

Cardiac Output - The amount of blood the heart can pump out of the left ventricle per minute.

Cardiorespiratory Fitness - A healthy functioning heart, lungs, blood vessels, and blood allowing the body to perform moderately strenuous activity over an extended period of time.

Cognitive Functioning - The operation of the mental process in which an individual becomes aware of thought and perception, including all aspects of perceiving, thinking, remembering, and moving.

Complex Carbohydrate - A form of carbohydrate consisting of three or more simple-sugar molecules bonded together in varying patterns.

Concentric Muscle Contraction - The characteristic of skeletal muscle to generate a force as the muscle fiber shortens.

Controlled Stretching - A procedure preformed prior to exercising for improved joint mobility during the following physical activity and consists of gently elongating the muscles that will be used.

Cool-down - A process of gradually allowing the exercised body to return to its pre-exercise resting state.

Coronary Vessels - The vascular system of the heart which supplies the heart muscle with blood.

D

Deep Breathing Exercises - A technique designed to reduce or alleviate stress through slow and held respiration.

Degenerative Disease - A disorder characterized by a change in the cell from a healthy functioning state to a less functionally active form.

Dehydration - A decrease in water content of the body below normal levels.

Delayed Onset of Muscle Soreness (DOMS) - A temporary muscle soreness and stiffness that occur 24 to 48 hours after performing unaccustomed eccentric muscle contractions and last for three to four days.

Diastolic Blood Pressure - The force of the blood against the artery walls during the relaxation period of the heart.

Dynamic Strength Training - A conditioning technique designed to improve skeletal muscle function by applying resistance to joint movements.

E

Eccentric Muscle Contraction - The characteristic of skeletal muscle to generate a force as the muscle fiber lengthens.

Energy Balance Equations - Three propositions that state what will happen to body weight if caloric intake is different than or equal to caloric expenditures.

Essential Fat - The lipid component of the body that is necessary for normal bodily functions and is found in cell membranes, bone marrow, nervous system, and etc.

Exercise Habit - A physical activity designed to promote health that has become an important part of the person's life.

F

Fiber - The portion of ingested food that cannot be broken down by intestinal enzymes and juices and functions to absorb organic wastes and toxins and make the stool softer.

Fibromyalgia - A complex multidimensional condition characterized by the presence of chronic diffuse pain and tenderness at specific anatomic locations.

Flexibility - The ability to move a joint through a full range of motion without discomfort or pain.

Flexibility Exercise - A technique or movement designed to improve or maintain joint range of motion.

Flexibility Training - A series of exercise movements designed to increase the joints range of motion in the body and alleviate muscle tightness.

Glossary of Terms

G

Glycemic Index - A rating of the increase in blood glucose after the ingestion of a standard amount of carbohydrate.

H

Health - A state of complete physical, mental, spiritual, and social well-being.

Health Fitness - The appropriate functioning body that allows quality living and longevity.

Heart Rate - The number of contractions per minute of the cardiac ventricles.

Hemoglobin - The oxygen-carrying pigment of the red blood cells.

Hydration - The absorption of water by the body.

Hydrostatic Weighing - A method of determining body composition using a water submersion technique.

Hyperglycemia - An excess of glucose in the blood.

Hyperhydrated - The increase in body water content above normal levels.

Hypertrophy - The increase in size of skeletal muscle due to the increase size of individual muscle fibers.

I

Individuality Principle - A conditioning effect that acknowledges the variation in the conditioning response from exercise due to a person's physical, psychological, and heredity makeup.

Insulin - A hormone secretion of the pancreas necessary to convert carbohydrates into energy and sometimes used therapeutically to control diabetes.

Ischemic - The diminished flow of blood to a tissue.

Isokinetic - A strengthening exercise that uses resistance at a constant velocity throughout the range of motion.

Isometric Muscle Contraction - The characteristic of skeletal muscle to generate a force without a change in muscle length.

Isotonic - A strength training exercise that involves a constant resistance throughout the range of motion.

L

Lean Tissue - The components of the body that is not fat.

Life Expectancy - The average longevity of a person from a specific population is projected to live from a given point in time.

Lifestyle - A method in which an individual chooses to live that includes dietary habit, physical activity level, personal hygiene, sleep pattern, social interaction, and spiritual commitment.

M

Medical Clearance - A physical examination by a physician to determine if there should be any limitations placed upon an individual starting an exercise program.

Meditation - A technique designed to reduce or eliminate stress by focusing on a non-stressful word, object, or location.

Minerals - The inorganic substances found naturally in food and play a vital role in the development and maintenance of the body.

Motor Neuron - A nerve fiber that transmits an impulse to a skeletal muscle fiber.

Motor Unit - A motor neuron and all of the skeletal muscle fibers it attaches to.

Muscle Development Exercise - An activity designed to improve the functioning ability of the muscles that control body movement and posture.

Muscle Relaxation - A technique designed to reduce or eliminate stress by alternating contracting and relaxing of skeletal muscles.

Muscular Endurance - The ability of skeletal muscle to contract repetitively or to maintain a contraction for an extended period of time.

Muscular Strength - The ability of skeletal muscle to exert maximal amount of force during a single contraction.

Myocardium - The thickest layer of the heart wall and is composed of cardiac muscle.

Glossary of Terms

O

Obesity - The excessive accumulation of storage fat in the body.

Osteoarthritis - A gradual destruction of the cartilage of a joint and overgrowth of bone in the joint.

Overfat - A condition of excess body fat as determined from body composition analysis.

Overload Principle - A conditioning process that uses an exercise workload greater than is normally performed to cause the body's systems to adapt and enable the body to function at a higher level.

P

Performance Fitness - The ability of an individual to successfully participate in sporting activities that requires good coordination, agility, and balance.

Physical Fitness - The ability to perform physical effort beyond normal daily activities without undue fatigue.

Physically Active Lifestyle - A method in which individuals will includes additional body movements into their normal daily life for reasons other than the specific development of fitness.

Posture - The natural and comfortable bearing of the body in normal, healthy persons promoting normal functioning of the body's organs and increasing the efficiency of the muscle to minimize fatigue.

Pregnancy - The condition of having a developing embryo or fetus in the body after union of an ovum and spermatozoon.

Protein - A major nutrient composed of carbon, hydrogen, oxygen, and nitrogen and is required in the growth, maintenance, and repair of body tissue.

Purging - An intentional emptying of the stomach and/or bowels by self-induced vomiting and/or use of laxatives.

R

Range of Motion (ROM) - The movement of a joint from full extension to full flexion.

Recommended Dietary Allowances (RDA) - The nutrient intakes suggested for the maintenance of health in people in the United States.

Repetition Maximum (RM) - The number of times a strengthening exercise can be performed before the muscle fatigues.

Rehydration - The process of returning fluids to the body during recovery from a dehydrated state.

Resistance - An external load used to oppose the contractile force of skeletal muscle.

Reversibility Principle - A deconditioning process that causes the physiological adaptations gained from exercise to be lost due to inactivity.

Rheumatoid Arthritis - An autoimmune disorder marked by severe inflammation of the joints and sometimes other organs.

Ruptured Disk - A herniated disk or pad of cartilage between vertebrae and pressing against the spinal cord causing excruciating pain.

S

Saturated Fat - A type of fatty acid in which all carbon atoms are joined by single bonds, allowing the maximum number of hydrogen atoms to bond to the molecule and are usually solid at room temperature.

Set - The number of times a particular strength training exercise is performed to muscle failure during a workout.

Skinfold Measurement - A technique for determining body fat percentage by assessing the amount of fat beneath the skin.

Slipped Disc - A rupture of a disk or pad of cartilage between vertebrae and pressing against the spinal cord causing excruciating pain.

Socio-Cultural - The interactions people have with each other and with their environment.

Specificity Principle - A process that causes adaptations to only occur within the bodily systems being used during exercise and is dependent upon the type of exercise performed.

Specific Warm-up - A procedure used to prepare an individual for participation in a physical activity by allowing them to become familiar with the playing or workout environment.

Static Strength Training - A conditioning technique designed to improve skeletal muscle function by using an immovable resistance that will allow no change in muscle length during muscle contraction.

Static Stretching - An exercise designed to increase flexibility in a joint by placing the muscles in an elongated position and holding that position for an extended period of time.

Stress - The body's response to a stimulus consisting of a mobilization of bodily resources for adaptation.

Stressor - A situation or event that elicits the stress response.

Storage Fat - The lipid held in adipose tissue.

Strength Training - A conditioning procedure that utilizes resistance exercises to improve muscle performance.

Stroke Volume - The amount of blood pumped from the heart per contraction.

Systolic Blood Pressure - The force of the blood exerted against the arterial walls during the contraction of the heart.

T

Tendons - A cord or band of strong white fibrous tissue that connects a muscle to a bone.

Triglycerides - A lipid that consists of three fatty acid molecules attached to a glycerol molecule and is stored in fat cells.

Trans Fats - A form of fatty acids derived from the process of hydrogenation and believed to increase a person's risk for coronary artery disease.

Type 1 Diabetes - A metabolic disorder caused by the destruction of the insulin producing beta cells of the pancreas.

Type 2 Diabetes - A metabolic disorder caused by changes in insulin secretion or sensitivity of the body to insulin.

Type I Muscle Fiber - A specialized contractile tissue in skeletal muscle that is highly aerobic, contracts slowly, and resist fatigue.

Type IIa Muscle Fiber - A specialized contractile tissue in skeletal muscle that contracts rapidly and has the capacity for both aerobic and anaerobic metabolism.

Type IIb Muscle Fiber - A specialized contractile tissue in skeletal muscle that contracts rapidly, is highly anaerobic, and fatigues quickly.

U

United States Department of Agriculture (USDA) - A governmental agency designed to provide protection, management of, and make public policy on issue regarding food, agriculture, and natural resources.

Unsaturated Fat - A type of fatty acid in which some carbon atoms are joined by double bonds, causing a fewer number of hydrogen atoms to bond to the molecule and are usually liquid at room temperature.

V

Valsalva Maneuver - An increase of intrathoracic pressure by forcible exhalation against the closed glottis.

Varicose Veins - The unnaturally and permanently distended, swollen, and knotted veins usually found in the legs.

Veins - The blood vessels that carry blood from various parts of the body back to the heart.

Ventricle - The lower chambers of the heart which pumps blood to various parts of the body.

Vitamins - The organic substances that are found naturally in food and play a vital role in the development and maintenance of the body.

W

World Health Organization (WHO) - The most widely recognized international agency responsible for studying and controlling disease on a global basis.

Index

A

Acclimatization, 73
Adipocyte, 80, 98, 102, 105
Aerobic, 19, 40, 41, 71
Aerobic Exercise, 19, 32, 38, 42, 44, 44, 55, 65, 72, 81, 90, 119, 131, 135, 139
Age, 39, 58, 88
Agility, 17
Aging, 20, 22, 89, 90
Aging Process, 91
Amino Acids, 102, 103
    Essential, 103
Anemia, 34, 84
Anaerobic, 19, 51, 55, 58
Anaerobic Exercise, 19
Anorexia Nervosa, 87
Antioxidants, 21, 109
Arteries, 30, 31, 36, 42
Arterioles, 30, 68
Arthritis, 105, 121, 133, 137
Asthma(tics), 70, 134
Atherosclerosis, 37, 39, 95, 97, 129
Atrium, 27

B

Back
    Flexibility, 123
    Problems, 125
    Strain/Sprain, 125
    Strengthening Exercises, 123
Balance, 17, 90
Ballistic Stretching, 70
Basal Metabolic Rate (BMR), 83
Binge Eating Disorder, 87
Bioelectrical Impedance, 81
Blood, 20, 25, 27, 30, 32, 46, 68, 96, 101
    Pressure, 32, 42, 81, 93
    Vessels, 18, 25, 29, 129
Body Composition, 16, 21, 41, 76, 82, 83, 90, 175
    Assessment, 77
Body Fat, 40, 76, 79, 81, 88
Body Mass Index (BMI), 75, 82
Body Weight, 84
Bones, 51, 53, 58, 76, 80, 88
Bran, 104
Bulimia Nervosa, 88

C

Caffeine, 111, 125
Calcium, 19, 35, 95, 103, 105,
Caloric Expenditure, 83, 179, 183
Calories, 83, 88, 101, 179, 183
Cancer, 4, 8, 19, 38, 75, 95, 99, 105, 136, 138
Capillaries, 20, 30, 68
Carbohydrates, 25, 51, 55, 68, 82, 96, 100, 102, 111, 129

Simple, 97
Complex, 97, 108
Carbon Dioxide, 29
Cardiac Output, 2, 32, 65
Cardiorespiratory (CR) Fitness, 15, 27, 41,
    44, 71, 93, 135, 155
Cardiorespiratory System, 19, 27, 40, 44, 69
Cardiovascular Disease, 37, 39, 54, 61, 78,
    87, 90, 97, 100, 102, 105
Carotid Arteries, 31, 44
Cell, 27
Cellulose, 105
Center of Disease Control & Prevention, 7,
    37
Cereals, 100
Cholesterol, 20, 37, 39, 89, 99, 101, 105,
    109, 112
Circulatory System, 31
Cognitive Functioning, 94
Concentric Contraction, 55
Cool-Down, 30, 61, 65, 173
Coordination, 17
Core, 68
Coronary Arteries, 29, 39
Coronary Vessels, 29

D

Death Rates, 11, 22
Death, Causes of, 4, 5, 8, 9, 95
Deep Breathing Exercise, 124
Degenerative Diseases, 6
Dehydration, 34, 71, 99, 103, 105
Delayed Onset of Muscle Soreness
    (DOMS), 60
Depression, 21, 47, 90, 95, 118, 133
Diabetes, 10, 42, 98, 112, 129-131, 137
Diaphragm, 32
Diarrhea, 103
Diastolic Blood Pressure, 32, 46, 89, 132
Diet, 83, 95, 98, 107, 113, 140
Dynamic Strength Training, 56

E

Eating Disorders, 87
Eccentric Contraction, 55
Endorphins, 122
Energy Balance Equation, 83
Environment, 2, 8, 28, 88, 140, 142
    Hot, 21, 46, 68, 69
    Cold, 74
Exercise Habit, 91

F

Fat, 14, 18, 27, 76, 82, 101, 105, 126
    Essential, 76
Fats, 25, 39, 46, 51, 55, 96, 104
    Saturated, 100, 112
    Unsaturated, 105
Fiber, 102
Fibromyalgia, 140
Flexibility, 16, 62, 71, 90, 123, 134, 136,
    169, 173
Flexibility Training, 65, 71, 90, 129, 132,
    137
Food and Drug Administration (FDA), 105
Food Guide Pyramid, 113
Free Radical, 109
Frequency, 41, 44, 55,
Fruit, 103, 108, 113

G

Gender, 37, 58
Genetics, 8, 9, 37, 58, 78,
Glucose, 40, 55, 68, 96, 97, 111, 131
Glycemic Index, 102, 111

H

Harvard School of Public Health, 111,
Health, 3-9, 15, 20, 95, 105, 107, 129
Health Care, 6, 9
    Costs, 6

Health Fitness, 15, 20, 26, 41, 46, 55, 65, 71, 76, 83, 87, 95, 187
Healthy Eating Pyramid, 115
Heart, 20, 27, 26, 30,
Heart Attack, 38, 87, 105
Heart Disease, 5, 17, 35, 95, 112
Heart Rate, 28, 42, 44, 46, 67, 153
    Measuring, 42
Heart Rate Training Zone, 43, 65, 159
Heat Illness, 72
Hemoglobin, 102
Heredity, 39
High-Density Lipoprotein (HDL), 41, 81, 101
High-Fiber Cereals, 102
High-Protein Diet, 106
Hydration, 71, 77, 183
Hydrostatic Weighing, 81
Hyperglycemia, 139
Hyperhydrate, 71
Hypertension, 32, 35, 37-38, 89, 129, 132-133, 141
Hypertrophy, 21, 61
Hypoglycemia, 139

I

Immune System, 21
Individuality Principle, 18, 60
Infectious Diseases, 9
Insulin, 100, 129
Intensity, 43, 69
Iron, 38, 106,
Ischemic, 29
Isokinetic, 53
Isometric Contraction, 55, 65
Isotonic, 55

L

Lactic Acid, 61, 65
Lean Tissue, 16, 76, 81
Life Expectancy, 5, 7, 9, 11, 21, 32, 40
Life Span, 4, 7, 21
Lifestyle, 4, 6, 7, 8, 20, 32, 45, 58, 66, 78, 80, 88, 122, 129, 140
Lifting Habits, 130
Ligaments, 18, 58, 66
Low-Density Lipoprotein (LDL), 37, 39, 101, 102
Lungs, 18, 25, 28, 30

M

Maximal Oxygen Uptake (VO2 Max), 76, 155, 156
Medical Clearance, 65
Meditation, 125
Menstruation, 34, 76
Minerals, 25, 81, 96, 105-107, 109
    Major, 105
    Trace, 105
Mitochondria, 48
Mormons, 9
Motor Neutrons, 54
Motor Unit, 54, 60
Muscle Relaxation, 124
Muscle Soreness, 59
Muscular Endurance, 16, 56, 71, 90, 132, 167
Muscular Strength, 15, 56, 71, 90, 136, 167
Myocardial Infarction, 31
Myocardium, 27, 46

N

National Sporting Goods Association, 5
Natural Killer Cells, 21
Nutritional Supplements, 6

O

Obesity, 38, 40, 99, 143
Osteoporosis, 22, 38, 58, 84, 103, 121
Osteoarthritis, 44, 75, 136
Overfat, 75, 78, 83, 90, 101, 140

Overload Principle, 18, 41, 46, 55, 65
Oxygen, 20, 25, 27, 32, 40, 46, 55, 65, 68, 95, 96, 121, 153

P

Perceived Exertion, 46
Performance Fitness, 15
Physical Fitness, 15, 41
Physically Active Lifestyle, 92
Plaque, 32, 38
Posture, 129
Power, 17
Pregnant, 38, 121, 144
Principles of Conditioning, 17, 55, 71
Protein, 25, 96, 102, 106, 109, 110
Psychological State, 21
Pulmonary System, 20
Pulse, 33, 42
Purging, 87

R

Radial Arteries, 33, 44
Range of Motion, 17, 54, 70, 90, 169, 173
Reaction Time, 17
Recommended Dietary Allowances (RDA), 81, 104, 108
Red Blood Cell, 30
Rehydration, 71
Relaxation Technique, 124
Repetition Maximum (RM), 58
Respiration, 34, 62
Resting Metabolic Rate, 84
Reversibility Principle, 18, 60
Rheumatoid Arthritis, 140
Risk Factors, 31, 132
    Controllable, 39
    Uncontrollable, 39
Ruptured Disc, 126

S

Sciatica, 125
Sedentary, 23
Sets, 58
Seven Basic Nutrients, 100
Seven Lifestyle Habits, 9
Seventh-Day Adventists, 9
Skeletal Muscles, 20, 29, 46, 51, 58, 65, 68, 81, 96
Skinfold Measurement, 81
Slipped Disc, 126
Smoking, 28, 38, 40
Socio-Cultural, 94
Specificity Principle, 18, 44, 59, 65
Speed, 17
Static Strength Training, 56
Storage Fat, 80
Strength Training, 53, 60, 65, 71, 81, 87, 90, 96, 135, 137
Stress, 42, 36, 45, 46, 68, 87, 117, 126
    Symptoms, 118
    Management, 119, 125
Stressors, 121
Stretching
    Controlled, 66
    Partner, 66
Stroke, 38, 75, 87, 95
Stroke Volume, 29, 46
Sweat, 32, 67
Systolic Blood Pressure, 32, 46, 89, 132

T

Tendons, 20, 53, 58, 66, 121
Thermogenesis, 83
Time, 43, 55, 69
Tooth Decay, 102
Trans Fats, 104
Triglycerides, 18, 35, 39, 97, 100
Type 1 Diabetes, 42, 131

Type 2 Diabetes, 42, 75, 95, 98, 111, 129, 141
Type I Muscle Fiber (Slow Twitch), 53
Type IIa Muscle Fiber (Intermediate), 53
Type IIb Muscle Fiber (Fast Twitch), 53, 58

U

United States Department of Agriculture (USDA), 113
United States Department of Human Services, 79

V

Valsalva Maneuver, 32, 54, 142
Vegetables, 35, 97, 99, 101, 105, 108, 113
Vegetarian, 107
Veins, 30
    Valves, 30
    Varicose, 30, 75
Ventricles, 27, 42
Venules, 32
Vitamins, 25, 39, 81, 96, 98, 103-105, 107, 108
    Fat-Soluble, 105
    Water-Soluble, 105

W

Walking, 7, 41, 44, 62, 65, 88, 90, 120, 123,
Warm-Up, 17, 61, 65, 124
    General, 66
    Specific, 69
Water, 25, 32, 67, 96, 103, 111
World Health Organization, 94